Jung Gyung Sung

Teachers' stance towards learning disabilities

Jung Gyung Sung

Teachers' stance towards learning disabilities
Empirical study among special education teachers in Korea

LIT

Gedruckt mit Unterstützung des Deutschen Akademischen Austauschdienstes (DAAD)

Bibliographic information published by the Deutsche Nationalbibliothek
The Deutsche Nationalbibliothek lists this publication in the Deutsche Nationalbibliografie; detailed bibliographic data are available in the Internet at http://dnb.d-nb.de.

ISBN 978-3-8258-1787-9

A catalogue record for this book is available from the British Library

©LIT VERLAG Dr. W. Hopf Berlin 2010
Fresnostr. 2   D-48159 Münster
Tel. +49 (0) 2 51-620 320   Fax +49 (0) 2 51-922 60 99
e-Mail: lit@lit-verlag.de   http://www.lit-verlag.de

Distribution:
In Germany: LIT Verlag Fresnostr. 2, D-48159 Münster
Tel. +49 (0) 2 51-620 32 22, Fax +49 (0) 2 51-922 60 99, e-mail: vertrieb@lit-verlag.de
In Austria: Medienlogistik Pichler-ÖBZ, e-mail: mlo@medien-logistik.at
In Switzerland: B + M Buch- und Medienvertrieb, e-mail: order@buch-medien.ch

In the UK: Global Book Marketing, e-mail: mo@centralbooks.com

In North America by:

Transaction Publishers
New Brunswick (U.S.A.) and London (U.K.)

Transaction Publishers
Rutgers University
35 Berrue Circle
Piscataway, NJ 08854

Phone: +1 (732) 445 - 2280
Fax: + 1 (732) 445 - 3138
for orders (U. S. only):
toll free (888) 999 - 6778
e-mail: orders@transactionpub.com

To my father,
you are my hero and inspiration in all I do.

To my mother,
whose love provided the foundation.

Contents

Acknowledgments 1

Part I. Introduction 3

1 Approaching the Concept of Learning Disabilities: An Overview 5
    1.1 Problem Statement 12
    1.2 Purpose of the Study and Research Questions 18

Part II. Literature Review 21

2 Korea's Education System and Special Education . . . 23
    2.1 Introduction to Korea 23
        2.1.1 Geographic, Historical, Cultural and Demographic Context 23
        2.1.2 Socio-Economics and Educational Context 27
        2.1.3 Educational Development and Historical Context . 27
    2.2 Education System 30
        2.2.1 School Education 31
        2.2.2 Special Education: Policy and Current Status . . 37
    2.3 Teacher Education 42
        2.3.1 Pre-Service Education 42
        2.3.2 In-Service Education 45

3 Social Construction of Learning Disability 49
    3.1 Social Construction of Disability 49
    3.2 Social Construction of Learning Disability 51
        3.2.1 Theoretical Perspectives 51
        3.2.2 Historical Perspectives 60
        3.2.3 International Perspectives 65

CONTENTS

3.3 Teachers' Perceptions of the Causes of Learning Disabilities. 71
    3.3.1 Consolidated View of Issues on Causes of Learning Disabilities 71
    3.3.2 Teacher Stance 79
    3.3.3 Relevant Background Theories 81
    3.3.4 Relevant Studies in Korea and Other Countries 87

PART III. RESEARCH DESIGN AND METHODOLOGY 97

4 Methods 99

4.1 Participants 99
    4.1.1 Population and Distribution 99
    4.1.2 Sampling 100
    4.1.3 Characteristics 105

4.2 Materials 106
    4.2.1 Development of Questionnaire 106
        4.2.1.1 Dimensionality. 107
        4.2.1.2 Item Revision 108
        4.2.1.3 Causal Factors of Learning Disabilities. . . . 108
        4.2.1.4 Reliability 110
    4.2.2 Procedure of Conducting Regression. 112
        4.2.2.1 Logistic Regression. 112
        4.2.2.2 Linear Regression 113
    4.2.3 Validity 114
    4.2.4 Pilot Study. 115
    4.2.5 Description of Scales and Questionnaire Construction. 115

4.3 Procedure 116

4.4 Research Design and Data Analysis 117

PART IV. RESEARCH RESULTS 123

5 Results. 125

5.1 Research Question 1 and Hypotheses 125
    5.1.1 Hypothesis 1.1 126
    5.1.2 Hypothesis 1.2 127
    5.1.3 Hypothesis 1.3 128
    5.1.4 Hypothesis 1.4 129

    5.2 Research Question 2 and Hypotheses 130
        5.2.1 Hypothesis 2.1. 130
        5.2.2 Hypothesis 2.2. 131
        5.2.3 Hypothesis 2.3. 132
        5.2.4 Hypothesis 2.4. 133
        5.2.5 Hypothesis 2.5. 134
    5.3 Research Question 3 and Hypothesis 135
        5.3.1 Hypothesis 135
        5.3.2 Descriptive Statistics: Collaboration Situation 135

Part V. Discussion and Conclusion 137

6 Research Findings and Discussion 139
    6.1 Summary of Findings. 139
    6.2 Comparison with Findings from Previous Studies. 143

7 Conclusion and Practical Implication 149
    7.1 Rethinking the Korean Concept of Learning Disability:
        The Need for a Broader Perspective 150
    7.2 The Need for Reform in Special Education Teacher
        Preparation Programs. 157
    7.3 Limitations of the Study 161
    7.4 Suggestions for Further Research 161

References 163

Appendix A 199

Appendix B 207

List of Figures

2.1	Chronological chart of Korean history	24
2.2	Map of Korea	25
2.3	History of education in Korea	26
2.4	School education system in Korea	32
2.5	National basic curriculum for all school levels	33
2.6	Issue of teacher's certificates as of 2005	43
3.1	Theoretical perspectives on LD: models of LDs and paradigm shift	52
3.2	Nested social contexts in the social system perspective	60
3.3	Historical perspectives of LDs: four major phases	61
4.1	Administrative divisions of South Korea	101
4.2	Educational offices in South Korea under the MOE & HRD	103
4.3	Research design	120
4.4	Data analysis	121

List of Tables

2.1	Overview: proportion of schools, students, and teachers	34
2.2	Primary revisions: current Special Education Promotion Act (SEPA) vs. revised version	39
2.3	Number of special education teachers who received in-service education by training program and institutions in 2006	47
4.1	Distribution of Korean special education teachers by their qualification and education offices	100
4.2	Distribution of samples by their education offices and number of e-mails sent to samples	104
4.3	Description of sample (Respondents)	105
4.4	Factor analysis – Rotated Component Matrix	109
4.5	Total Variance Explained	110
4.6	Item-Total Statistics – Teacher related school items	111
4.7	Item-Total Statistics – Student's personality items	111
4.8	Item-Total Statistics – Student's cognitive items	112
4.9	Correlations as indicator of component 4 (Student's family items) homogeneity	112
4.10	Overview of questionnaire structure	116
4.11	Research questions and corresponding hypotheses	118
5.1	Predicted logit of *normal or above average intelligence*	126
5.2	Predicted logit of *disorder in basic psychological processes*	127
5.3	Predicted logit of *exclusion clause*	129
5.4	Predicted logit of *central nervous system dysfunction*	130
5.5	Predicted logit of *interviews*	131
5.6	Predicted logit of *standardized test*	132
5.7	Predicted logit of *observation in regular classroom*	133
5.8	Predicted logit of *error pattern analysis*	133
5.9	Predicted logit of *alternative assessment methods*	134
6.1	Overview of findings	140
6.2	Summary of findings	141
6.3	Descriptive summary of findings	142

Acknowledgments

I wish to extend my heartfelt appreciation to a number of people who contributed significantly to the preparation and completion of this book and the research on which it is based.

My heartfelt gratitude to my *Doktormutter, Prof. Dr. Rosemarie Mielke* at the University of Hamburg, for her great supervision, advice in academic and personal aspects and endless support over the years, especially during the hardest times of my doctoral study in Germany. I am deeply grateful to her for providing me with many valuable suggestions and for empowering me to drive the research towards success. Without her enthusiasm, it would not have been possible to complete my dissertation at the University of Hamburg. I am truly thankful to her for being my supervisor.

My sincere gratitude to my *Doktorvater, Prof. Dr. Thomas Hofsäss* at Leipzig University, for his support from the beginning of my stay in Hamburg, his encouragement, patience and gentle guidance in all phases of my doctoral study in Germany. I am greatly indebted to him for giving me the opportunity of being part of the Institute for Special Education at Leipzig University and for integrating me in his team, which allowed for me to experience a different mentality and culture, working day by day in a German environment. Thanks as well to the staff of the Institute of Special Education at Leipzig University for their care and concern. Thanks to my friend and colleague Dr. Conny Melzer who supported me with her kindness and friendship.

Special thanks to *Prof. Dr. Meinert Meyer* at the University of Hamburg for his great insights, perspectives, guidance and sense of humor. I want to personally thank him for letting me take part in a wonderful doctoral colloquium where I gained valuable experience and insight into the field of education.

My sincere thanks and appreciation to *DAAD* (*Deutscher Akademischer Austausch Dienst*, German Academic Exchange Service), which awarded a scholarship for my doctoral study in Germany. I am much indebted to DAAD for their great help by supporting the whole dissertation writing and publishing process at the University of Hamburg and Leipzig University. Financial support for this book was also provided by the DAAD.

Dr. Phil. Sung, Jung Gyung

Part I.

Introduction

1

APPROACHING THE CONCEPT OF LEARNING DISABILITIES: AN OVERVIEW

A good teacher is one who empowers her/his students and is empowered by them. Being a teacher myself, I believe that teachers have far more positive influence over their students than they may realize. I always say this to students in my course who are prospective or practicing teachers. It is the power of teachers to help children build upon their strengths and learn to compensate for their weaknesses.

All children progress at different rates and have different ways in which they learn best. Children with learning disabilities (LDs), whatever the cause, are more like their peers in the classroom than unlike them. They learn, like others, based on their own strength and weakness; they have a natural ability to compensate for their weakness; and they will learn more when teaching is effective, meeting their strengths and learning needs. It is important for teachers to be aware and reflect in their practice that good learning and good performance cannot be forced, but only facilitated – by realizing the importance of the child being actively involved in learning and taking the child's background into account in teaching. This applies to all children, but especially to those with LDs. As a special education teacher, I have come to appreciate that every child learns differently and progresses at her/his own rate. Children with LDs are special with their own combination of gifts, skills, needs and difficulties for learning. They may need additional or different support from that given to other children of the same age in the classroom, since they differ somewhat in the ways in which they relate to others and interact with their environment, and considering the rate and manner in which they learn. Within the school curriculum, children with LDs may excel in some areas but often struggle in others when their peers don't – in most cases, these areas concern the acquisition of basic skills such as language, literacy and numeracy. Often, these uneven learning profiles and unexpected weaknesses make it hard for teachers to identify LDs and plan instruction, which in turn can make it harder for the children with LDs to learn at school. Essentially, the teacher and the child are involved in learning from each other both as actors and reactors during a round of teaching and learning – the *Möbius* strip as in its unbroken flow. This entails that what happens in the classroom is affected by – or affects – the child as well as the teacher. Nobody behaves/acts mindlessly; we behave as we do because of our beliefs. It is our beliefs towards ourselves and others that shape what we do and have impact on others' beliefs, which in turn cause their behavior towards us, which again will influence our beliefs and subsequently reinforce our behavior. Each child comes to school with her/his own understandings, values, assumptions, learning styles and motivations. On the other hand, teachers also possess personal beliefs and values that provide an unconscious foundation for their teaching behavior in the classroom. Thus, it is essential that the teacher and the child develop an awareness of each other's viewpoint and, more importantly, that teachers reflect on their own beliefs and practice. Teacher belief has long been accepted as an important factor in teaching and learning in terms of students' academic achievement and behavior. Knowing the basic, underlying beliefs behind teacher action gives us valuable insights into what occurs in the classroom, thus providing a better understanding of teacher practice. The stance (*Haltung*) that teachers take about how and why their students are failing and how they might be helped serves as a lens of understanding for classroom events and provides an understanding of the factors that influence classroom practice by teachers. Answering the question what teachers believe about LDs and how those beliefs shape teacher decision-making and behavior, would help us deal with the barriers in the way of further improving LD education.

The argument that is being built in this chapter is firstly that any attempt to change teacher practice needs to take into account teacher stance; any reform in LD education (a reform by itself may bring some temporary changes, but finally) will fail unless changes are made in teachers' stance towards LD. Relatively few efforts have been made to address teachers' stances with respect to basic issues in the field of LD and taking it into account in policy-making, whereas researchers' stance and opinion have often been widely known and developed. An argument is made for a renewal of confidence in practitioners' stance as teachers in understanding the children's learning, success and failure at school – teacher stance [1] towards LD. This will be discussed further on in this chapter. Secondly, and importantly, LD is a relational concept [2] that cannot be understood in isolation (i.e. isolated individual and isolated occurrence) and needs to be framed in a broader context of social relations (*Soziale Beziehungen* [3]). The point being made here (and further discussed in chapter 3) is that LD cannot be fully understood by examining an

---

[1] According to Berghoff (1997, 9), "stance is a relational concept. One can only assume as stance in relationship to something or someone. As teachers we assign students a position relative to ourselves when we assume a stance. We deliver curriculum and pedagogy with conscious and unconscious assumption about 'who' the students are, 'what' they need to learn, and 'how' we should support them in learning it".

[2] cf. Relational concept, Nagi (1991), 317; see also, Wunderlich, Rice, & Amado (2002), 54f.

[3] cf. *Soziale Beziehungen,* Henning (2006), 62, 52f.

individual (e.g. deficit perspective). Rather, 'having LD' is a social construction which emerges from complex interaction of people, places and activities. Moreover, it is also important to understand that LD is not merely produced in a social context; rather it is itself part of the context that gives meaning to the participants' actions (Dudley-Marling, 2004, 485).

From the systemic-constructivist perspective *(systemisch-konstruktivistische Perspektive*[4]*)*, the theoretical framework underlying this book and the research on which it is based, learning and also disability in learning *(Behinderung des Lernens)* is to be understood within the social context in which it occurs (Werning & Lütje-Klose, 2006, 76). This allows for the focus to be extended from the individual to a broader context, understanding LD within the complex of social interactions performed in a place called school, which is itself situated in a broader social, political and cultural context (Dudley-Marling, 2004, 485). This perspective acknowledges that LDs emerge within a complex network, among factors which interact and mutually influence each other in a circular way; maintains that particular factors such as good teaching and caring as well as support for the child can compensate for others (such as low cognitive ability and/or social disadvantages of the child) (Werning & Lütje-Klose, 2006, 77). In turn, however, this also means that teachers' negative and stigmatizing attitude towards the child and/or bad teaching can accelerate the child's learning difficulties (Werning & Lütje-Klose, 2006, 77). The use of the systemic-constructivist perspective forces us, as experts, to seek above and beyond the relationship between the causes of LDs (what is wrong with the child, "in-the-head-perspective", Dudley-Marling, 2004, 482), and instructional strategies to repair or fix ("fix-it-and-get-better treatment", Thomas & Loxley, 2007, 44). Rather, this perspective demands that we recognize the complexity of the many issues related to these children who are being educated in regular school setting, regardless of whether they are officially identified as having LD or not. Inclusive education – of children with and also of children at risk for LDs is one of the most discussed issues in the field of special education. In fact, inclusion has become an international buzzword and terms like 'inclusive education' and 'inclusive school' are used generically in our society (e.g. Moser & Sasse, 2008; Thomas & Loxley, 2007; Segal, 2005; Westwood, 2007; Avissar, 2005). Schools strive to be inclusive by educating the full range of children, and, by implication, teachers are encouraged and expected to address and respond to the diversity of needs of all learners. The move towards inclusion has entailed changes in schools and has had an impact on the role of teachers as facilitators of learning *(Förderer des Lernens*[5]*)*. In practice, inclusion has required changes in how teach-

---

[4] cf. *Soziologisch-systemtheoretische Perspektive*, Luhmann (1977), (1993); *System Heilpädagogik*, Speck (2003); *Mensch-Umwelt-System*, Sander (2003), (1999).
[5] The role of the teachers has many facets (e.g. Hack & Williams, 1984) but that of facilitators of learning *(Förderer des Lernens)* (Rogers, 1974; Zimring, 1994) is perceived as the most essential

ers teach, as well as changes in how students with and without disabilities interact with and relate to one another in the classroom. The role of teachers and schools of facilitating learning encompasses teaching and learning practices that recognize diversity provide for active and deep learning (e.g. Entwistle, 1981; Prosser & Trigwell, 1999; Ramsden, 1992) that provide opportunities for social learning (e.g. Bandura, 1977) and that provide supportive learning environments. From the systemic-constructivist perspective, 'school' is to be understood as a democratic institution, a place where experience is enriched by diversity and where the right to be different is ensured – a school for all children (*"eine Schule für alle Kinder"*, Moser & Sasse, 2008, 105). This implies legitimizing diversity and dealing with problems of equality and equity, and involves empowering[6] those from disadvantaged and minority backgrounds. Diversity encompasses sex, race, age, disability, religion, ethnic origin and a wide variety of other factors and characteristics such as socio-economic status, social/cultural background and so much more. This will be further discussed in this chapter with regard to LDs. In the inclusive education practice, students are not labeled within or excluded from the learning environment because of any of these characteristics. Inclusive education practice, therefore, is about human rights and is the practical way in which we can put our equality and diversity agenda into action.

Importantly, inclusive education practice relies on teachers – it depends on teachers' attitudes towards the students with disabilities, on their capacity to enhance social relations, on their view on differences (that is, diversity as previously above) in the classrooms and their willingness to deal with these differences effectively (European Agency for Development in Special Needs Education, 2003, 4). In other words, as Miles (2005, 13) put it, "teachers are arguably the most valuable human resources available to promote inclusive practices. If they do not believe in inclusion, they can become a major barrier to progress". The point to be made here is that, as written by Thomas & Loxley (2007, 43): "When children are excluded from the mainstream it is because someone feels that they will not fit. To examine why people don't fit, and to help organizations to enable them to fit, we have to understand them as people and to understand the people in the organizations that accept or reject them".

The following section discusses some of the major characteristics associated with LD, taking a closer look at recent literature (for more literature review see chapter 3). Students with or also at risk for LDs (*"Risikokinder"*, Schründer-Lenzen, 2007, 181) are those who do not make adequate progress within the school

---

role for a teacher.

[6] By definition, empowerment is aimed at the disadvantaged with the aspiration of creating the transition from a state of powerlessness to a state of power -in which they feel responsible for their fate, take responsibility for their action, and actively participate in the process of change- at both the individual and collective levels (Al-Haj & Mielke, 2007, 2).

curriculum, particularly in basic skill areas covering language, literacy and numeracy (Westwood, 2004, 53). And apart from these difficulties, many (although not all) of them present social, emotional or behavioral problems (e.g. Wiener & Tardif, 2004; Bauer & Shea, 1998). They often exhibit difficulties in building and retaining social relationships (e.g. Al-Yagon & Mikulincer, 2004; Wiener & Schneider, 2002) and in acquiring age-appropriate social skills (e.g. Forness & Kavale, 1996). Such problems (may) have a negative influence on their self-concept (e.g. Bear & Minke, 1996), since it is derived from experiences with the social environment, which is based on the messages conveyed by their parents, teachers and peers who are significant others in the home, school and community (e.g. Bear, Minke, Griffin, & Deemer, 1998, 91f.; see also Cole et al., 2001). It is important to understand that students with and at risk for LDs run a greater risk than their non-disabled peers of having such problems. According to studies, students with LDs have been found to manifest motivational problems, and it has been suggested that this is a common characteristic of LDs (e.g. Pintrich, Anderman, & Klobucar, 1994; Fulk, Brigham, & Lohman, 1998; Sideridis & Scanlon, 2006). With regard to motivational problems, students with LDs are often referred to as having learned helplessness (Maier & Seligman, 1976, 3ff.; see also Black, 1977, 41) and are more likely to exhibit negative attributions and have an external locus of control when compared with their non-disabled peers (e.g. Rogers & Saklofske, 1985). More to the point, students with LDs much depend on outside influences that affect them and tend not to believe that they control their success and failure in learning. In learning situations, they attribute failure as well as success not to their own efforts but to situations or events beyond their control (Pierangelo & Giuliani, 2008, 39), and due to their experience of continuous failure over time, they do not expect to succeed with any task they are given and feel powerless to change this outcome (Westwood, 2007, 13). Unfortunately, these problems are likely to establish a "vicious cycle where academic failure and negative affective characteristics are mutually reinforcing" (Rogers & Saklofske, 1985, 276), in which the student with LD becomes poorer in school achievement, self-concept, motivation, social relationships with their peers/teachers and attitudes towards school. Moreover, students with LDs not only possess those characteristics that constitute risks, but may also experience common risk factors such as poverty and parental conflict. In fact, several studies have indicated that students' socio-economic status (SES) correlates with students' school performance (e.g. Chatterji, 2006; Werning & Wischer, 2002; McLoyd, 1998). Students from low SES backgrounds are considered at high risk for LDs, because for the most part they experience prenatal stress, are born into chronic poverty and live in unsettled family environments. Indeed, not all students who come from disadvantaged socio-economic backgrounds are doomed to negative school outcomes (e.g. Masten, 1994); however, many of those students exhibit poor school performance and behavioral problems (e.g. McLoyd, 1998). Particularly, many students with or at risk for LDs – an increasing number of whom is being educated in regular primary schools – come from disadvantaged SES and family structures (Werning, Löser, & Urban, 2008, 50; see also Klein, 2001; Hengst, 2008; Zander, 2008; Wocken, 2000). These students enter school with different levels of school readiness (*"Schulfähigkeit"* and *"Schulbereitschaft"*, Keller & Novak, 2000[7], 312), and many of them begin school with less prior knowledge or skills in certain domains (e.g. Werning & Wischer, 2002; Vernon-Feagans et al., 2001; Storch & Whitehurst, 2001). For the most part, students with LDs lack the experiences that prepare them for learning in school, particularly regarding literacy and numeracy (e.g. Westwood, 2004), which are the key elements of school readiness and the strongest predictors of later school achievement (e.g. Ducan et al, 2007). Especially for primary school students, prior knowledge (*Vorwissen*), which strongly predicts later school success (e.g. Helmke & Weinert, 1997), is also highly associated with family socialization[8] (*"Vorwissen"*, Werning & Lütje-Klose, 2006, 55; see also Makin & McNaught, 2001). With regard to literacy in particular (as for the field of LD, much research has been done on this area and thus also the impact of SES on children's early literacy), for instance, children supported by their parents in language development are mostly literate before they learn to read, and this may have a strong impact on their language and literacy competencies in school further on (e.g. Painter, 1999; Emmitt, Pollock, & Komescaroff, 2003). There is considerable evidence that family practices differ according to income[9] and social status levels (that is, SES) and that children from low SES are at greater risk for school failure as a consequence of the literacy practices in their homes (Stone et al., 2006, 160; see also Storch & Whitehurst, 2001; Vernon-Feagans et al., 2001). Some researchers have argued that the unfortunate link between low SES backgrounds and LDs can be explained by communication problems at school, particularly concerning the relationship between the student with LD and the teacher. In this regard, there have been discussions concerning the 'mismatch' of children's language milieu at home and at school, which makes it harder for them to learn and access the general education curriculum than it is for most students of the same age at school (*"Miß-Deutungen der Sprache"*, Begemann, 1996, 135). In fact, some researchers believe that communication barriers do exist between many students with LDs and their teachers (Belusa et al., 1992,

---

[7] The term *"Schulreife"* (school readiness) is to be understood as *"Schulfähigkeit"* in the objective sense and *"Schulbereitschaft"* in the subjective sense (Keller & Novak, 2000, 312).
[8] cf. *Primäre Sozialisation,* Hurrelman & Ulich (2002); Hurrelman (2002)
[9] In comparison with middle income parents, factors that impede low income parents' ability to provide children with literacy-rich home environments were for example a lack of financial resources, family support, educational background and available time (Vernon-Feagans et al., 2001 cited in Stone, Silliman, Ehren, & Aple, 2006, 160).

162). Thus most students with LDs struggle and fail in school settings since they (may) differ in the ways in which they relate to others and interact with their environment, or the rate and manner in which they learn while their 'normal' peers' behavior is in congruence with the norms of the environment (i.e. school) (Shea & Bauer, 1994, 8). Hence the "congruence", the 'match' between the student and his/her environment, is the major factor that impacts whether a student is identified as having an LD or not (Thurman, 1977, 329).

The point being made here is that many students with LDs come from disadvantaged SES backgrounds (or vice versa). Thus they may suffer from economic and social distress, and from continuous discrimination and stigmatization. Clearly, teachers have little control over these factors. Nevertheless, it is important that teachers are aware of and understand the impact that such emotional strain, engendered by poverty and social insecurity, can have on students' learning (Al-Haj & Mielke, 2007, 2). Because teachers' ways of thinking and understanding affect the way in which they shape their teaching practice (e.g. Nespor, 1987; Shavelson & Stern, 1981). As mentioned above, a teacher's stance towards the student guides teacher decision and classroom management (e.g. Allington, 1996 as cited in Berghoff, 1997, 5; Ainscow, 1998), hence generally reflects on her/his teaching behavior towards the student – and towards students with disabilities in particular (e.g. Poulou & Norwich, 2002; Brophy, 1985; Schechtman, Reiter, & Schanin, 1993). Particularly, special education teachers play a key role in the achievement of students with LDs. In regular school settings, special education teachers not only provide support (develop and suggest accommodation) in instructional planning and actual teaching, but also provide others, such as teachers, parents and peers who are 'significant others' in the home, school and community, with explanations of the student's disability, learning style and strengths. In other words, the special education teacher is an "inclusion facilitator" in regular school, who serves as an 'adaptor' and 'collaborator' (Ferguson, Meyer, Jeanchild, Juniper, & Zingo, 1992 as cited in Bauer et al., 2001, 342) for the welfare of students with LDs who are perceived as varying from their peers. Obviously, special education teachers are the key persons of inclusive practice, and hence we may conclude that a successful inclusive practice for students with LDs largely depends on special education teachers' stance towards students with LDs.

Today, as the move towards 'more inclusive education' (in terms of qualitative enhancement rather than quantitative growth) gains momentum, it is increasingly important to understand the stance of special education teachers towards students with LDs. Because they serve as inclusion facilitators in regular school (as mentioned above), knowing the commonalities and differences between special education teachers and regular teachers would allow us to add to the knowledge base on which collaborative relationships among teachers are built in inclusive settings

(Clark, 1997, 78). Furthermore, knowing the approaches and methods used by special education teachers and obtaining reliable data on special education teacher opinions would lead us to conclusions concerning the assessment [10] of LD (Prücher & Langfeldt, 2002, 409), which has been a long-standing issue in the field of special education (Kavale, Holdnack, & Mostert, 2005, 2).

1.1 Problem Statement

What do special education teachers think about students with LDs? A simple question with complex answers, which need to take into account the impact that special education teachers' beliefs, their assumptions and perceptions about students with LDs have on teacher-student interaction in instructional and learning situations. It should be noted that special education teachers' beliefs, by affecting the way in which they perceive 'reality', guide both their thoughts and their behaviors – a belief is an attitude consistently applied to an activity (Eisenhart, Shrum, Harding & Cuthbert, 1988, 54). Despite this, little attention has been drawn to the thoughts of special education teachers. Although acknowledged as being important in inclusive education for students with LDs (see above Clark, Prücher & Langfeldt), it must be stated that relatively little research has been conducted on the stance of special education teachers towards LDs than on that of regular teachers and parents. As yet, relatively few efforts have been made to explore and develop special education teachers' stance towards basic issues and problems (such as definition and assessment) in the field of LD, whereas researchers' opinions have often been known and developed. For that matter, do researcher and special education teachers share a common stance on LD?

The question is crucial, particularly with respect to defining LD and identifying students with LDs, because firstly, although it has been debated over many years, choosing the appropriate definition and criteria for LD eligibility has remained debatable (Proctor & Prevatt, 2003, 459), and due to this dissension (Mercer, 1997, 14f., see also Doris, 1993; Kavale & Forness, 1985; Keogh, 1986; Mercer, 1997; MacMillan & Siperstein, 2002) the inhomogeneity of definitions has continued to plague the field of LD (e.g. Brinkerhoff, Shaw, & McGuire, 1992; Gregg, 1994; Mellard, 1990; Siegel, 1999). While the academic field has failed to reach consensus, in practice, the vagueness of definitions of LD has provoked varying estimations of when and where LD occurs, which consequently has lead to different rates of LD (Prücher & Langfeldt, 2002, 399, see also Lauth, 2000). Secondly, and importantly, if researchers (academics) and practitioners (teachers) arrive at sharing a common stance on LD, many problems may be resolved based on a

---

[10] Educational assessment serves five primary purposes: first, screening and identification; second, eligibility and diagnosis; third, IEP and placement; fourth, instructional planning; and, finally, evaluation (Berdine & Meyer, 1987 as cited in NICHCY, 1997).

consensus. However, if the two parties differ in their stance, positive changes are more difficult to achieve, because actions are not based on a consensual decision, and consequently the parties may work at cross-purposes (Kavale & Reese, 1991, 141). Unfortunately, it seems that researchers and practitioners/teachers are not likely to agree on who students with LDs are and subsequently how many students with LDs there are – a gap between research and practice (for example, the distinction between 'school identified (SI)' and 'research identified (RI)' students with LDs, MacMillan & Siperstein, 2003 [11], 3, see also MacMillan, Gresham, & Bocian, 1998). All too often, teachers' perspectives have been disregarded when compared to researchers in spite of its importance (Gerber, 2000 [12], 40). Instead of making an effort to understand how schools function and to acknowledge the diverse factors teachers have for identifying students with LDs, the research community (academic field) have tended to interpret the discrepancy between SI LD and RI LD as an error on the schools' part, showing a preference for RI LD over SI LD (MacMillan & Siperstein, 2002, 3). The point being made here is that despite the extensive literature and work on definition and identification of LD, it will fail to provide adequate service to students with LDs, if the research does not inform practice ("much of our research base, particularly regarding effective intervention and classroom integration, may not apply", Gerber, 2002, 341). If the discussion continues to be confined to 'what LD ought to be' rather than 'what LD is' (this may happen if the discussion takes place exclusively among academics), this divergence of stances will be widened instead of narrowed, and it will become more difficult to close the gap between research and practice in the near future.

In Korea, efforts have been made to reach consensus on how to operationalize the authoritative definition of 'LD', since the relatively new concept of LD, compared to other disability categories (cf. Ch. 2), was officially included as a category of special education under the Special Education Promotion Act [13] (SEPA) of 1994. For years, there has been debate among researchers, practitioners and policymakers about the proper way of operationalizing the definition for purposes of assessment, identification, placement and service (e.g. Jung DY, 1991; Kim YO, 1992; Park HS, 1992; Kang WY, 1992; Baek WH, 1993; Hwang JW, 1995; Lee SH, 1999; Shin JH, 1999). The latest revision of SEPA (Individuals with Disabilities Special Education Act, IDSEA) which took effect in 2008, was one of

---

[11] According to MacMillan & Siperstein (2002), over half of the SI students with LD failed to meet the definition criteria of the authoritative definition (employed in RI LD) for reasons that can be found in the operation of schools.

[12] "Demonstration that schools identify problem learners with markedly different characteristics than those proposed by formal models... too often has led to premature conclusion that the models must be right and the schools wrong" (Gerber, 2000, 40)

[13] The SEPA definition of LD states that "pupils with special educational needs identified as learning disabled are pupils with disabilities in specific academic learning areas such as mathematical calculation, speaking, reading, and writing".

those efforts to work out the obscurity and oversimplification of the SEPA's definition and criteria for LD (Byun CS, 2007, 56), which pose difficulties to the identification of LD. For a comparison between SEPA and IDSEA, see chapter 2. Much has changed and yet so little – while Korea has achieved a remarkable quantitative growth, the situation concerning the qualitative improvement in LD education is less clear. Unfortunately, such rapid quantitative expansion has often been achieved at the expense of quality. In this aspect, LD education has actually changed very little over the past decade. For instance, LD definition and criteria is one of the important indicators reflecting on the quality of LD education. Despite the efforts to settle the issue, the definition of LD has become articulated in many different operational definitions, and LD identification criteria vary across educational institutions and by researchers (e.g. SEPA, 1994; KEDI, 1990 as cited in Kim DI, Lee DS, & Shin JH, 2003, 28; MOE & HRD, 2006 as cited in Jung DY, 2007, 186; KISE, 2001). As a result, the reported prevalence rate of LD ranges from 0.83% to 14% (Kim DI, Lee DS, & Shin JH, 2003, 45; see also Korea Inclusive Education Association, 2006). It might therefore be difficult to ascertain the real prevalence of LD in Korea, as McGrady (1980, 510) puts it: "No one seems to be able to agree on a definition, but everyone knows it when they see it". According to the latest government report, there are 8,447 students with LDs enrolled in schools, which represents 14.5% of the number of students with special educational needs (SEN) enrolled in special education (MOE & HRD, 2005b, 7). Experts, however, assume that there is a large number of students at risk for LDs or who have LDs uncovered – students who have learning difficulties in one or more learning areas, but who are not receiving any support, because they have not been identified as eligible for special education and related services (e.g. Jeong KS & Kim AH, 2006; Park HS & Cho JK, 2004; KISE, 2001). Notably, it is the students who suffer most from the lack of appropriate instruction and opportunity for differentiated learning, while we continue to debate, persuading our theories and failing to reach consensus while widening the divergence between our stances. Special education [14] is free and compulsory throughout all school levels [15] in Korea. Principally, students with LDs are being educated in regular schools; while about 8.16% of them receive special educational support in regular classes, most of the students with LDs are taught in special classes [16] by special education teachers (MOE &

---

[14] In most cases, special education is provided in one, or a combination, of the following forms across school levels: regular class at regular school, special class at regular school, special school (cf. IDSEA Ch. 3, Article 17).

[15] In present Korea, special education is free and compulsory in primary and middle schools, while it is free in kindergartens and high schools. As from May 26th, 2008, it becomes compulsory in kindergartens and high schools, too (cf. IDSEA Ch. 3, Article 17).

[16] Special education is provided in one, or a combination of regular classes and special classes at regular schools. Special classes run on either fulltime or part time basis and the special education services are provided by special education teachers.

HRD, 2005b, 7). Thus, along with the promotion of inclusive quality education, followed by a period of quantitative expansion, increasing demands are currently posed upon special education teachers in Korea. Because, firstly, the way teachers teach is of critical importance to any education reform setting out to enhance quality. Secondly, as previously mentioned, special education teachers as 'inclusion facilitators' (see above, p. 7) have foremost influence on regular teachers' practices and attitudes – be it towards students with LD, (learning) disability itself or inclusive education.

In fact, considering the current situation of LD education in Korea, much depends on special education teachers and their capacity for inclusive practice. This is particularly true concerning the professional capacity to collaborate effectively with regular teachers and the professional capacity in subject matter, classroom pedagogy and decision-making strategies essential for participating in decisions that directly affect classroom practices (such as IEPs, FBAs or BIPs) [17]. This does not only mean physical proximity, but also academic and social inclusion of students with LDs in education. In Korea, students with LDs constitute the majority in special education classrooms at regular schools (MOE & HRD, 2005b, 7). However, in recent years, several studies have revealed that although the enrolment rates of students with LDs in regular primary schools are up in most regions, the quality of LD education has been suffering (Jeong KS & Kim AH, 2006, 30; see also Park HS, 1999; Cho KS & Whang IK, 2003; Kang KS et al., 2000). It might be assumed that truly individualized instruction and intervention through IEP, FBA or BIP for these students rarely occurs, and that placement decisions are often not based on students' needs; instead they are inserted into established programs. In many primary schools, students with LD may share the regular classroom (in this sense, described as the same physical space at school) with their non-disabled peers with minimal accommodation or modification necessary for them. Whereas some students with mild LDs may participate in the traditional core academic content areas (such as mathematics, language, arts, science, history etc.), the majority of students with LDs may be only included in physical education, music, arts and/or vocational programs; other students with more severe LDs may stay in their special education classrooms for most of their school days. These results demonstrate that the responsibility for LD education still remains with special education teachers, and that students with LDs are considered to belong into special education classrooms. In this regard, it seems that little has changed – special education (and related services) in Korea have traditionally been a subsystem of the general educational system, and have therefore been considered to be beyond the regular teachers' area of responsibility (e.g. Park SH, 1999; Kang KS et al., 2000; Cho

---

[17] Individualized Education Program (IEP), Functional Behavioral Assessment (FBA) or Behavior Intervention plan (BIP) (e.g. Van Acker, Boreson, & Gable, & Potterton, 2005).

KS & Whang IK, 2002). Hence, for facilitating responsible inclusion for students with LDs [18], there are many questions that need to be asked and answered in Korea. Concerns have arisen particularly over the special education teachers' capacity in the assessment of LD (Park HS & Cho YG, 2004, 129). Numerous studies have demonstrated that the assessment process of LD in regular schools has been chiefly – or rather solely – implemented by special education teachers (e.g. Jung DY & Kim JY, 1999; Kim JY, Lee MS, Lee YH, & Choi SM, 2001; Cho KS & Whang IK, 2003; Lee MS, 2001 as cited in Lee MR & Kown YH, 2006, 230). Researchers have observed that special education teachers use SEPA's definition when identifying LD and tend to shorten the procedure under the prevailing circumstances in school settings instead of using various assessment methods (Kim YO & Bong WY, 2004, 100). Also, researchers have concluded that the vagueness and obscurity of SEPA's definition and criteria for LD much contribute to these problems and to the lack of guidance for practitioners on how to assess students with LD and thereby collaborate with regular teachers (e.g. Kim YO & Bong WY, 2004; Byun CS, 2002a, 2002b). Further, it has been reported that IEP (and FBA/BIP) development, which are of crucial importance to the assessment process, are often carried out solely by special education teachers (Cho KS & Whang IK, 2003, 127). With regard to this shortcoming, Choi SS (2006, 131) addressed the need for administrational support to build a collaborative climate in schools for an effective regular and special education teacher collaboration. A collaborative school climate is requisite because, although regular teachers say they think special education teachers are helpful in IEP planning for students with LDs, collaboration and communication are in many cases encountered rather infrequently for various reasons (Schumm, Vaughn, Haager, McDowell, Rothlein, & Saumell, 1995, 335f.). Researchers assume that the most common barrier to teacher collaboration is that teachers initially perceive teaming as an increase to their workload; a significant amount of time and (mental) effort is needed for planning as a team and for building a collaborative work relationship (Bauwens, Hourcade, & Friend, 1989, 18). Despite the growing awareness of the importance of collaboration between regular and special education teachers in the assessment process, little research has been conducted on the topic in Korea as yet. To make teacher collaboration possible and effective for identifying LDs and developing IEPs and instructional planning for students with LDs, teachers need a clear and precise operational definition which specifies the operation and procedures by which the construct of LD can be recognized and measured (Swanson, 1991, 242). First of all, there is a need for reaching

---

[18] "Responsible inclusion of students with LDs in regular education involves putting the student first, allowing teachers to self-select their involvement in inclusion, providing adequate resources, developing school-based inclusive models, maintaining a continuum of services, offering professional development, developing an inclusion philosophy, and refining curriculum approaches and service delivery to meet all students' needs" (Vaughn & Schumm, 1995, 264).

a consensus on the LD definition on a national level which suits the Korean context. Otherwise researchers, teachers, parents and administrators will be confused; as Hammill (1990, 74) puts it, the study of a field cannot begin in earnest until involved individuals have agreed on the definition. Conclusively, Korea's probably most urgent task in the field of LD is to provide a consensual definition as well as unified (diagnostic) criteria for LD on a national level.

Much of the Korean research on LD is based on US theories and concepts thus far (e.g. Kang JG, Kim JH, & Foley, 2004; Jung DY, 2007). It has been criticized that many Korean researchers have mainly just introduced or cited the IDEA (Individuals with Disabilities Education Act) definition of LD (Kang JG et al., 2004, 293), and that most of them have merely utilized translated or re-standardized assessment methods developed in and for the US in their research (Jung DY, 2007,186). The lopsidedness of current approaches justifies looking for alternative aspects which can carry implications for Korea. However, solely adopting the definition concept from other countries or changing assessment formats is not likely to bring about meaningful reform in LD education. Western methods of identification do not align with curriculum, subjects, teaching methods, home education and other factors in Korea (Jung DY, 2007, 186). It appears that Korean researchers tend to focus on introducing and adopting study findings from other countries during the initial phase, rather than deducing from their own investigations which would suit the educational, social and cultural background in Korea. On the positive side, however, the field of LD in Korea has developed dramatically fast within a short time. Extensive work has been done in recent years on the development of a new definition and criteria of LD as well as identification methods appropriate for the Korean context (e.g. Kim AH, 2006; Kim AH & Lee DM, 2005; Kim JK, 2001; Lee DS, 2001). There has also been an increasing awareness of the need to close the gap between theory and practice. It is obvious that efforts to resolve this issue are presently underway in Korea, and that more attention is being paid to the perspective of teachers in the field of LD (e.g. Jeong KS & Kim AH, 2006; Park HS & Cho YK, 2004; Kim YO & Bong WY, 2004; Kim DI & Lee IH, 2003; Byun CS, 2002a). Nevertheless, there is insufficient research available to bridge the gap that currently exists between research and practice of LD education (Byun CS, 2007, 57). It is a fact worthy of notice that, whilst there is a need for theory to underpin practice, there is also a need for research to deliver answers to practical questions. Although some studies supporting the link between teacher perception and practice might have provided insight into LD definition and identification, current literature regarding special education teachers' stance on this topic is rather void or merely inferential in Korea. Although the problems related to the assessment process are apparent in the regular school setting and – as previously mentioned – special education teachers are intricately involved in the assessment of LD, little is known about special education teachers' perception of and practice on LD.

1.2 Purpose of the Study and Research Questions

The research on which this book is based focused on Korean special education teachers' stance towards LDs. The main purpose of the research was (a) to access information pertaining to special education teachers' perceptions of the causes of LD and (b) to examine the way in which these perceptions influence their assessment practices. The most important perceptions that teachers have about their students are those that deal with the causes of students' failure [19] – those summarized under the term of causal perception (e.g. Mavropoulou & Padeliadu, 2002, 192, see also Clark & Peterson, 1986; Georgiou, Christou, & Stavrinides, 2002; Gottfredson, Marciniak, Birdseye, & Gottfredson, 1995; Madon, Jussim, & Eccles, 1997; VanOudenhoven, 1985; Babad, 1993). Several studies have suggested that such causal perceptions of teachers have crucial implications for teacher referral and the types of methods teachers implement in the assessment process (e.g. Jordan, Kirkaali-Iftar, & Diamond, 1993; Podell & Soodak, 1993; Soodak & Podell, 1994).

Hence, this research intended to explore and determine the relationship between 'what' special education teachers perceive as the 'main causes' of LD and 'how' these perceptions shape their decision-making in the assessment of students with LDs. How do special education teachers make decisions about the ways in which they assess student with LDs? What factors and considerations, particularly regarding the causes of LD (perceived by them) were given priority in these decisions? This may be an important addition to the existing body of knowledge, and may provide an interesting focus for the future theoretical debate in the field of LD. Additionally, this study provided an opportunity to look into special education teachers' self-competence in using assessment methods and to capture the collaboration situation, particularly when interpreting the students' assessment results, from the special education teachers' viewpoint. The goal thereof was to provide a basis for describing the status quo of LD assessment in regular schools.

The *main research questions* were as follows:

---

[19] Such causal perceptions of teachers regarding students' failure/success were found to influence the expectations teachers hold for the students' future academic achievement (Clarkson & Leder, 1984, 413) and also to impact the students' own attributions (Fennema, Peterson, Carpenter, & Lubinski, 1990, 55).

Research question 1 Do special education teachers' definitions of LD differ due to their perceptions of the causes of LD and their demographic background?

Research question 2 Do special education teachers' assessment methods used for the assessment of students with LDs differ due to their perceptions of the causes of LD?

Research question 3 Do special education teachers' self-competences to use assessment methods differ in their frequency of use?

Part II.

Literature Review

2

KOREA'S EDUCATION SYSTEM AND SPECIAL EDUCATION

2.1 INTRODUCTION TO KOREA

This chapter presents an overview of Korea's education system. In order to elucidate the Korean context of LD, it was felt necessary to introduce the nature of the education system and the current status of special education. Much of this chapter is based on information and material provided by the MOE & HRD and KOIS.

2.1.1 GEOGRAPHIC, HISTORICAL, CULTURAL AND DEMOGRAPHIC CONTEXT

Korea is a constitutional republic, located in the eastern section of the Asian continent, and has 5 thousand years of history and culture (Figure 2.2; Figure 2.3). The Korean population is homogeneous. Ethnically, the Koreans originate from the Mongolian race, and their language, part of a Ural-Altaic variant, uses a unique phonetic alphabet called *Hangul*. They are thus primarily one ethnic family and speak one language. It is important to mention that as early as in the 7th century, the various states of the Korean peninsula were unified under the *Silla* Kingdom (Figure 2.1). Such homogeneity has enabled Koreans to be relatively free of ethnic issues and to maintain a firm solidarity with one another (KOIS, 2007b, 13).

As shown in Figure 2.2, Korea lies adjacent to China and Japan. As a consequence of its unique position, Chinese culture filtered through Korea and into Japan. Eventually, a common Buddhist and Confucian cultural sphere formed among the three countries (KOIS, 2007a). Typical Korean folk customs are deeply rooted in shamanist beliefs and ancestor worship. Influences such as Buddhism, Confucianism, and Taoism were introduced from outside Korea. Hence the first salient feature of Korean culture lies in integration and complexity. While Buddhism and Confucianism flourished and blended harmoniously with Korean traditional thoughts and folk customs, Western culture, introduced during the late *Joseon* dynasty period, conflicted with those same traditional folk customs and beliefs[1]. Today Korea's religions are Buddhism, *Cheondoism*, Protestantism,

---

[1] At that time, there were movements against Western influences, and this resistance was reflected in

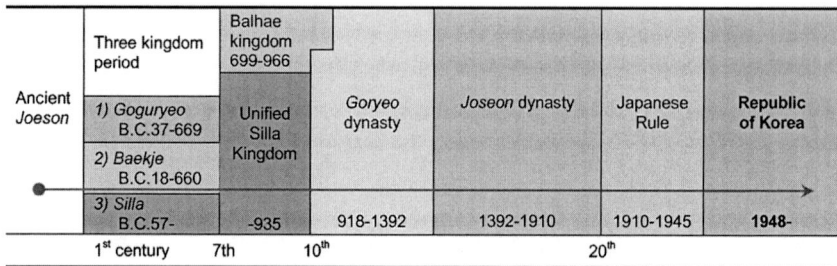

Figure 2.1   Chronological chart of Korean history[a] *(MOE & HRD, 2007, 5)*
a) According to the written history of Korea, the earliest state was the Ancient Joseon. This tribal state ended around 100 B.C. with the advent of the Three Kingdoms (Goguryeo, Baekje, andSilla) which were followed by the Unified Silla and Barhae kingdom in the 7th century. In the 10th century, the Goryeo dynasty succeeded the Unified Silla kingdom to reign over the Korean peninsula. Goryeo was, in turn, succeeded by the Joseon dynasty in the late 14th century (MOE & HRD, 2007, 4).

Catholicism and many others. Religious freedom is a right guaranteed to all citizens of the Republic of Korea, and there is no state religion (MOE & HRD, 2007, 4f.).

At the end of World War II in 1945, Korea was liberated from Japan's colonial domination, but the Korean peninsula was divided into a northern and a southern zone (38th parallel) occupied by Soviet and U.S. forces. Democratic elections were thereafter held in the South, in accordance with a U.N. resolution, and the government of the Republic of Korea was inaugurated in 1948. However, the national division and establishment of separate governments in the North and the South eventually led to a civil war, the Korean War (1950-1953) (MOE & HRD, 2007b, 5). After all, at the end of the Korean War in 1953, a new border was fixed along the Demilitarized Zone (DMZ) between North and South Korea, and has remained stable to this day (KOIS, 2007a).

As of the end of 2005, South Korea's (hereafter Korea) total population was estimated at 48,138,077 and the population density of the country was about 476 persons per square kilometer, which is relatively high in comparison to world levels (MOE & HRD, 2007, 9). A notable trend in Korea's demographics is that, with a low birth rate and extended life expectancy, the population is growing older (as of 2005, 9.1% of the total population of Korea was 65 years or older); also, the population growth (0.21% in 2005) is decreasing and is expected to further decline (KOIS, 2007b, 14).

---

the Donghak (Eastern Learning) and Wijeong cheoksa (defending orthodoxy and rejecting eterodoxy) doctrines. The philosophy of Donghak (Eastern Learning) is based on a doctrine, uniquely Korean, which embraces Confucianism, Buddhism and Taoism (MOE & HRD, 2007, 4). The uniquely Korean religion Cheondoism was derived from the above mentioned Donghak doctrines.

Map of Korea

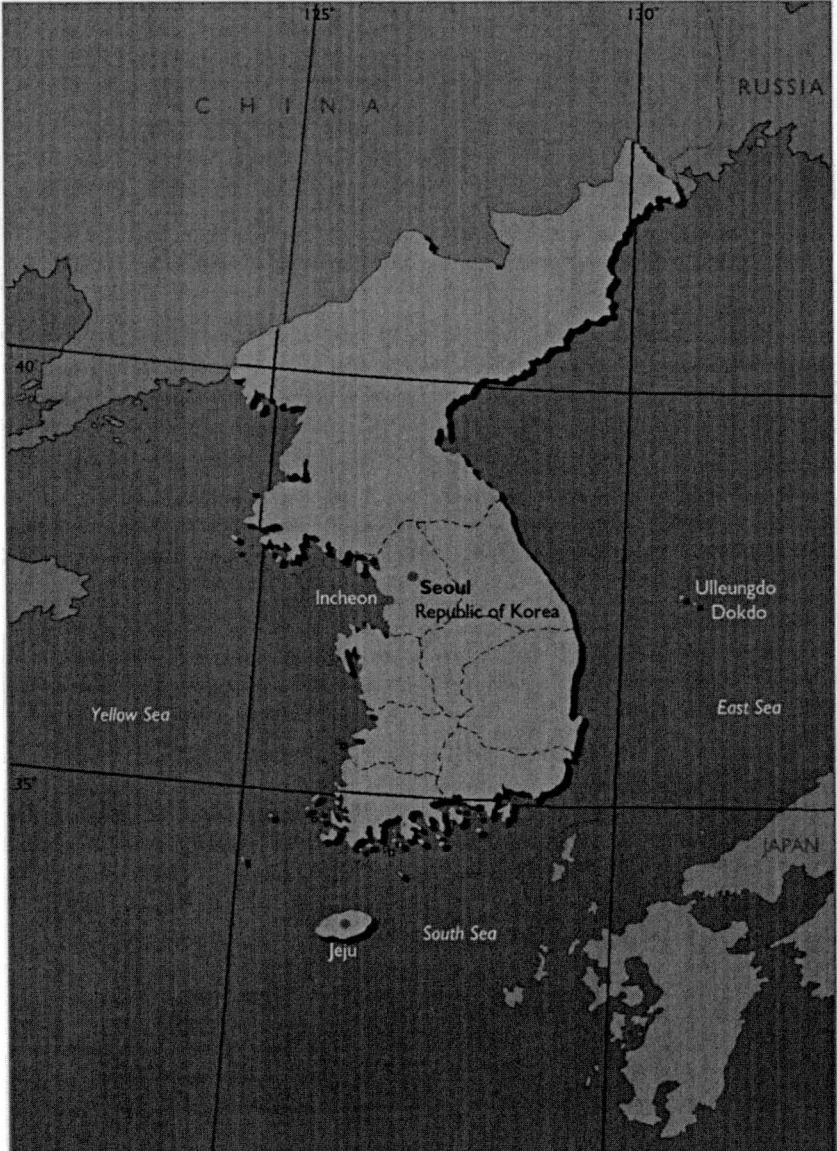

Figure 2.2   Map of Korea (MOE & HRD, 2005a, 6)

2 KOREA'S EDUCATION SYSTEM AND SPECIAL EDUCATION

Figure 2.3   History of education in Korea (MOE & HRD, 2005a, 6)

2.1.2 Socio-Economics and Educational Context

Until the early 20th century, Korea was a society based primarily on agriculture. From the 1960s, Korea has been able to join the leading group of developing countries and developed rapidly by means of high savings and investment rates as well as a strong emphasis on education. The nation became the 29th member country of the Organization for Economic Cooperation and Development (OECD) in 1996. As of 2005, the nation's per capita GNP stood at $16,291, and the annual trade volume was recorded at $314.6 billion. At that point, Korea had emerged as the world's 13th largest trading country (MOE & HRD, 2007b, 8). The rapid economic growth has also produced various side effects, and drastic social changes have brought about changes in social structure (KOIS, 2007b, 14). The population concentration in urban areas is one of those changes. The nation's rapid industrialization and urbanization in the 1960s and 70s were accompanied by continuing migration of rural residents into the cities, particularly its capital Seoul, resulting in heavily populated metropolitan areas. In addition, the shift from the traditional extended family system to the concept of the nuclear family led to a lack of housing capacities. Consequently, numerous apartment complexes are being constructed, particularly in large cities. Moreover, the nation is expected to cope with this and other problems arising from the rapid development. The social security system, including retirement grants, medical insurance, industrial accident compensation and various other types of insurance, is in place. Efforts are also undertaken to protect economically disadvantaged people, produce jobs for the poor, provide vocational training and job opportunities and help increase their income (MOE & HRD, 2007, 9f.).

2.1.3 Educational Development and Historical Context

Koreans have traditionally put great importance on education as a means of self-fulfillment as well as for social advancement. Today, Korea boasts one of the highest literacy rates in the world; Koreans are aware that well-educated people are the primary source of their rapid economic growth (KOIS, 2007, 112). In effect, education has contributed to forming a modern value system, and it has enhanced social mobility. The quantitative expansion of education created a high demand for teachers, educational facilities and equipment, and the increased educational opportunities impacted the hierarchic structure of society, extending the middle class and promoting so-called upward mobility. Eventually, the qualitative improvement of education has enhanced peoples' overall living standards and welfare (MOE & HRD, 2007, 11). Ever since the modern education system was introduced in the late 19th century, there have been five noteworthy education reforms that restructured Korea's education paradigm. The first abolished the traditional education system to pave the way for a western-oriented education system; the second converted the nation's education system to a colonial-era education system the third reform was placed right after liberation to build a democratic education system; the fourth focused on vocational training to emphasize the role of education in contributing to economic growth and productivity during the 1960s; and the fifth aimed at resolving the problems accumulated as a result of rapid quantitative growth regarding the number of students and schools as well as the problems resulting from the popularization of education after liberalization (MOE & HRD, 2005a, 138).

Education in Korea has undergone numerous transformations and streaks of development through changing objectives according to the needs of the times (cf. Figure 2.3).

Pre-modern education (4th-19^{th}century): The informal education in Korea began in the prehistoric times. The historical onset of formal education was the establishment of *Taehak* in the year 372 during the *Goguyreo* era, which focused on ethics education, aimed at educating the public based on Confucianism and Buddhism. While there were state-operated institutions to prepare the young upper class people for future government service (e.g. *Taehak, Gukhak, Gukjagam*), there were also private schools (*Sahak*) in the capital and provincial schools (*Hyanggyo*) in the countryside for children of lower ranking officials and commoners. Private schools (e.g. *Sib-i-do, Seowon*) provided a high level of education almost equal to that of the state-operated, highest institute. There were also institutes (*Gyeongdang*) for commoners in the *Goguyeo* era already, which taught material and scripture reading. This developed into the basic education institute (*Seodang*) and spread to nearly every village during the late *Joseon* dynasty, contributing greatly to education and enlightenment of the general public (MOE & HRD, 2007b, 12). Out of ancient Korean tradition, people with disabilities have always been provided with help and aid by the government (e.g. *Seodang hunyuk bangchim*; basic education notion of *Seodang*) (Gu BG, Kim DY, Kim YU, Kim WG, Park HM, Seok Di, Yoon JR, Jeong JK, Jeong JJ, Cho IS, 1996, 34f.). Although formal education may not have catered for disabled people until the late 19^{th}s century, they did receive support from their family and neighbors, emotionally and physically.

Modern education (1880-1945): Modern schools, as introduced in the 19th century, comprised private schools established by western Christian missionaries and national schools. In 1910, not long after a number of modern schools were established and before education had reached the masses, Korea was annexed by Japan. Korean education during the colonial period remained undeveloped. At that time, when many private schools established by western missionaries began to appear nationwide, the first special schools for the visually impaired (1903) and hearing impaired (1909) were established by missionaries such as Alice Moffet and Rosetta Sherwood Hall (e.g. Jung DY, 2007, 184). Thereafter, the first special school established by a Korean opened in 1935 (*Gwang Meong* school for the visually impaired, founded by *Lee Chang Hoo* pastor). The first special class established in regular school (1937) aimed at sick children. Initially, the primary beneficiaries of special education in Korea were those with visual and hearing impairments (Gu et al, 1996, 35f.).

Expansion of democratic education (1945-1950s): After liberation (1945) and with the establishment of the Republic Korea (1948), the Education Law was enacted and promulgated followed by the provision for educational autonomy and the implementation of compulsory education (MOE & HRD, 2007b, 15f.). However, although the establishment of special schools and special classes in each province and regular school were mandated by the Education Law, in practice the education of students with disabilities was not properly implemented in public institutions, but rather delegated to private institutions (e.g. Gu et al, 1996, 38). At that time (in the 1950s), education continued to endorse the role of reconstructing the nation after the Korean War (1950-1953).

Quantitative expansion of education (1960s-1970s): As previously mentioned, Korea developed rapidly from the 1960s onwards, and the rapid economic progress triggered a quantitative expansion in Korean education. The rapid growth in student population, however, also resulted in overcrowded classrooms and schools, a shortage of fully qualified teachers and educational facilities as well as intense competition in the university entrance system (MOE & HRD, 2007b, 18f.). Education for students with several disabilities started in the 1960s, when the first personnel preparation program for special education professionals was established at *Daegu University* (1961). Also, the first special schools for the physically impaired (1964) and mentally retarded (1966) were established in the 1960s, as were the first special classes in regular schools for the visually impaired (1969) and the mentally retarded (1971) at that time (Gu et al, 1996, 37). Also, efforts were made within in the scope of educational policy in order to improve the government's passive role in special education (e.g. the Five-Year Special Education Plan, 1967). However, in the majority of cases, the government gave higher priority to economic growth at that time. In 1977, the Special Education Promotional Act was enacted, which mandated free special education and related services for children with disabilities in compulsory education.

Qualitative improvement of education (1980s-1990s): The 1980s and 90s were a period of qualitative development and normalization in the education system. During this period, the need for lifelong education was first stipulated, and the Social Education Act and Early Education Promotion Act were established (MOE & HRD, 2005a, 17). In the 1990s, Korean education emphasized people-centered education, and educational policies focused on the expansion of mandatory education and opportunities for higher education. Since the enactment of the new law for the promotion of local autonomy (1991), the educational administration has become decentralized, and more money has been transferred to local authority budgets (MOE & HRD, 2007b, 23f.). Based on the SEPA (1977), special education in Korea progressed rapidly in the 1990s (cf. Ch. 2.2.2 for current status and policy).

2.2 EDUCATION SYSTEM

In Korea, the Ministry of Education and Human Resources Development (MOE & HRD) is the central body of educational administration. The MOE & HRD plans and coordinates educational policies, formulates policies that govern the elementary, secondary and higher educational institutes, publishes and approves textbooks, provides administrative and financial support for all levels of the school system, supports local education offices, operates the teacher education system and is responsible for overseeing lifelong education and developing human resource policies (MOE & HRD, 2007b, 28). Otherwise, with the enactment of the local autonomy law (1991), the educational administration has tended to become decentralized in Korea, and currently, a total of 16 city/provincial education offices and 182 county education offices have been put in place as of 2004 under the local autonomy system (MOE & HRD, 2005a, 24). Regarding the budget of education, primary and secondary education is under the jurisdiction of local authorities, including city/provincial offices of education, while higher education is under the jurisdiction of the central government (i.e. MOE & HRD). Primary and middle school education, mostly financed by the state, is free and mandatory. High school and college/university education are financed by the state, tuition payment and local governments. In sum, education funding in Korea consists of those funds from the central and local governments as well as the independent resources of private schools. The central government's education budget provides funding for local education offices, which oversee primary and secondary school education, and the operation of national and private universities; educational administrative and research organizations complete the line-up. Most of the central government's education budget comes from tax revenues. The local governments' education budget is funneled into primary and secondary education. The central government's grants and subsidies take up about 75% of the budget, with the remaining 25% financed by local governments and tuition payments. Private schools are in place on every level of education. In particular, private schools account for more than 85% of colleges and universities in Korea. The major source of financing for private schools are entrance and tuition fees, central or local government subsidies and school foundations, but dependence on tuition fees still remains high (MOE & HRD, 2007b, 32).

2.2.1 SCHOOL EDUCATION

The school ladder system in Korea (Figure 2.4) is an overall inter-school structure. It is a single-track 6-3-3-4 system which requires 1 to 3 years in kindergartens (preschool), 6 years in primary school, 3 years in middle school, 3 years in high school and 4 years in college/university. Higher educational institutions include graduate schools, 4-year colleges/universities and 2 or 3-year junior colleges (MOE & HRD, 2007b, 38). Primary schooling is compulsory with an enrollment rate of nearly 100% in Korea, and 3 more years of compulsory middle school education have been implemented nationwide since 2002. Although preschool education is not yet compulsory, its importance has been increasingly recognized in recent years (KOIS, 2007b, 114).

The national curriculum (Figure 2.5) serves as the basis for educational content at each level and for textbook development. The MOE & HRD oversees the national school curriculum pursuant to Article 23 of the Primary and Secondary Education Act. The current 7th national curriculum as revised in 1997, which gradually applied to kindergarten and all schools (graders) from 2004, focuses on strengthening basic education, student-oriented education and local/school autonomy expansion. Under the 7th national curriculum, students are required to learn ten basic compulsory subjects, elective and extracurricular activities for ten years from the first year of primary school through to the first year of high school. During the second and third years in high school, students are given the opportunity to choose their curriculum and courses they wish to take (MOE & HRD, 2007b, 38). Textbooks under the 7th national curriculum are classified into three types (i.e. type I: copyrights held by the MOE & HRD, type II: authorized by the MOE & HRD and published by private publishers, type III: recognized by the MOE & HRD). Currently, totals of 721 type I and 1,575 type II textbooks are in use across all school levels. Particularly, textbooks for kindergartens, primary schools and Korean language/history, ethics for middle and high school, as well as for the advanced levels in high school are developed as type I, whilst all other textbooks are developed as type II or III (MOE & HRD, 2007b, 39).

As of 2005, there were 5,647 primary schools (with enrollments of 4,023,000), 2,947 middle schools (2,015,000) and 2,156 high schools (1,783,000) across Korea. There were a total of 381,000 teachers, which in proportion breaks down to primary schools (160,000), middle schools (104,000) and high schools (117,000). The average number of students per class in 2005 was 31.8 in primary schools, 35.3 in middle schools and 32.7 in high schools (MOE & HRD, 2007b, 136). For an overview, Table 2.1 shows the proportion of schools, students and teachers.

With regard to special education, as of 2006, there were 143 special schools (with enrollments of 23,291) and 5,204 special classes (32,506) at 4,171 regular schools across school levels including kindergarten. In addition, there were a total

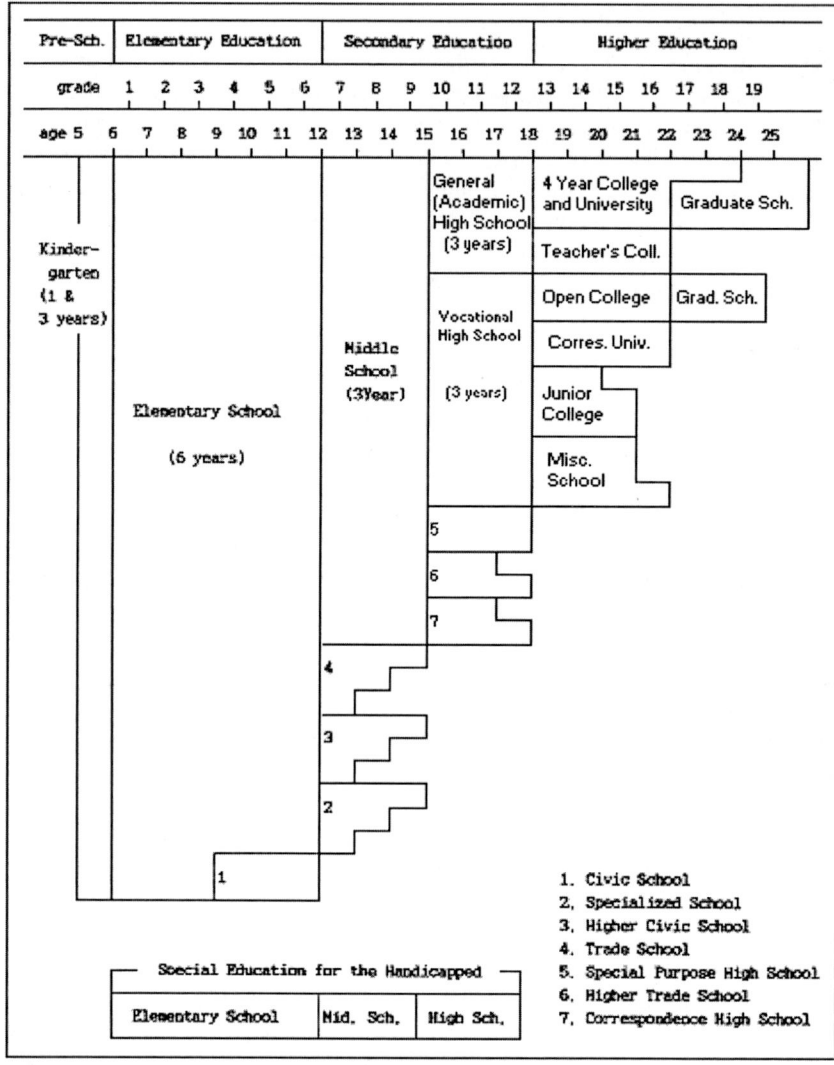

Figure 2.4 School education system in Korea

National Basic Curriculum

Time Assignment for Each Subject

Subject		School Year	1	2	Elementary School 3	4	5	6	Middle School 7	8	9	High School 10	11	12
Curriculum	Korean language arts		Korean Language Arts 210	Korean Language Arts 238	238	204	204	204	170	136	136	136	Selected Subject	
	Ethics				34	34	34	34	68	68	34	34		
	Social Studies				102	102	102	102	102	102	136	170 (Korean History 8)		
	Mathematics		Mathematics 120	Mathematics 136	136	136	136	136	136	136	102	136		
	Science		Ethics 60	Ethics 68	102	102	102	102	102	136	136	102		
	Practical Course		Wise Living 90	Wise Living 102	-	-	68	68	Technical education / Home economics					
			Pleasant Living 180	Pleasant Living 204					68	102	102	102		
	Physical Education		We are 1st Grade 80		102	102	102	102	102	102	68	68		
	Music				68	68	68	68	68	34	34	34		
	Arts				68	68	68	68	34	34	68	34		
	Foreign Language (English)				34	34	68	68	102	102	136	136		
Independent Activity			60	68	68	68	68	68	136	136	136	204		
Special Activity			30	34	34	68	68	68	68	68	68	68	8 units	
Annual Class Time			830	850	986	986	1,088	1,088	1,156	1,156	1,156	1,156	144 units	

1. Number of class hours proposed above shows the minimum number of hours of 34 school weeks as the National Basic Education Period.
2. Number of hours for curriculum for the 1st grade, independent activities and special activities are based on a 30 week period. The number of hours for 'We Are 1st Grade' is that for March only.
3. One class period for elementary school, middle school and high school is 40 minutes, 45 minutes, and 50 minutes, respectively. The periods, however, may be adjusted depending on weather conditions, seasonal conditions, academic achievement level, and nature of learning.
4. The number of hours for special activity and annual class hours for 11th and 12th year are to be completed in two years.

Figure 2.5 National basic curriculum for all school levels (MOE & HRD, 2005a, 43)

Table 2.1 Overview: proportion of schools, students, and teachers (MOE & HRD & KEDI, 2005, 11f.)

Institutions /units	Schools	Students	Teachers
Kindergarten	42.3%	4.5%	6.4%
Primary school	28.8%	33.7%	33%
Middle school	15.1%	16.9%	21.5%
High school	11%	14.9%	24.1%
Special school	0.7%	0.2%	1.2%
University/college	1.1%	20.2%	10.9%
Junior college	0.8%	7.2%	2.5%
Graduate school	0.2%	2.4%	0.4%
	Total (100%)	(100%)	(100%)

of 38,640 students integrated in regular schools, which break down to 6,741 for full-time inclusion (11%; receiving 100% special education service provided by regular class) and 31,899 for part-time inclusion (52%; special education service partly provided by both regular and special class) (MOE & HRD, 2006a, 11). The numbers of students per class in special schools and special classes at regular school were similar to each other (i.e. the number of students per class was 5.9 for special school and 5.8 special class in primary school level, 8.3 and 6.5 in middle school level, and 9 and 8.7 for high school level). As of 2006, there was a total of 5,911 special education teachers for special schools and 5,348 for special classes at regular schools (MOE & HRD, 2006a, 29).

PRESCHOOL EDUCATION

In Korea, preschool education is regarded as very important when it comes to measures of pulling up the low birth rate, resolving social polarization and allowing a greater number of women to work outside their homes. As of 2005, 45% (based on 5-year-old children) of preschool age children attended 8,275 kindergartens nationwide. In particular, the government has carried out nationwide projects since 1999 to provide the preschool education opportunity to children of low-income families (e.g. subsidize kindergarten tuition for 5-year-olds from 1999, finance free education for 5-year-old children from 2002, provide differential tuition aid to 3- and 4-year-old children in 2004, and extend support to families with two or more children attending kindergarten simultaneously from 2005) (MOE & HRD, 2007b, 40). Pre-school education had been led by religious, social and other private organizations until the Education Act provided the legal basis of kindergarten education in 1949. Today national, public and private kindergartens provide preschool courses for children in the 3- to 5-year age brackets. Teaching materials for children as well as guides for teachers and parent education are annually developed by the government and distributed freely to kindergartens nationwide. As for the private kindergartens, besides the financial support for materials and facilities at private schools, the government has, since 2006, also extended allowances to class teachers to help improve the treatment of private kindergarten teachers in rural areas. Currently, more than 15,000 volunteer workers are trained every year to promote the efficiency of preschool education by reduction of the student/teacher ratio (MOE & HRD, 2007b, 41).

PRIMARY EDUCATION

The 6-year primary education and three years of middle school education are compulsory in Korea. As of 2005, Korea had 5,647 primary schools with a total enrollment of more than 402 million students (MOE & HRD, 2007b, 42). In 1960, the average number of students per teacher in primary schools stood at 58.8 (KOIS, 2007b, 114), as the rapid population growth increased the demand for education, and the migration of the rural population into cities in line with the rapid economic development during the 1960s resulted in overcrowded schools and classes. These obstacles to the qualitative improvement of education induced the government in 1982 to create an education tax to finance the expansion and modernization of facilities and to improve the socioeconomic status of teachers. Overcrowded schools were divided into smaller ones and the double-shift class system was terminated. As a result, the number of students per class dropped from 65 in 1965 to 32 in 2005. In addition, with the revision of the regulation prohibiting children under 6 from entering primary school, even 5-year-olds who used to be judged as able are now eligible for entry if there is a place for them (MOE & HRD, 2007b, 42).

SECONDARY EDUCATION

In Korea, free compulsory middle school education began in 1985, and gradually expanded to cover the entire country in 2004. Since 1969, when the entrance examinations for middle schools were abolished, primary school graduates enter middle schools without a competitive examination, and they are assigned to the school nearest to their respective residences. Further, graduates of middle schools or the equivalent may enter high schools (Article 47 of the Primary and Secondary Education Act). The period of study is three years, and students bear the expenses of education (MOE & HRD, 2007b, 43). Admission into high school was formerly based on entrance examination grades, but since 1974, applicants for general high schools are assigned to a school in their residential district (equalization policy for high schools). In the equalization areas[2], students make multiple applications

---

[2] There is some variance in the admission process between equalization-applying areas and non-equalization areas in Korea since 1974, when the equalization policy for high schools went into operation.

and are then assigned to general high schools through a lottery, while applicants for vocational high schools are given the opportunity to choose their school and to be selected through a competitive examination or based on achievement in middle school. This system has been in place since 1996, in order to integrate some of the school districts and thereby to reduce the total number. The so-called 'independent private high schools', which have clear founding principles and rely on school foundation support and tuition, without government funding, have been given the right to determine tuition fees and select students at their discretion since 1998. Meanwhile, 99.7% of middle school graduates advanced to high schools in 2005 (MOE & HRD, 2007b, 44), and the ratio of high school graduates who advanced to institutions of higher education was 88.3% for general high schools and 67.6% for vocational high schools (KOIS, 2007b, 117).

Higher education

Institutions of higher education in Korea are divided into seven categories (colleges and universities, industrial universities, universities of education, junior colleges, broadcast and correspondence universities, technical colleges and other miscellaneous institutions). The education period is between four and six years (MOE & HRD, 2005a, 47). The government sets basic minimum requirements for universities regarding the student selection process to normalize the public education system and to alleviate the burden of private tutoring costs. The application process has been divided into three methods (special selection, regular selection and additional selection), offering students broader opportunities to apply (MOE & HRD, 2005a, 49). In selecting students, colleges and universities may exercise independent authority in utilizing students' high school records and national standardized test results (scholastic aptitude test scores[3]). Since 1996, universities are also administering separate entrance essay tests (KOIS, 2007b, 117). Colleges and universities in Korea operate under strict enrollment limits, therefore, in order to expand the entrance opportunity for all students; paper-and-pencil tests, accepting donations from students and the high school classification system are prohibited (MOE & HRD, 2005a, 48). As of 2005, there were 419 institutions of higher education in Korea, with a total of 3.55 million students and 66,862 faculty members (MOE & HRD, 2007b, 46f.).

---

[3] The scholastic aptitude test consists of five areas: language (Korean), mathematics, foreign language (English), social studies/science/vocational training, and second foreign language/Chinese characters. Students may choose the subjects to be taken in the test, based on the basic principles of the 7th curriculum, allowing students to take either part or all the tests in the subjects available.

2.2.2 SPECIAL EDUCATION: POLICY AND CURRENT STATUS

SPECIAL EDUCATION POLICY

Special education is based on the Basic Education Act, the Primary and Middle School Education Act, and the Special Education Promotion Act (SEPA). The SEPA, established in 1977, was thoroughly revised with an emphasis on the selection, admission and integrated education of candidates for special education in 1994 (MOE & HRD, 2007b, 51). In 2006, the revision of SEPA ("Individuals with Disabilities Special Education Act"), which will take effect on May 26th, 2008, was sought to make primarily kindergarten and high school education compulsory, offer free education to challenged infants under three years of age, guarantee life-long education, expand integrated education by increasing the number of special classes at regular schools across all school levels, and extend related services and support in order to meet the diverse needs of students and respond to rapid social changes (cf. Table 2.1 for a comparison of the current SEPA and the revised version) (Kim EJ, 2007, 3).

In 1994, to improve the quality of special education, the government established the Korea Institute for Special Education (KISE), which has been responsible for conducting research experimentation, distributing information on special education as well as developing and supplying teaching and learning materials, offers training to both regular and special education teachers, and serves as the information center for special needs students (KOIS, 2007b, 118). In 2005, the Special Education Policy Division was established at the MOE & HRD for the purpose of strengthening administrative support for special education. Later in the same year, Special education support centers were set up at 182 education offices across the country, They offer counseling service for local parents of special needs students, supporting the assessment-evaluation of the students, and helping hospitals and related facilities with transportation. A special education teacher and a therapist teacher each were allotted to 18 rural areas as part of the efforts to bolster operations at special education support centers in 2005. The number of centers, 60 as of 2006, will continue to increase.

From 2004, special education assistants were assigned to special schools and regular schools in special and regular classes to help special needs students with mobility, learning and behavioral issues. In 2006, a total of 2,400 special education assistants, including 874 public interest service personnel individuals, were allotted. The number of special education assistants will continue to increase gradually. In 2005, the SEPA and the Enforcement Decrees of the Primary and Secondary Education Act were revised to allow for therapist teachers to be allotted to not only special schools, but also to special classes. Under the revised laws, 130 itinerant teachers in charge of therapeutic education were assigned to special classes in 2006. In addition, the government began to support full-day and after-school operation of the special education institutions for the first time in 2005, in order to help special needs students through full-day education and edu-care service, alleviate their parents' financial burden and to promote their economic activities (MOE & HRD, 2007b, 196). In addition, under the Master Plan of Special Education Development (2003-2007), 15 major tasks involving four areas have been undertaken with a view to maximizing the efficiency of special education by sharing the responsibilities of general and special education. The four areas are meant to guarantee opportunities for special education to each region and level of school education in a balanced way, improve the social and physical environment of regular schools to make them suitable for special education inclusion programs, establish a community-based special education support system, and expand support for special education (MOE & HRD, 2007b, 52).

Further, continued efforts are being made in Korea to promote the welfare and well-being of individuals with disabilities and to ensure an appropriate free public special education and related services. Subsequently, the Disability Service Plan (2007-2010; Master plan for disability support) was developed, and the SEPA was revised in 2006. Under the revised law (i.e. "Individuals with Disabilities Special Education Act", hereinafter referred to as IDSEA), which will take effect on May 26th, 2008, special education for kindergarten and high school become compulsory and education for infants with disabilities under three years of age becomes free. In addition, the law stipulates a new standard of special class establishment, the operation of disability student support centers at universities, support for life-long education, and therapeutic education to be included in related services; Table 2.2 describes the primary revisions concerning the contents (Kim EJ, 2007, 3).

CURRENT STATUS OF SPECIAL EDUCATION

In present Korea, special education is free and compulsory in primary and middle schools, while it is free in kindergartens and high schools. However, as from May 26th, 2008, as mentioned above, it becomes compulsory in Kindergarten and high school, too. In most cases, special education is provided in one, or a combination, of the following forms across school levels: regular class at regular school, special class at regular school, special school (cf. IDSEA Ch. 3, Article 17). Special classes at regular schools run on either a full-time or a part-time basis, the special education service being provided by special education teachers. A special class contains a maximum of 12 students; however, according to the revised law, this standard is to be changed as follows: 1 to 4 students per class for Kindergarten, 1 to 6 students per class for primary and middle school, and 1 to 7 students per class for high school (cf. Table 2.2; cf. IDSEA Ch. 4, Article 27). In addition, itinerant education is provided by special education teachers and related service personnel from regular school as well as special education support centers for pupils with SEN at all school levels who receive inclusive education. Also, itinerant education

Table 2.2 Primary revisions: current Special Education Promotion Act (SEPA) vs. revised version (Individuals with Disabilities Special Education Act)

Classification	Current SEPA	Revised version ("Individuals with Disabilities Special Education Act")
Compulsory education,	Primary, middle school (Free education: Preschool, high school)	Kindergarten, primary, middle, high school
Infant with disabilities	–	Free education for under 3-year-old infants with disabilities
Higher education	–	Operation of disability student support center at universities
Life-long education	–	Support of life-long education for individuals with disabilities
National survey on special education status	Every 5 years	Every 3 years
Establishment Special class	1-12 person: 1class (if beyond 13, more than two classes established)	For kindergarten, 1-4 person: one class (if beyond 4, more than two classes established)
		For primary and middle school, 1-6 person: one class (if beyond 6, more than two classes established)
		For high school, 1-7 person: one class (if beyond 7, more than two classes established)
Special education support center	–	Establishment of special education support center in region
Therapeutic education	Therapist teacher assigned to special schools	Therapeutic education Article removed, included in special education related service

is provided, in case of long-term or indefinite absence from school due to severe disabilities, for pupils who are committed to welfare facilities, medical facilities or home (cf. IDSEA Ch. 4, Article 25).

Pupils with special educational needs (SEN) are classified into the following categories: visually impaired, hearing impaired, mentally retarded, physically impaired, emotional disturbance/behavioral disorder, autistic disorder (including related disorders), communication disability, learning disability, health impaired, and developmental delay (cf. IDSEA Ch. 3, Article 15).

According to the revision, the Special Education Support Center conducts the assessment process of pupils with SEN. The statement on educational support, implemented by an education support center, should be comprised of special education, vocational education, and special education related service. As yet, the local committee on special education (hereinafter referred to as local committee), and otherwise the national committee on special education under the MOE &

HRD, have implemented the assessment and enrollment of pupils with SEN. The city/provincial local committee, which is responsible for the high school level, is composed of eight to twelve members including a chairman, while the county local committee, which is responsible for primary and middle school level, is composed of five to eight members including a chairman. The local committees consist of members such as school principals, special education teachers, experts in the field of special education from university and government agencies, medical doctors, social workers and parents etc. (cf. SEPA Ch. 2, Article 10).

While there are special school curriculums for students with visual, hearing, physical impairments and the mentally retarded, special education teachers follow the general education curriculum with Individualized Educational Program (IEP) for students in special classes. The general education curriculum consists of academic subject activities and extracurricular activities (cf. Figure 2.5, National basic curriculum for all school levels). In addition to these general education curriculum activities, special education related services are provided to pupils with SEN, according to their individual needs. Related service contains therapeutic education programs (e.g. psychological, linguistic, physical and operational treatment and training) and vocational and rehabilitation training activities. Vocational training is particularly emphasized on the middle and high school levels.

As of 2006, 32,506 pupils with SEN were being educated in 5,204 special classes, which were established at 4,171 regular schools across school levels. 5,348 special education teachers were working in special classes at regular schools. Following the expansion of inclusive education, the number of special classes at regular schools is continuously increasing; special schools, in comparison are increasing to a lesser extent. Between the years 2005 and 2006, 507 special classes and 523 special education teachers has been increased, while 1 special school, 95 classes and 307 special education teachers in special schools have been increased (cf. Table 2.1, Ch. 2.2.2) (MOE & HRD, 2006a, 5). In addition, 6,741 pupils with SEN were being educated in 5,763 regular classes at 3,347 regular schools across school levels (MOE & HRD, 2006a, 6).

In sum, 38,640 pupils with SEN received inclusive education in 2006, which break down to 6,741 for full-time (only regular class) and 31,899 for part-time basis (combination of special and regular class) (MOE & HRD, 2006a, 7). In average, about one-fifth (18.7%) of regular schools in Korea offer special classes, among them about half (45.3%) of the primary schools. Many (63% of 62,538) of the pupils with SEN are being educated in general education settings (i.e. special classes: 52%, regular classes: 11% at regular schools) (MOE & HRD, 2006a, 11). The number of pupils with SEN per special education teacher is 5.6; this number meets the OECD (Organisation for Economic Cooperation and Development) average standards (MOE & HRD, 2006a, 9).The majority of special education teachers working in special classes are primary school level teachers (3,413), of which most (92.5%) held special education teacher certificates (MOE & HRD, 2005b, 13). With regard to teacher education for special education teachers (see also Ch. 2.3.3 Teacher education for regular and special education teacher), in Korea, special education teachers are trained on four routes: certificates for undergraduates of four-year special education programs (most), supplementary in-service education for teachers [4], special education degree holders at graduate level and qualifying examination in special education. However, as yet, it can be stated that there is no national standard curriculum of pre-service teacher education for special education teachers in Korea. Even though a basic guideline is provided by MOE & HRD (2000) [5], in fact the curriculums vary by the departments of special education at the universities; also, the number of compulsory/optional courses and their credit hours differ by universities (Kim YW, Kim DY, & Kim SS, 2002, 109). For years, in the field of special education, efforts have been made in this regard (e.g. Kim, 1995; Kim, Kim, Park, Shin, Kim, & Jeon, 1998; Kim DY & Lee TS, 2000; Kim, YW, Kim, DY, Kim, SS, 2002). However, not much has changed. The period of teaching practice has remained 4 weeks in general. This is an integral part of pre-service education (bachelor degree) of which the standard period of study is 8 semesters. From 135 to 150 total credit hours are required to graduate, of which teaching practice usually varies to consist of an average between 2 and 4 credit hours, differing by university. Thus, apart from the shortage of practical and subject studies, it has been argued that the teaching area of inclusive education should be strengthened in particular. For instance, the mild disability education course was only offered at a small number of universities, although it was a required basic course (Kim DI & Lee TS, 2000, 63f.), considering the rapid growth in student population integrated in the general education settings, which inevitably resulted in an increased demand of special education teacher (cf. Ch. 2.3.3 for further information of teacher education for special education teachers).

Accordingly, the government has been making efforts to develop a teacher education model for pre-service teacher education for special education teachers: standard requirements for courses in universities, curriculum reconstruction for the purpose of recruiting and training highly qualified special education teachers (e.g. MOE & HRD, 2004, 2005b, 2006a). In this regard, according to the Annual Report on Special Education, the planned and renewed emphasis on educational

---

[4] The requirement and qualification for a special education teacher in Korea is a fully certified special education teacher or a fully certified regular education teacher, who subsequently becomes fully certified or licensed as a special education teacher.

[5] The guideline demands that at least 5 courses with a minimum of 14 total credit hours must be earned in 11 required basic courses: special education, special class management (or mild disability education), learning disability, visual impairment, hearing impairment, mental retardation, physical impairment, emotional-behavioral disorder, speech impairment education, early special education and special education technology (MOE & HRD, Notification 2000-1, 28.01.2000).

policy focuses on: (a) expansion of educational opportunities for pupils with SEN in inclusive settings, (b) enhancement of special education service through the improvement of teaching, particularly improvement in the quality of school instruction, and (c) enhancement of professional development for special education teachers (MOE & HRD, 2006a, 109f.).

2.3 TEACHER EDUCATION

2.3.1 PRE-SERVICE EDUCATION

The classification and qualifications of teachers are defined in Section 2 of Article 21 of the Act on Elementary and Secondary School Education. According to the provisions, teachers are classified into (regular) teachers (Grade I and Grade II), assistant teachers, professional counselors, librarians, training teachers and nursing teachers. In Korea, teacher education is offered by universities of education, colleges of education, departments of education or teachers' certificate programs in colleges and universities, junior colleges, the Korea National Open University (broadcast and correspondence university), and graduate schools of education (MOE & HRD, 2005a, 76).

GENERAL EDUCATION TEACHERS

Most primary school teachers are trained in national institutions; that is, eleven national universities of education located in metropolitan cities and provinces. In addition, Seoul National University of Education offers a bachelor degree to students after their completing a 4-year training, and departments of primary education at the Korea National University of Education, and one private university; Ewha Woman's university. Currently, about 77% of the freshmen at universities of education are female, and incentives to recruit competent male students are needed (MOE & HRD, 2007b, 62). While secondary school teachers are mainly trained by teachers' colleges, some are also trained by departments of education or through teacher training courses at ordinary universities and graduate schools of education. A total of 13 national and 27 private colleges of education and departments of education at universities see off approximately 16,000 prospective teacher graduates annually. About 46,000 teachers are also trained by graduate schools of education, whose main purpose is to give in-service training to teachers. Overall, more than 25,000 prospective teachers are trained annually (MOE & HRD, 2007b, 64). The curriculum of colleges/universities of education requires a total of 130-150 credits for graduation, of which 20% must be in liberal arts, 60% in the major subject, and the remaining 20% in electives. The curriculum for major courses consists of subject study, subject teaching, general education and a teaching practicum. Teacher's certificates are awarded to the graduates of the colleges upon completion of certain courses, as prescribed by the Primary and Secondary Education Act. They do not have to take an examination to obtain a teacher's certificate. Public school teachers are selected and appointed based on a teacher qualification examination conducted by metropolitan/provincial offices of education. In the case of private schools, teachers are selected by each school. The examination for public school teachers is two-tiered: the primary examination is a written test on pedagogy (20%) and the special areas (80%), and the secondary examination consists of a practical test, essay writing and interview (MOE & HRD, 2007b, 65).

Figure 2.6 Issue of teacher's certificates as of 2005 (MOE & HRD, 2007b, 66)

School Level	Kinder-garten	Primary	Second-ary	Special				Sub-total
				Kinder-garten	Primary	Second-ary	Sub-total	
2nd grade regular teacher certificate	10,960	6,005	33,554	337	925	519	1,781	52,300

SPECIAL EDUCATION TEACHERS

Special education teachers are mainly trained by ordinary universities, at the departments of special education, which offer a bachelor's degree to students after their completing a 4-year training. Others are trained by graduate schools of education, which offer special education teacher training courses, and graduate schools designated by the Minister of Education and Human Resources (MOE & HRD, 2007b, 51). Primary education applicants to special schools/classes must complete the courses necessary for primary school education, and those who apply for special school/class as secondary education teachers must complete the courses necessary for secondary school education in addition to their majors. Classification and qualification of special education teachers are defined in the attached Table 2 related to Section 1 Article 21 of the Act on Elementary and Secondary School Education, and they are similar to those of regular teacher education. Special education teachers are classified into special school teachers (Grade I and Grade II), assistant teachers, kindergarten (Grade II) and kindergarten assistant teachers (Jung JJ, 2002, 130). In the same manner as the regular teacher classification, there are also (special school) professional counselors, librarians, training teachers and nursing teachers. According to the Special Education Promotion Act (SEPA), Article 16 and 17, there are also therapeutic education teachers and vocational education teachers (Jung JJ, 2002, 132).

As of 2006, a total of 42 universities finalize training of approximately 1,812 prospective special education teachers annually, which break down to 190 for special kindergarten, 771 for primary special education and 851 for secondary special education. Also, about 260 special education teachers are trained by three graduate schools of education (majoring in special education), and there are further 34 graduate schools of education which offer courses related to special education (MOE & HRD, 2007b, 89).

The curriculums vary across programs in the universities. According to the standard provided by the MOE & HRD (notification-2001), merely five compulsory courses with a total of 14 credits must be achieved from eleven basic courses suggested as follows: special education, special class management or education of mild disability, visually impairment education, hearing impairment education, physically impairment education, speech impairment education, education of mental retardation, education of emotional disturbance and/or behavioral disorder, education of learning disability, early childhood special education and special education technology) (e.g. Kim DI & Lee TS, 2003). As a result, the minimum credit required for graduation, which is constituted of major subject, liberal arts and electives, varies from 135 to150 between universities; for example, liberal arts vary from 15 to 30 and electives vary from 36 to 58, depending on the university (Kim SS, 2000 as cited in Jung JJ, 2002, 135). Particularly with regard to the major subject (e.g. learning disability), which in turn consists of subject study, subject teaching, general education and teaching practicum, the required credits for the teaching practicum differ from 3 to 8 across universities. In addition to this, course names are very different across the universities, rendering them impossible to be compared (Jung JJ, 2002, 135). Even so, most programs and courses in curriculums provide introductions to each disability category and on teaching strategies for children with special needs (Park JY, 2002, 31).

In the same manner as the regular teachers, as mentioned above, special education teachers' certificates are awarded to the university graduates upon completion of certain courses, as prescribed by the Primary and Secondary Education Act. Thus, they do not have to take an examination to obtain a special education teacher's certificate. Public school teachers, including public special schools and special classes at regular schools, are selected and appointed based on a special education teachers' qualification examination conducted by the city/provincial offices of education. In the case of private special schools, special education teachers are selected by each school.

Since the inauguration of the Participatory Government, the MOE & HRD has sought to modify the curriculum of teacher training universities in order to produce highly qualified teachers. Efforts are being made to strengthen the specialization of teacher training and to design the teachers' examination to differentiate qualification levels among applicants. En route to that goal, universities of education have been advised to increase the ratio of 'subject teaching' in the curriculum, reinforce subjects of study involving teacher ethics, computer and other IT applications, class management and counseling, as well as other student services, and increase the credits and duration of the teaching practicum. Since 1998, teacher training institutes have been evaluated from the perspective of encouraging competition among the institutes. Intensive support is extended to the universities, evaluated as 'outstanding', so as to help facilitate their development through specialization (MOE & HRD, 2007b, 65).

2.3.2 IN-SERVICE EDUCATION

TYPES OF IN-SERVICE EDUCATION PROGRAM

In-service education programs are for certificates, professional job training (including overseas in-service training) and special training. First, the *certificate training* program is for teachers who want to obtain new or higher grade certificates. Certificate training programs are available for Grade I and Grade II teachers, vice-principals and principals, professional counselors, librarians and nursing teachers. The training period is 30 days (180 hours) or longer. Second, the *professional job training* aims at improving teachers' effectiveness and their ability to teach subjects and help guide students. Diverse programs are available to this end, with curriculums determined by the president of each training center. The training period and hours differ according to students and courses, and the programs are offered by city/provincial education training institutes, training centers attached to or associated with universities and online education training institutes. Third, *overseas in-service training*, a part of the professional job training, is divided into *training through experiences* and *field training*. Under the training through-experience programs, teachers visit educational institutes, schools and cultural facilities in other countries for about two weeks. Currently, the programs are operated autonomously by each city/provincial office of education. *Field training*, introduced in 1978, is offered by foreign universities and training institutes for four to eight weeks to help teachers acquire advanced knowledge, teaching methods and science & technology. *Special training* is a long-term (up to two years) type of training, offered by domestic or foreign training centers designated by the MOE & HRD. Assessment is conducted on those who complete 60 hours or more of the training program. The distribution curve has a range of 80 to 100 and reflects the performance of teachers with 60 points or higher out of the total 100 points. As of 2004, it was indicated that around 9% of all teachers (454,050) participated in certificate training, while most of the teachers (91%) received professional job training.

SPECIAL EDUCATION TEACHER TRAINING PROGRAMS

The types of special education teachers' in-service education are implemented, as mentioned above, in the same manner as regular teachers'. As from 1994, the Korea Institute for Special Education (KISE) was established and began to offer certificate training and professional job training for special education teachers. Besides the KISE and city/provincial education training institutes, as from 1996, training centers are also attached to or associated with universities, and online education training institutes offer various training programs for special education teachers and other teachers such as vocational and therapeutic education teachers as well as, further, for parents (Kwak SC, Baek EH, Jeon BW, Lee BI, Lee YH, 2002, 30). Currently, the KISE offers eleven 62-hour programs of professional job training, five 16-hour programs of professional job training (including online education), three programs of certificate training, one 60-hour program of oversea-training, and five 30-hour programs of general training (MOE & HRD, 2007a, 93). As of 2006, 1,898 special education teachers, regular teachers and parents participated in the in-service education programs offered in KISE (Table 2.3).

Table 2.3 Number of special education teachers who received in-service education by training program and institutions in 2006 (MOE & HRD, 2006a, 94)

Types	Professional job training (62 hour)	Professional job training (16 hour)	Certificate training (182 hour)	Oversee training (60 hour)	General training (30 hour)	Total
Number	895	145	117	21	720	1,898

Region		Institution	KISE (Government)	City/province education office	Associated universities
Capital (trainee)		Seoul	204	1,354	55
City		Pusan	66	1,266	–
		Daegu	59	353	–
		Incheon	33	1,050	35
		Kwangju	115	467	–
		Daejeon	62	573	6
		Ulsan	9	309	–
Province		Geongi	223	7,569	42
		Gangwon	71	640	18
		Chungbuk	48	245	50
		Chungnam	70	707	84
		Jeonbuk	55	651	10
		Jeonnam	17	72	40
		Gyeongbuk	84	160	10
		Gyeongnam	5	278	–
		Jeju	69	46	–
Total			1,190	15,740	350

3

SOCIAL CONSTRUCTION OF LEARNING DISABILITY

"Behinderung ist keine objeckitve Realität sondern eine in die soziale Kommunikation eingebrachte Kategorie" (Moser & Sasse, 2008, 92).

3.1 SOCIAL CONSTRUCTION OF DISABILITY

The term 'disability' has been diversely defined across societies and in various social contexts (e.g. Lindemann & Vossler, 1999; Bogdan & Taylor, 1998; Richardson, 1997; Burch & Sutherland, 2006; and e.g. Oliver, 1989; Oliver, 1986; Oliver, 1993; Oliver & Zarb, 1989; Finkelstein, 1993; Swain, 1993). Disability is to be properly understood as a social construct, since disability is not an objective reality (*"objeckitve Realität"*), but rather a quite versatile category brought in by the social communication (*"Soziale Kommunikation"*) (Moser & Sasse, 2008, 92). Its definitions have been interpretational within the social context rather than scientific fact (Albrecht & Levy, 1982, 11f.). In the field of disability studies, it has been argued that disability is often less about physical or mental impairments than it is about how society responds to impairments (Burch & Sutherland, 2006, 129). The concept of 'Disability' may be described by the response of society to the individual – as either able or disabled, rather than such as physical or mental ability within an individual (Lindemann & Vossler, 1999, 107; see also Holbrook, 1999, 341f.). For instance, Vygotsky (1983, 102) saw disability as a socio-cultural developmental phenomenon rather than a psychological consequence. Thus, from the social (system) perspective Vygotsky regarded the primary problem of a disability not as the sensory or neurological impairment itself, but much more as the sum of its social implications. As Benkmann (2003, 444) puts it: "results of a complex process of construction under particular social conditions".

Any physical handicap [...] not only alters the child's relationship with the world, but above all affects his interaction with people. Any organic defect is revealed as a social abnormality in behavior. [...] However, the teacher must deal not so much with these biological factors by themselves, but rather with their social consequences (Vygotsky, 1983 as cited in Gindis, 1999, 335).

One may conclude that what it means to be disabled in the society is understood through the lens of the social construction. As 'disability' is recognized as a social construct created by the physical and social barriers evident in a world adapted solely for the non-disabled (e.g. De Jong, 1979; Stone, 1985; Finkelstein, 1980; 1993; Oliver, 1993). In this regard, broadly speaking, there have basically been two perspectives of disability competing for attention; the individual and the social model of disability (Thomas & Woods, 2003, 14) – as Borsay (1986, 180) puts it: "personal troubles" and "public issue". Models of disabilities such as medical, functional and environmental/cultural models (e.g. Bleidick, 2000a; McDermott & Varenne, 1995; Oliver, 1996; Smart & Smart, 2006; Smart, 2006; Shakespeare, 2006; Siebers, 2001; Smart, 2002; Stone, 1985) have been underpinned during particular periods and convey the perspectives of the society they originate from. The medical model came about as modern medicine began to develop in the 19th Century, along with the enhanced role of the physician in society. Under this model, the problems that are associated with disability are deemed to reside within the individual. The medical aspect mainly regards disability as an individual problem or a personal tragedy – *"individualtheoretisch-medizinischen Paradigmas"* and does not consider factors such as family, school, social aspects, stigma, or the coping resources of the disabled (Bleidick, 2000a, 185). Rather it serves to deliver diagnosis, prognosis and treatment for the disabled individual (Fowler & Wadsworth, 1991, 19f.). Thus, within this model, disabilities are labeled and categorized based on physical or mental diagnosis. The functional model is, more or less, similar to the medical model. It defines disability as an impairment that must be rehabilitated, on this occasion, in order to meet the social expectations – the economic and functional needs of society (Oliver, 1996, 18f.). Within this model, disability is graded by the degree of impairment and is defined according to one's ability to meet the basic earning capacity and sustain daily living activities within a particular environment (e.g. Stone, 1985). In this framework, the implemented intervention and the imposed treatment are to adapt the individual's functions to the particular environment (e.g. Smart, 2002). On the other hand, the environmental/cultural model regards disability not as "an individual category" (Bleidick, 2000b, 190) and rejects the notion that persons with disabilities are in some inherent way, implying that disability is defined by the social and cultural environment (Beck, Duee, & Wieland, 1996, 9). According to the environmental cultural aspect, the environment of the individual can cause and exacerbate a disability either socially or physically (Smart & Smart, 2006, 29f.). Under this model, disability becomes not a physical or mental diagnosis but a social, cultural response (Hursch, 1995, 303ff.). In this regard, the tolerance- and expectation levels within the schools are to determine students' learning and behavioral problems (e.g. Shakespeare, 2006; Siebers, 2006; Algozzine, Serna, & Patton, 2001). And because teachers have different tolerance levels (Love, 2003, 1), this may generate different interpretations of the student's disability among teachers.

3.2 SOCIAL CONSTRUCTION OF LEARNING DISABILITY

LD is no less socially constructed than other disabilities (e.g. Klotz, 2004; Bogdan & Taylor, 1989; Taylor & Bogdan, 1989). There have been numerous attempts to construct models of LD and frame paradigms (e.g. McDermott, Goldberg, Watkins, Stanley, & Glutting, 2006; Ahrbeck, Bleidick, & Schuck, 1997; Poplin, 1988b, 1984b; Proctor & Prevatt, 2003; Stanovich, 1999; Brackett & McPherson 1996; Fletcher, Francis, Shaywitz, Lyon, Foorman, Stuebing, & Shaywitz, 1998; Fletcher, Foorman, Boudousquie, Barnes, Schatschneider, & Francis, 2002).

3.2.1 THEORETICAL PERSPECTIVES

Models of LD have continued to develop in various separate traditions and literature (e.g. Balgo, 2002; Werning & Luetje-Klose, 2003; Bleidick, 2000c) and some of these models may have more historical than current significance. Brendtro & Van Bockern (1994, 1ff.) suggested that these approaches for LDs have become more eclectic over time. Also Bauer, Keefe, & Shea (2001, 37) suggested that cross-fertilization has occurred as practitioners pragmatically apply interventions which have emerged from once pure models. This section attempts to cover the major approaches to LD: first, the individual-centered perspective (*"Individuumzentrierte Perspektive"*, Werning, 2002, 135), suggested to be forming the student problem approach (Bauer, Keefe, & Shea, 41), the medical biological model (*"Biomedizinische Modell"*) and the psychological model (*"Psychologische Modell"*). And second, the individual-environment-interaction perspective (*"Individuum-Umwelt-Beziehung orientierte Perspektive"*, Werning, 2002, 136), suggested to be forming the problem solving approach (Bauer, Keefe, & Shea, 2001, 41), the ecological model (*"Ökologische Modell"*), the holistic model (*Holistisches, Ganzheitliches Modell*) and the postmodern model (Figure 3.1). The individual-centered perspective assumes that LD resides in-the-heads of individual students (Dudley-Marling, 2004, 482) and is based on the belief that a disability (wherever it comes from, whether from genetic defects or difficult early socialization) must be hardwired in the body of the child (e.g. Varenne & McDermott, 1999). Whereas this perspective views LD as an individual category, the individual-environmental-interaction perspective assumes that LD is not an etiological but a relational concept in the context of social interaction processes. This perspective views learning as an inherently social activity (see for example Vygotsky, quoted in Gindis, 1999, 335; Holbrook, 1999). Currently, the focus in the field of LD is shifting to describe, interpret and understand LD, rather than to predict and control variables – this is the postmodern approach. The previous modern approach and the postmodern approach regarding the nature of special education and related outcomes should naturally blend together (Hallahan & Mercer, 2002, 33). However, the position of these approaches foster extreme viewpoints and minimum common ground. As Hallahan & Mercer (2002, 33) puts it: "Educators must join to stop yet another education war that deters special education from being the helping profession it was created to be, if students with LDs are to receive the best possible education and be accepted by the society. In this context, application of a single model is limited. In order to fully understand the nature of students with LDs, there is a need for an "integrated perspective" (Bauer, Keefe, & Shea, 2001, 50), which recognizes the contribution of each of the various models. Bauer, Keefe, & Shea (2001, 50) suggested the social systems perspective as an alternative approach – this perspective emphasizes that the behavior cannot be understood as a simle cause and effect relationship, but must be interpreted within the context in which it occurs. The following section presents the models which have underpinned the field of LD and also discusses the social system perspective in some detail.

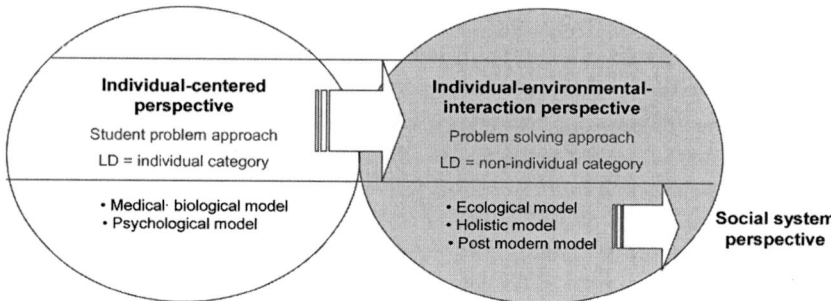

Figure 3.1   Theoretical perspectives on LD: models of LDs and paradigm shift

MEDICAL BIOLOGICAL MODEL *(Biomedizinische Modell)*
In the early investigation of brain research, causes and definitions regarding the term of LD stem from the medical biological model; terms such as word blindness, brain injury, central nervous system dysfunction, aphasia and minimal brain dysfunction (cf. Ch. 3.2.2 Historical Perspectives) were used in order to define LD (e.g. Brantlinger, 2004; Dudley-Marling & Dippo, 1995; Poplin, 1988a; Reid & Valle, 2004; Torgesen, 1986). The medical biological model assumes that learning problems mainly occur neurologically by a brain dysfunction. Therefore, in this model the individual with LD is viewed as a result of physical deficits of malfunction or developmental challenges. For example, (a) Schroeder

& Schroeder (1982) discussed the deficit sub-type (genetics, temperament, neuro-psychopharmacology, nutrition, neurological dysfunction) and the developmental sub-type (neurological organization, perceptual motor learning physiological readiness, sensory integration and development); (b) Orton (1928) spoke of the term strephosymbolia; he discussed a whole range of developmental disorders including dysgraphia and developmental word deafness; and, (c) Hewett (1968) described a classroom model built on the early beliefs about neurological functioning (as cited in Bauer, Keefe, & Shea, 2001, 37). Applying the medical biological model, objective and standardized diagnosis and the measurement of intelligence assessment dominated the field of LD (Proctor & Prevatt, 2003, 459f.). These early remedial- and treatment-oriented efforts have been the subject of scientific scrutiny and have been found ineffective in improving academic skills of LD students (e.g. Hallahan, Kauffman, & Lloyd, 1999). One of the key reasons is, as Illich (1984 as cited in Balgo, 2002, 22) suggested, that the medical biological aspects only focus on the superficial problem regardless of the suffering student. Nevertheless, recently, medical and biological aspects of learning problems are drawing attention; for example, Sylwester (1997, 75f.) explored the relationship between neurobiology and self-esteem.

PSYCHOLOGICAL MODEL *(Psychologische Modell)*

The psychological model is based on the assumption that learning and behavior are determined by dynamic intra-psychic relationships (Poplin, 1988b, 401f.). This model also views the causes of learning and behavior as being within the student (individual). There are two main lines in the psychological model according to Balgo (2002, 27): behaviorism and psychoanalysis. While the psychoanalyst focuses on why students behave as they do, the behaviorist focuses on what behavior students demonstrate. The behaviorist assumes that what the student do is influenced by what follows what she/he does (Sarason, Glaser, & Fargo, 1972, 10). According to the behaviorist, in order to facilitate the student's learning process the teacher must modify the environment and methodology (Torgesen, 1986, 399f.). These intervention methods and strategies for student's behavior modification has been the predominant aspect in special education until recently. However, the emphases on managing undesirable behaviors rather than desirable behaviors among teachers have called into question these behavioral interventions without consideration of the context in which the interventions are applied. With regard to the cognitive acknowledgement (*im Zeichen der kognitiven Wende*), there have been significant changes, and the emphasis has been placed on the student's viewpoint the way the student thinks and cognitively processes information (Balgo, 2002, 33). Hence, topics such as meta-cognition processes rather than ability problems are considered (Poplin, 1988b, 401f.). The psychoanalysis within the psychological model can be delineated as psycho-education ("*Psychoedukation*" or "*verste-*

hende Erziehung", Balgo, 2002, 37). The psychoanalyst's concern is based on understanding and helping approach (Palmowski, 1996, 70). Unlike the behaviorists, the application of the psycho-educational aspect would be reflected in an accepting atmosphere in which the teacher tolerates and interprets the student's behavior (e.g. Berkowitz & Rothman, 1967). The psychoanalyst suggests that in order to support students with LDs the teacher must provide a specialized environment, in which the student can be successful at his/her present level, through understanding how the student perceives, thinks and feels in the setting, and recognizing the student's vulnerability to competition, sharing and testing (Bauer, Keefe, Shea, 2001, 40). Husslein (1983 as cited in Balgo, 2002, 38) suggested the possible positive influences of these psycho-dynamic and psycho-educational aspects in the special educational context regarding the teacher-student relationship and especially teachers' understanding of disabilities. On the other hand, Benkmann (1989, 83) pointed out that the one-sided individual-centered perspective on personality-structural deficits of the student leads to an underestimation of actual environmental influences. Similarly, Belschner (1976, 43) argued that there is a risk for the student with disabilties to be isolated in his/her social relations and constricted by individual (e.g. teacher) procedures. Nevertheless, the psychological model is useful as an overall educational fundamental concept (Palmowski, 1996, 67).

ECOLOGICAL MODEL *(Ökologische Modell)*

The ecological model emphasizes the interrelation between an organism and its environment – the environment is understood in a broader sense of "existential condition" (*"Existenz-Bedingungen"*) (Haeckel, 1866 as cited in Balgo, 2002, 65). The ecological aspect assumes that the individual is an inseparable part of a social system, which is made up of the individual and his/her school, family, neighborhood, and community (Hobbs, 1966, 1105f.). Hence, within the ecological model LD is a product of the student's response to the environment in which the student with LD functions, as these interact with the student's personal traits and experiences (Bauer, Keefe, & Shea, 2001, 41). From this aspect, the causes of LDs are not located in the individual but far more in the ecological system in which the student and his/her environment exist. In this regard, topics such as learning environment and school and classroom climate have been dealt with in the educational context (e.g. Ortner, 1979; Saldern, 1987). Thus, within the ecological model the teacher must be aware of the impact of the environment on the individual and/or group, and manage the classroom to create a supportive environment concerning the social and physical classroom environment. However, Werning (1996, 1989, 89) argued that the ecological model neglects the role of the observer category (*"die Beobachterkategorie"*), as it remains unexplained who determines from which ecological environmental context.

HOLISTIC MODEL *(Holistisches, Ganzheitliches Modell)*

The holistic model assumes that the universe is a self-organizing, self-regulating place, and that students can only construct meaning in their own ways (Poplin, 1988b, 401f.). Learning within the holistic model does not take place inside a person's head, but is largely a result of social and cultural interaction with persons and symbols (e.g. Heshusius, 1984; Poplin, 1984a, 1984b). The holistic model suggests that the whole is more than the sum of the parts, different from the sum of the parts and cannot be accounted for or reduced to the sum of the parts (Heshusius, 1995, 166ff.). Within this aspect, the reason why people have LD can be explained by their developmental un-readiness, inactive teaching methods, insufficient previous and current experiences, insufficient interest and mismatch of previous experiences. The most frequently assumed reason of students' learning failure has been their developmental un-readiness (Poplin, 1988b, 412). Poplin (1988b, 414) pointed out that most teachers believe bits of the holistic and reductionism *(Reduktionism)* theories each, but they are supported in mostly using reductionist practices (e.g. sequentially ordered material, rigid methods of control, reinforcement). Therefore, the learning and teaching process of the holistic model would shake the foundation and challenge the previous models in the field of LD. The implications of the holistic model for the field of LD are, as Poplin (1988b, 405) addressed, the principles of the teaching and learning process. The holistic aspect maintains that the whole of the learned experience is greater than the mere sum of its parts. Under this aspect, the interaction of the learned experience transforms both the individual's whole and the single experience (part). These transformations related to teaching aspects such as curriculum, method, material and instruction also cause knowledge to be personalized. In addition, this model views all people always as active learners, as our old and new experiences are constantly interacting. Generally, people acquire information from their external environment by initially judging its personal value and its relation to what is already known. And what is known predicts what is learned; that is, the best predictor of what and how someone will learn is what they already know. It will therefore be difficult for teachers to teach students present new experiences without knowing what is already known and perceived by students. The holistic model considers that experiences connected to the learner's present knowledge and interests are learned best[1], and that learners learn best from people they trust. Unfortunately, in this regard, Poplin (1988b, 409) pointed out that the critical role of trust is ignored in schools in which fairness is defined as random student assignment and the school rarely asks the student with LD about her/his opinion about the placement, despite

---

[1] cf. Poplin (1988b, 407): a personal connection to new learning experiences almost guarantees what we have come to call generalization and maintenance -learning (see also Belenky, Clinchy, Goldberger, & Tarule, 1986, on ways of knowing).

its impact on the possible success/failure of the student. Finally, the holistic model believes that integrity is a primary characteristic of the human (learner's) mind. These principles will lead teachers and schools to different attitudes about how to involve children in learning, and those with LDs. The values and beliefs inherent in the holistic aspect change the focus of diagnostics and assessment from seeking disabilities (e.g. unlearned sub skills – part) to interest and strengths (e.g. successful school experiences upon which to build a healthy self-concept – whole).

POST-MODERN MODEL

Whereas the previous approach (such as modern) states that the disability is owned by the individual and needs to be treated, accommodated, and/or endured and is consistent with the medical biological model, the emerging direction of the post-modern approach views disability primarily as a social construction that is based on incorrect immoral assumptions about difference (Hallahan & Mercer, 2002, 33). The postmodern approach assumes that reality (disability) is constructed and intended, and that the reality (disability) we experience is a process of social construction (e.g. Ferguson & Ferguson, 1995; Andrews, Carnine, Coutinho, Edgar, Forness, Fuchs, et al., 2000). That is, if two individuals (e.g. special education teachers) experience the same event (e.g. student's learning failure), they may interpret it differently. Within the postmodern model, there is no dualism of subjective and objective, as the postmodernist assumes that subject and object cannot be separated (Ferguson & Ferguson, 1995, 104ff.). According to this, to make sense, both subjective and objective aspects (e.g. mental and physical) must be considered simultaneously and thus, it is impossible to separate fact from value. Rather, the production of social construction is recognized to occur within the context of moral values (Bauer, Keefe, & Shea, 2001, 43). In sum, the postmodern approach values the outcome of creating a caring adaptable society that treats differences and needs without labels, stigmas, or exclusion (Andrews et al., 2000, 258f.). This aspect focuses on changing social constructions that limit individuals with disabilities despite mentioning the importance of enhancing performance in the special educational context (Hallahan & Mercer, 2002, 33). Hence, the vital point of the postmodern aspect is 'what the experiences of students with LDs are' instead of 'what LDs are'. Skrtic (1991, 163) suggested that the successful school in the 21th century must promote a sense of social responsibility in students and an awareness of interdependency. In order to fulfill this, schools must develop students' capacities for learning through collaborative problem solving and reflective discourse within a community of interest (e.g. Dudley-Marling & Dippo, 1995[2]).

---

[2] cf. As Dudley-Marling & Dippo (2005, 413)put it: "[...] work daily to remove the stigma of difference, to create classrooms in which relationship and dialogue, as opposed to treatment and training, are central, and to create a conception of community based not on normalcy, competitiveness, and 'just deserts,' but rather on diversity, mutuality, and social justice".

On the other hand, he argued that teachers' professional behavior in schools (e.g. towards the students with LDs) is more governed by institutionalized social and cultural norms than by rational, knowledge-based actions. The student's disability (respectively the student with LD), then, is an organizational pathology that results from the ways a school works (Skrtic, 1999, 193f.). According to Dudley-Marling (2004, 484), when understanding LD in the context of the institution that created it, then LD will be defined in terms of skill deficits in an institution that sorts differential rates of learning. In particular, to the point that the rate of learning rather than the learning is the total measure of the learner (McDermott, 1993, 272) and equates learning with the mastery of skills. In an institution that valorizes the individual, LD will be defined in terms of the individual, situated in the head of the individual. According to Sleeter (1986, 46f.), it thus avoids placing any blame on the home or school for the student's learning failure. After all, special education removes students with LDs from the general education system, as LD is a matter of not fitting the standard program at school, an organizational pathology (Bauer, Keefe, & Shea, 2001, 43). Deno (1970, 229f.) argued that special education accepts regular education's fallout. Similarly, Lyon was quoted (Colvin & Helfand, 2000, 1) as saying "LD has become a sociological sponge to wipe up the spills of general education [...] it is where children who were not taught well go in many respects". Finally, Sleeter (1995, 153f.) remarked that important questions about education and the inequities within the educational experience were avoided by developing the category LD.

Social system perspective

The social system perspective consider each individual as developing in dynamic relationships with, and as an inseparable part of, the several social contexts or settings in which the individual either functions directly or is affected by throughout his or her life (Bauer, Keefe, & Shea, 2001, 61). Within this perspective, emphasis is given to the dynamic relationship between the individual and forces in the larger social and physical environment. The dynamic relationship involves the individual and the environment as both actors and reactors (Thomas & Marschall, 1977, 16f.). And the behavior of an individual (student) is assumed as the expression of these relationships between the individual and environment (Scott, 1980, 279ff.). Hence, in the social system perspective, in order to change the student's behavior, initially the environment in which the student functions must be changed. Also, it is assumed that the student (or the family) can be affected by events that occur in settings where the student is not present (Bauer, Keefe, & Shea, 2001, 62); that is, even settings in which the student does not directly engage may have an impact on his/her behavior. Thurman (1977, 329) addressed that, from the social system perspective, "congruence" (i.e. the match between the individual and his/her environment) is the major factor that impacts on whether a student is identified as having LD or not. Hence, students identified as having LD are those whose behavior is not congruent with the norms or standards of their environment. In addition, Bauer, Keefe, & Shea, (2001, 62) argued that the crucial concept in the social system perspective is that of "roles". According to Bronfenbrenner (1979, 6; 83ff.), a role is a set of activities and relations expected of a person occupying a particular position in society (the expectation for behavior associated with particular positions in society), and of others in relation to that person. Roles have a magic-like power to alter the way a person is treated, how the person acts, what the person does, and thereby even what the person thinks and feels. The principle applies not only to the developing person but to the others in the person's environment. Thus, an individual acting in a role (e.g. teacher) will tend to evoke perception, action, and interpersonal relationships consistent with the expectation of the role from both the person occupying the role, and others with respect to that person, as the role becomes more established in the institutional structure of society (e.g. Dudley-Marling, 2004; Dudley-Marling & Dippo, 1995) and a consensus forms regarding the expectations of that role. Speck (1996, 283) argued that the ecological and the social system approach are related together and in particular replenish each other. Both approaches regard the individual as an inseparable part of a social system (e.g. Hobbs 1966; Speck, 2003). Lesar, Trivette, & Dunst (1995, 197) addressed that Bronfenbrenner's approach to the ecology of human development is useful as a framework for research involving students with disabilities and their families, among the ecological approaches (e.g. Baacke, 1980; Walter, 1981; Hurrelmann & Ulich, 2002). According to Bronfenbrenner (1979, 16ff.; 56ff.), development is a lasting change in the way in which a person (e.g. child) perceives and deals with his/her environment. Bronfenbrenner (1978, 35, 36) suggested that the ecological environment is conceived as a set of nested structures: at the innermost level (Mikrosystems) is the immediate setting containing the developing person (growing individual); this can be the home, the classroom. The second level (Mesosystems) is the interaction among settings. Bronfenbrenner (1979, 3) argued that such interconnections can be as decisive for development as events taking place within a given setting. For example, a child's ability to learn to read in primary grades may depend no less on how he is taught than on the existence and nature of ties between the school/classroom and the home. The third level (Exosystems, an extended Mesosystem) is made up of the formal/informal social structures such as community, school, family and relatives, parents' field of work, and social network. Bronfenbrenner (1979, 4) argued that the individual's development is profoundly affected by events occurring in settings in which the person is not even present (e.g. the conditions of parental employment). The final level is the Makrosystems, it includes spheres such as the cultural (tradition, religion, ideology), political, economic system. According to Bronfenbrenner (1979,

4), there is a striking phenomenon pertaining to settings at all three levels of the ecological environment outlined above. Within any culture or subculture, settings of a given kind (e.g. home, office) tend to be very much alike, whereas between cultures they are distinctly different. It is as if within each society or subculture there existed a blueprint for the organization of every type of setting. Furthermore, the blueprint can be changed, with the result that the structure of the settings in a society can become markedly altered and produce corresponding changes in behavior and development. While Bronfenbrenner referred to ecological contexts outside the individual, Belsky (1980, 320f.) pointed out that individual differences (i.e. the personal characteristics of each individual) within the ecological context should be taken into account. According to him, individual differences of the growing individual include the cognitive, communicative, social, physical, and personality characteristics that the individual brings to his/her relationships in ecological contexts. Thus, for example, the individual strengths and weaknesses of the student identified as having LD should be taken into account, since these are the ways in which the student learns best, and personality traits which contribute to his/her learning styles (Bauer, Keefe, Shea, 2001, 64). The social system perspective is primarily concerned with the dynamic relationship between the growing individual and its environment and examines the ways the relationships are formed and reconciled by forces from the individual's various social contexts. These social contexts include in the innermost level the individual; in the second level, one-to-one relationships; in the third level, interactions among contexts; in the fourth level, community, work and school; in the last level the society (Bauer, Keefe, & Shea, 2001, 63) (Figure 3.2).

According to Bronfenbrenner (1979, 209ff.), the interaction among contexts includes, at a practical level, parent and teacher collaboration, family and community service involvement, and also transitions of the individual between home to school and from school to work. In addition, transitions are enhanced if role demands in the different settings are compatible, and if the individuals engage in mutual trust, a positive orientation and goals consensus between settings. In this regard, teachers must consider that the problems a student exhibits do not originate from a single cause. Therefore, teachers must recognize that a single intervention will probably not be sufficient to support the student and not be effective in order to solve the problem (Hanson & Carta 102ff.). As previously mentioned, the social system perspective assumes that the behavior is not linear but is composed of transactions among the individual and social contexts. Also, events occurring in the school setting are affected by, or affect, the individual student. Thus, teachers' beliefs have an impact on the education of students with LDs. For example, the behavior of the student in the classroom is influencing the teacher's behavior while the teacher's behavior is influencing the student's behavior. According to

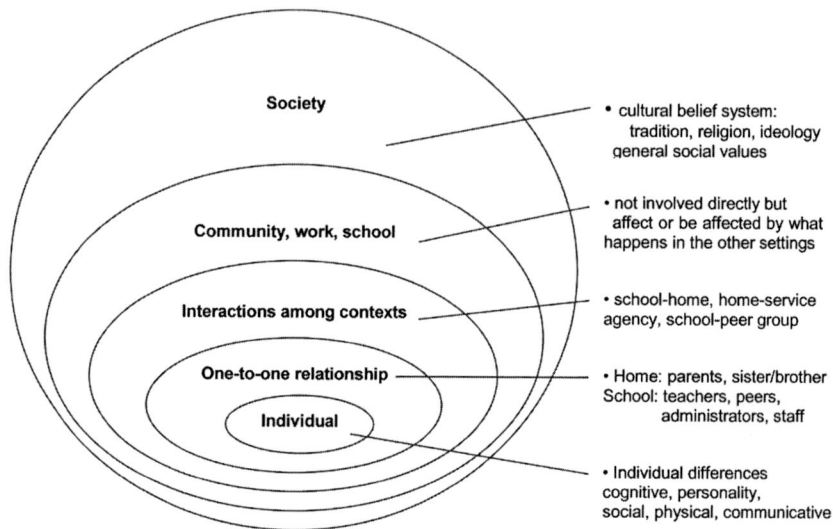

Figure 3.2   Nested social contexts in the social system perspective

Sameroff & Cahndler (1975, as cited in Bauer, Keefe, & Shea, 2001, 69), teachers with similarly behaving students may vary in their responses towards the students, and thus, cause different developmental outcomes. A student's development cannot be explained entirely by either biological or environmental factors, but rather by the reciprocal interactions between the individual and the environment.

3.2.2 Historical Perspectives

Although the Korean government's involvement in matters of LDs through legislation and funding has been evident since the mid-1990s, and LD may be one of the latest categories officially recognized as special education categories by the special education promotion law in 1994, the roots of LD theory can be traced back to the early 1800s; thus, the origins of the conceptual foundation of LD are long-standing, like many of the other disability categories (Hallahan & Mercer, 2002, 1). Moreover, the field of LD is often thought of as having come into being in the early 1960s, with regard to the period when the term LD was introduced and included by the US government on its agenda, though there is a long history of investigations which have influenced the development of the field of LD (Opp, 1994, 10). This section attempts to summarize the history of LD theory, divided into four major phases; foundation phase, transition phase, LD phase, and current phase (Figure 3.3), referring to research and researchers such as Hallahan & Mercer (2002), Lerner (2000), Mercer (1997), Opp (1994, 1992), Bleidick (1985) and Beschel (1980).

Figure 3.3   Historical perspectives of LDs: four major phases

Foundation phase 1800s -1930s	Transition phase 1930s-1960s	LD phase 1960s-1980s	Current phase 1990s-present
Early investigation:	Terminologies:	Integration of LDs:	Qualitative enhancement:
Brain research Reading disability, Word blindness, Dyslexia	Brain injured child (1947) MBD (1966) LD (1963)	Quantitative expansion Implementation in the schools- intervention, learning strategies	Efforts to facilitate Educational/social integration of students with LDs
School for slow learning children (1867) *Neben Klasse* (1898)	Clinical studies		Definition, identification, placement issues

FOUNDATION PHASE: EARLY INVESTIGATION OF BRAIN RESEARCH AND READING DISABILITY

The foundation phase (1800s to 1930s) goes back to research in Europe on acquired brain research; during this period, neurology underpinned the early investigation of brain research (e.g. nervous system functions). Towards the end of this period, research on reading disability increased (Hallahan & Mercer, 2002, 1). In the early investigation on brain research, researchers attempted to match up areas of the brain to particular forms of behavior. A German physician, Franz Joseph Gall, is credited as the first major figure to explore the relationship between brain injury and mental impairment; Gall and Spurzheim (1809) termed the brain the organ of the mind (Simpson, 2005, 475f.). Of particular relevance to LD, Gall is known for noting the effect of brain damage on what today would be termed Broca's aphasia (Hallahan & Mercer, 2002, 1). The investigation of Broca (motor aphasia) and Wernicke (sensory aphasia) in the 1860s and 1870s was the beginning of the scientific debate between the holistic versus the localistic theory of brain functions (Cappa, Moro, Perani, & Piattelli-Palmarini, 2000, 27). Wernicke's studies were engrossed further on by researchers such as Lichtheim, Liepmann, Berlin, Grashey and Goldscheider; Lichtheim (1885) extended his model to the functions of reading and writing, he called disturbances of reading 'alexie' (Opp, 1994, 10). Following Lichtheim's clarifications for the diagnosis of aphasia, Berlin (1887) introduced the term 'dyslexie' to describe a specific disturbance of reading in the absence of pathological conditions in the visual organs and spoke of word blindness (*Wortblindheit*) (Opp, 1994, 10). Also, Ogle (1867) was among the first to use the term 'agraphia' to describe writing disorders and link it to aphasia (Roeltgen & Heilman, 1984, 811f.). In 1877, Kussmaul spoke of word-blindness and word-deafness to describe symptoms like the inability to read despite normal intelligence and sensory functions. This shifted the focus from aphasia to reading problems (Anderson & Meier-Hedde, 2001, 9ff.). Hinshelwood (1917) extended the work on acquired word-blindness in adults to congenital word-blindness in children. He suggested the potentially inherited aspect of reading disability and the preponderance of males with the condition, and advocated for intensive, individualized one-on-one instruction for these children (Hallahan & Mercer, 2002, 2). The educational achievements of the investigations of brain research during the 19th century can be seen in the focus shifted from aphasia to reading problems, and the expansion of special education efforts (Opp, 1994, 10). As early as 1867, Heinrich Stötzner, a German teacher of the deaf, founded a school for slow-learning children *(Schule fuer Schwachsinnige Kinder)* (Stötzner, 1864, 38). These children were not mentally retarded but, as Stötzner described, their difficulties in learning resulted from poor memory and motor coordination. Thus, at that time, remedial teaching efforts were suggested (Opp, 1994, 10). Likewise, Fuchs (1898) addressed this issue by means of the *Nebenklasse* for mentally retarded children *(Nebenklasse fuer geistig schwache Kinder)* (Fuchs, 1922, 72). In school, Still (1902) observed a child with a quite abnormal incapacity for sustained attention, entirely unable to spell words correctly from dictation. This resulted in backwardness in school acquirements despite average achievements in all other school accomplishments (Opp, 1994, 10). Morgan (1896) and Hinshelwood (1900) found children who could not learn to read or write despite good intellectual capacities [3] (Hallahan & Mercer, 2002, 2).

Transition phase: brain injury, minimal brain dysfunction to learning disability

According to Mercer (1997, 5), the study of LD began, in part, with the work of Strauss and Werner in the late 1930s and early 1940s. They studied children with brain injuries and differentiated the characteristic of exogenous retardation (e.g. shortage of oxygen during birth, extremely high fever during infancy or injury to the head) and endogenous retardation (inherited brain structures) although both etiologies recognized learning impairments. Strauss and Werner based their research and descriptions on children with mental retardation, they also focused on rehabilitation. Their work prompted Cruickshank to initiate studies regarding the effects on brain injury on children with normal intelligences (e.g. Cruickshank, 1976; Hallahan & Cruickshank, 1973; Cruickshank & Hallahan, 1973). Further researchers such as Kirk (1966), McCarthy & Kirk (1968), Kephart (1975), and Cruickshank (1975) elaborated their work and suggested educational concepts referring to these as psycholinguistic abilities, perceptual-motor and psycho-motor

---

[3] While Kavale & Forness (1985, 17) addressed this as the dyslexia branch of the field of LD, another major branch in the foundation of LD is the work of Strauss and Werner (e.g. Opp, 1994; Kavale & Forness, 2000).

match (Opp, 1994, 10.). Lerner (2000) identified this period as a transitional phase while Mercer (1997, 7) described it as a learning disability phase. During this period, emphasis was given on language and reading disabilities and perceptual, perceptual-motor, and attention disabilities (Hallahan & Mercer, 2002, 4). Thus, an increased concern with neurological psychology became manifest. At that time, as research focused on clinical assessment and remediation strategies, some children with learning difficulties were, mistakenly classified as mentally retarded or emotionally disturbed (Silver, 1990, 243f.). During the 1960s, a shift in terminologies occurred with the introduction of the term minimal brain dysfunction (MBD) recommended by Clements in 1966 and the term learning disability (LD) by Kirk in 1962 (e.g. Mercer, 1997; Hallahan & Mercer, 2002; Silver, 1990). The term MBD embraced genetic variations, biochemical irregularities, perinatal brain insults or other illnesses or injuries sustained during the years which are critical for the development and maturation of the central nervous system, or from unknown causes (Clements, 1966 as cited in Hallahan & Mercer, 2002, 16). However, MBD has not been accepted widely in comparison with the term LD. In this regard, Mercer (1997, 7) pointed out that special education teachers found that labels connoting a medical etiology were not useful in planning educational intervention.

LEARNING DISABILITY PHASE: QUANTITATIVE EXPANSION OF INTEGRATION

From about 1960s to 1980s, the population of LD in public school grew rapidly and LD began its emergence as a formal category. During this period, education for LDs evolved and organizations for LD founded by parents and professionals (Hallahan & Mercer, 2002, 14). Thus Mercer (1997, 7) described this period as a learning disability phase. According to Lyon (1996, 390f.), there were two reasons that promoted the progression of the field of LD. One was the response to the need to understand individual differences in academic performance among children who displayed specific deficits in the learning process despite normal intelligence; and the other was the need to address social and political forces that emerged as educators were pressured to provide services to students experiencing significant difficulties in learning. During this period, the vast majority of the educational approaches assumed that children with LDs suffered from psychological processing and/or visual-perceptual processing deficits; hence, emphasis was given on psychological processing and perceptual training. Hallahan & Mercer (2002, 16) divided these educational approaches into those focused on language disabilities and those focused on visual and visual-motor disabilities. Researchers such as Kirk (e.g. diagnostic tests), Myklebust & Johnson focused (e.g. remedial techniques for receptive and expressive language) on language disabilities whereas researchers such as Kephart, Frostig, Getman, and Barsch focused on visual and visual-motor disabilities. However, Cohen (1969, 1970) argued that the educational approaches on perceptual training were ineffective in improving academic performance, although they sometimes were effective in improving perceptual and/or perceptual-motor development. The use of perceptual and perceptual-motor training hung on for a period of time, but by the mid-1980s its use had waned considerably (Hallahan & Mercer, 2002, 19). From the mid-1970s to 1980s, efforts were made by experts to reach consensus on the definition of LD and to develop methods of identifying students with LD (Keogh, 1983, 123). During this period, in several works of research, emphasis was given on information processing problems of students with LDs, strategies and interventions for LD (e.g. Connor, 1983 for information processing of LD; Bryan, Pearl, Donahue, Bryan, & Pflaum, 1983 for social competence and attribution about success and failure of LDs; Ysseldyke, Thurlow, Graden, Wesson, Algozzine, & Deno, 1983 for curriculum based assessment and decision making in identification; Hallahan, Hall, Ianna, Kneedler, Lloyd, & Loper et al., 1983 for cognitive behavior modification, self-monitoring of attention). In particular, with respect to identification, differently from other researchers above, Ysseldyke et al. (1983) raised concerns about whether students identified as having LD could be reliably differentiated from low achievers. They suggested that assessing students' progress in the curricula (CBA) provides more educationally useful information than the typical, standardized tests.

CURRENT PHASE: EFFORTS AND ATTEMPTS FOR QUALITATIVE ENHANCEMENT OF INTEGRATION

During the current phase, from about the 1990s to the present, there have occurred important shifts regarding the field of special education and LD. Among them are legislation amendments and developments towards integration. Although the movement towards integration begun earlier in the previous phase and this led to a quantitative expansion of the integration of LD, the qualitative enhancement of integration; facilitation of educational and social integration of LD (e.g. Avramidis, Bayliss, & Burden, 2000 for placement of students with LDs in regular classroom and their special education service; see also Avramidis, Bayliss, & Burden, 2002) has ensued in recent years. During the current phase, several themes have emerged that influenced the field of LD. Referring to Hallahan & Mercer (2002, 25), research on definition of LD have solidified the field while issues on identification procedures and placement of LD have contributed to the turbulence in the field of LD. They also added research on phonological processing and biological causes of LDs as having solidified the field of LD; first, since the majority of students with LDs exhibit reading difficulties, research on phonological awareness has the potential to improve the assessment practices for LDs, but in order to improve reading skills of poor readers, phonemic awareness training must be combined with other types of reading instruction. Second, evidence has begun to mount that LD may be the result of neurological dysfunctions, and hereditary factors are implicated in many cases of LD.

3.2.3 INTERNATIONAL PERSPECTIVES

Whereas it is said that a definitional consensus is near (e.g. Hammill, 1990, 1993; Mercer, Jordan, Allsopp, & Mercer, 1996), it is suggested that the inhomogeneity in the definition continues to plague the field of LD (e.g. Brinkerhoff, Shaw, & McGuire, 1992; Gregg, 1994; Mellard, 1990; Siegel, 1999). As Klotz (2004, 93f.) mentioned, several terms synonymous with LD have been applied to a condition that exists or a problem that appears in practice. It is argued that LD has depended upon arbitrary and changing criteria over periods of time since the ongoing discussion of LD concerning the definition and criteria have failed to reach consensus (e.g. Doris, 1993; Kavale & Forness, 1985; Keogh, 1986; Mercer, 1997; MacMillan & Siperstein, 2002). Moreover, Proctor & Prevatt (2003, 459) argued that choosing appropriate criteria for LD definition and identification is one of the most debated tasks in the fields of special education. They suggested that the ambiguity in LD criteria originate from the heterogeneity concerning the LD definitions provided in the ICD-10 (International Statistical Classification of Diseases and Related Health Problems-10th Revision), IDEA (Individuals with Disabilities Education Act), and in the DSM-IV (Diagnostic and Statistical Manual of Mental Disorders; American Psychiatric Association). This section presents several aspects of the LD definition and identification in the ICD-10 (World Health Organization, WHO), amendment of the IDEA in 2004 (U.S Department of Education) and the Recommendations of KMK, the Standing Conference of the Ministers of Education and Cultural Affairs in Germany (*Die Ständige Konferenz der Kultusminister der Länder in der Bundesrepublik Deutschland*) in 1994 and 1999.

ICD-10 (INTERNATIONAL STATISTICAL CLASSIFICATION OF DISEASES AND RELATED HEALTH PROBLEMS. TENTH REVISION)

In the ICD-10, LD is referred to as specific developmental disorders of scholastic skills (F81) included in mental and behavioral disorders (F00-F99) under Chapter V. Disorders of psychological development (F80-F89). The definition reads as follows:

> Disorders in which the normal patterns of skill acquisition are disturbed from the early stages of development. This is not simply a consequence of a lack of opportunity to learn, it is not solely a result of mental retardation, and it is not due to any form of acquired brain trauma or disease (WHO).

In addition, the ICD-10 delineates subtypes of LD such as specific reading disorder (F81.0), specific spelling disorder (F81.1), specific disorder of arithmetical skills (F81.2), mixed disorder of scholastic skills (F81.3), other developmental disorders of scholastic skills (F81.8), and developmental disorder of scholastic skills, unspecified (F81.9). In ICD-10, these disorders are considered to have in common: an onset invariably during infancy or childhood; impairment or delay in development of functions that are strongly related to biological maturation of the central nervous system; and a steady course without remissions and relapses. Within this statement, it is commented that in many cases the functions affected include language, visuo-spatial skills, and motor coordination. Usually, the delay or impairment has been present from as early as it could be detected reliably and will diminish progressively as the child grows older, although milder deficits often remain in adult life (WHO).

INDIVIDUALS WITH DISABILITIES EDUCATION ACT (IDEA) IN U.S

IDEA provides for the funding and establishment of student rights within the public school system (Ysseldyke & Algozzine, 2006, 25). Through the reauthorization of IDEA 2004, student with disabilities are expected to participate in the state and district wide assessments, use of accommodations where appropriate, and results are to be reported in the same way as other students are reported (e.g. Kossar, Mitchem, & Ludlow, 2005; Council for Exceptional Children, 2002). The background philosophy is that if an individual is to be competitive in today's global society, everyone must reach his or her full potential. The IDEA 2004 supports the mandate for highly qualified teachers and assessment to determine annual yearly progress through high-stakes-testing for approximately 95% of students in special education (Ysseldyke & Algozzine, 2006, 29; Kossar, Mitchem, & Ludlow, 2005, 66). In addition, the necessity was felt to mention the No Child Left Behind (NCLB) Act regarding the impact on special education and the field of LD. NCLB is the reauthorization of the Elementary and Secondary Act of 1965. NCLB provides for four categories of reform; accountability, flexibility in local control, parent option and teaching methods (see also Ysseldyke & Algozzine, 2006; Marschak, 2003). These goals are to be accomplished through results-based and standards-based accountability methods (Beaver, 2004, 1f.). NCLB, thereby, aims to improve the instruction methods and the teacher quality, to therewith enhance students' achievements. Concerning the education of students with LDs, basically special education certification is required for the 'highly qualified teacher' condition, as further is a professional knowledge of the subject and curriculum. This may bring changes and reforms in the current special education teacher education and special education certifications concerning the primary and secondary education.

IDEA'S DEFINITION OF LD

The conceptual definition of LD in IDEA (P.L. 94-142) has been amended through 1975, 1983, 1986, 1990, 1992, 1997 and 2004. The definition of LD is referred to as Specific learning disability (SpLD) and reads as follows:

A disorder in one or more of the basic psychological processes involved in understanding or in using language, spoken or written, which disorder may manifest itself in the imperfect ability to listen, think, speak, read, write, spell, or do mathematical calculations.

Included disorders are such conditions as perceptual disabilities, brain injury, minimal brain dysfunction, dyslexia, and developmental aphasia. Such term does not include a learning problem that is primarily the result of visual, hearing, or motor disabilities, of mental retardation, of emotional disturbance, or of environmental, cultural, or economic disadvantage (P.L.108-446 Status TITLE I /A/602/30).

This definition, with relatively minor modification, has been the basis for policies in a majority of states (e.g. Mercer, Jordan, Allsopp, & Mercer, 1996). Kavale & Forness (2000, 240) argued that this definition outlines a generic concept rather than a description of the specific condition; thus, it is not clear if one can answer what LD is after reading this statement. According to them, the most concrete perspective is the indication about process disorders (disorder in basic psychological process), particularly in the language area that interfere with basic academic achievement. Even so, the descriptions and relationships are vague and no explicit conceptualization emerges. Furthermore, there is a statement likening LD to other known conditions such as dyslexia. However, indications about how similar and how different they are from LD are not presented. Finally, there is a perspicuous statement about what LD is not; that is, the 'exclusion clause', the problem is that such a statement is not appropriate to define what LD is. Adelman (1971, 528f.) contended that even though outlining the form of a specific learning disability, this definition is rather a nonspecific description of the elements contributing to LD.

IDEA'S IDENTIFICATION OF LD
In section 614. Evaluations, eligibility determinations, individualized education programs, and educational placements b) Evaluation Procedures (6) Specific learning disabilities, it is stated that the use of a severe discrepancy between intellectual ability and achievement must not be required; the use of a process based on the child's response to scientific, research-based intervention and other alternative research-based procedures may permitted for LD determination (Statute: TITLE I /B/614/b, U.S. Department of Education). That is, the amendment of 2004 included the Response to Instruction (RTI) model as eligibility criteria of LD besides the previous IQ-achievement discrepancy model. In addition, IDEA (2004) addressed significant changes from preexisting regulations to the final regulatory requirements regarding the identification of LD compare it to 1997 are as follows (Office of Special Education Programs, 2006): (a) add procedures for identifying children with specific learning disabilities; (b) require additional group members parents and a team of qualified professionals; (c) add criteria for determining the existence of a specific learning disability; (d) describe the required observation; (e) specify documentation required for the eligibility determination.

To summarize, the definition of LD in IDEA is referred as Specific learning disability (SpLD). The SpLD articulates the presence of disorder in basic psychological processes, and adds other included disorders (e.g. perceptual disabilities etc.), at the same time, it also declares the exclusion clauses [4]. Since the amendment of 2004, IDEA encourages the Response to Instruction (RTI) model as eligibility criteria besides the IQ-achievement discrepancy model. It should be mentioned that several methods have been utilized in the states based on the discrepancy model and RTI model to determine LD in the assessment process (Bauer, Keefe & Shea, 2001, 241). Although the IDEA definition of LD includes the exclusion clause, the exclusion criteria are used less consistently than that of the discrepancy model, which in many cases some states include in their definition or criteria for determining LD (e.g. Fletcher et al. 1998; Reschly & Hosp, 2004).

STANDING CONFERENCE OF THE MINISTERS OF EDUCATION AND CULTURAL AFFAIRS IN GERMANY *(Die Ständige Konferenz der Kultusminister der Länder (KMK) in der Bundesrepublik Deutschland)*

The *Grundgesetz* (Basic Law) is the framework for the education system in Germany. The rights of disabled children are enshrined in the Basic Law (*Grundgesetz*, Article 3-R1) and in the *Länder* constitutions (R14-29). The educational legislation and administration of the education system are primarily the responsibility of the *Länder*. This particularly applies to the school system, higher education and the continuing education sector, more detailed provisions are set out in the school legislation of the *Länder* (e.g. *Hamburgisches Schulgesetz; Schulgesetz für den Freistaat Sachsen*). In 1994, the German Basic Law (*Grundgesetz*) was changed and developed through the introduction of one new article (i.e. Art. 3, Abs. 3, Satz 2):

Niemand darf wegen seiner Behinderung benachteiligt werden (nobody must have disadvantages due to his/her handicap (Die Grundrechte Art 3, Abs.3, Satz 2, Bundesministerium der Justiz).

Based on this Article in the *Grundgesetz* (Basic Law), the new Social Welfare Code IX (SGBIX) has come in force in 2001, which summarizes the legal bases of the medical and vocational rehabilitation. The development and organization of special education in the *Länder* was harmonized by several resolutions adopted by the Standing Conference of the Ministers of Education and Cultural Affairs (KMK) of the *Länder* and especially by the Recommendations on the Organization of Special Schools (*Empfehlung zur Ordnung des Sonderschulwesens*, Resolution of 1972 as cited in KMK, 2006) and recommendations for the individual

---

[4] "Such term does not include a learning problem that is primarily the result of visual, hearing, or motor disabilities, of mental retardation, of emotional disturbance, or of environmental cultural, or economic disadvantage (Public Law 108-446 Status TITLE 1/A/602/30)

types of special education. Thus, the current situation is documented in the Recommendations on Special Needs Education in the Schools of the Federal Republic of Germany (*Empfehlungen zur sonderpädagogischen Förderung in den Schulen in der Bundesrepublik Deutschland*, Resolution of 1994).

SPECIAL NEEDS EDUCATION (SNE)
Since the school year 1999/2000 all *Länder* agreed in a joint definition of Special Needs Education (SNE). Considering the increasing number of multiply handicapped (which may be due to the complexity and difficulty in practice to clearly classify disabilities), consensus was reached to use the term "pupil with needs for special education or special educational needs relating to development" (*Schüler mit sonderpädagogischem Förderbedarf*) in Germany. SNE relating to development is to be presumed for children and adults who are disabled or have limited possibilities for education, development and learning. Further, therapy and social aids from additional external school services may be included as necessary. Above all, the key-element in SNE is the ability of each school to promote pupils' development by meeting the necessary special education tasks and requirements. This is the key for all didactic and methodical measures as well as the framework of conditions for each individual pupil inside school (KMK, 1994).

RECOMMENDATIONS ON SPECIAL NEEDS EDUCATION IN DEVELOPMENT AREA LEARNING (*Empfehlungen zum Förderschwerpunkt Lernen*)
This recommendation (1999) of KMK was an amendment statement of the *Empfehlungen zur sonderpädagogischen Förderung in den Schulen* (1994) (Recommendations on Special Needs Education in the schools, 1994). This recommendation (KMK, 1999) stated that for students who have difficulties in learning (learning difficulties), the relationship between the individual and its environment is permanently or temporarily aggravated, so that they may not reach or may achieve only to some extent the goal and the curricular content of a regular school. Thus SNE is provided for students who have significant impairments (difficulties) in their learning development and performance development, and thus can not be supported in the regular school to meet their needs, in spite of additional support for learning.

KMK'S IDENTIFICATION OF LD (*Feststellung und Ermittlung des Sonderpädagogischen Förderbedarfs*)
The Recommendation passed by the KMK (1994) (*Empfehlungen zur sonderpädagogischen Förderung in den Schulen der Bundesrepublik Deutschland*, 1994) clarified the need to improve the traditional disability categories with respect to more differentiated approaches of support and individual development. Overall, qualifications and perspectives of basic developmental levels were suggested to be involved in the analysis of child and environment (*Kind-Umfeld-Analyse*). Thus,

eight key elements for identification and diagnosis of pupils with SNE have been established as follows; motor, perception, cognition, motivation, communication, interaction, emotion and creativity. The recommendation (1994) stated that the diagnosis of special educational needs must be a precise definition of individual special needs and must guide the decision of educational process and placement. Moreover, the need of a qualitative and quantitative profile of the pupil was addressed in order to ensure appropriate support measures. The information which is required to be included in the profile is as follows: development of learning and behavioral strategies; perception and the process of perception; social relationships; communication and interaction; individual and educational circumstances in life; the school environment and the possibilities for change; the vocational environment and the necessary supporting factors. In addition, the assessment for a "pupil with needs for special education or special educational needs relating to development" is based on syllabus requirements and the knowledge, abilities and skills acquired in a particular class or learning group. Procedures within the assessment process are to be performed by the teacher in charge of lessons, who is educationally responsible for the student's decision. In all *Länder*, the establishment of IEP (Individualized Education Program) is compulsory in some degree, meaning that the standardized achievement tests to assess student's performance and learning development in certain subjects or grades are not given on *Länder* level. Continuous assessment of performance for students with special educational needs is based on multi-disciplinary reports. Parents are able to make applications for assessment. If an institution makes an application, the parents have to be informed and consulted; moreover, parents are able to object to a placement decision. In addition, special education is divided into categories relating to the particular requirements of the pupils concerned, and operates on the basis of special educational principles. It seems that the overall tendency of special education in Germany regarding the identification and assessment of students with disabilities is going to be less institution-related than before. It is noticeable that emphasis is given on individual and ecological aspects of learning and the living environment. The *Deutscher Bildungsrat* (1973) (as cited in Eberwein, 1997, 16) suggested to consider the causes of LD not only as arising from the student personally but also associated to school situation, school curriculum, and the interaction of teachers and peers. Eberwein (1997, 16) argued that LD is considered as a normative, relative and school related organizational definition referring more to the expectation of the teaching and school environment. According to him, LD is not a fixed deficitary criterion of a person according to the school frame conditions and the requirements of efficiency. Rather, it is preferred to exchange the terminus by individual learning and development provision, team consultancy, parental work and living-environment-related measures. It depends on the school administration, and the normative expectation varies from school to school, from teacher to teacher, from place to place and from culture to culture. As stated above, the KMK focuses on individual and ecological aspects of learning [5] and living environment (e.g. *Kind-Umfeld-Analyse*) within the scope of SNE (Special Needs Education). As mentioned previously, SNE means specific support for disabled pupils. Since the school year 1999/2000 all *Länder* agreed on a joint definition of SNE. The area of responsibility of SNE in Germany with respect to all organizational aspects refers to the special needs within the context of disability exclusively. The European Agency for Development (2003), in SNE remarked that there has been a noticeable trend in practice; there are many problems in dealing with the disability/special education categories, since many disabled children can not be clearly classified. It must be considered that there is an increasing number of multiply handicapped children. Conclusively, Germany came to an agreement using the term *Schüler mit sonderpädagogischem Förderbedarf* (pupil with needs for special education or special educational needs relating to development) (KMK, 1994). After all, with regard to more differentiated approaches of support, the focus is laid on the individual's successful and independent life within the family, community, and society.

3.3 TEACHERS' PERCEPTIONS OF THE CAUSES OF LEARNING DISABILITIES

3.3.1 CONSOLIDATED VIEW OF ISSUES ON CAUSES OF LEARNING DISABILITIES

This section briefly covers the consolidated view of issues on causes of LD. Differentiation among students with LDs and learning difficulties has always been problematic (Gresham, 2002, 471). While some researchers have argued that a separate type of LD; qualitatively and etiologically separate from general learning difficulty does not exist (e.g. Shaywitz, Fletcher, Holahan, & Shaywitz, 1992; Swanson, 2000b; Ysseldyke, Algozzine, & Thurlow, 2000; Hoskyns & Swanson, 2000; Moats, 2002), some have pointed out that there are differences in the domain of reading disability (e.g. Grigorenko, 2001; Fuchs, Fuchs, Mathes, Lipsey, & Roberts, 2002; Bailet, 2001). Over the years, researchers have debated the similarities and differences between these two groups (e.g. Epps, Ysseldyke, & McGue, 1984; Fuchs, Fuchs, Mathes, Lipsey, & Roberts, 2002; Kavale, Fuchs, & Scruggs, 1994; Ysseldyke, Algozzine, Shinn, & McGue, 1982). Shaywitz et al. (1992) concluded that there are more similarities than differences between students with LDs

---

[5] "*Unter Lernen soll vor allem eine selbstständige und entwicklungsfördernde Auseinandersetzung des kindes und Jugendlichen mit seiner Umwelt verstanden werden*" (Schlichting & Schulz, 2000, 317-318).

and other learning difficulties. Likewise, Swanson (2000b) suggested that students identified as LD share very many characteristics with students with learning difficulties. In their recent study, Ysseldyke et al. (2000) argued that there are 96% overlap between the two groups on measures of intelligence, achievement, perceptual motor skills, classroom behavior and self concept. More recently, Moats (2002) cited the meta-analyses of Hoskyns & Swanson (2000) to suggest there are no significant differences between the two groups, particularly in phonological awareness and rapid naming. In most countries, the term 'learning difficulty' is applied to students who are not making adequate progress within the school curriculum, particularly in basic skill areas, language, literacy and numeracy. Their difficulties may be associated with one specific school subject or evident across all subjects in the academic curriculum (Westwood, 2004, 53). The intellectual level of these students is often somewhat below average, and disproportionate numbers come from lower socio-economic and disadvantaged backgrounds (Westwood, 2004, 53; see also Westwood & Graham, 2000, 24f.; Waldron & McLeskey, 2000, 171ff.). How, then, is LD different from other learning difficulties? The question may center on the degree to which LD can be differentiated from learning difficulty and the extent to which these two groups overlap in intellectual, academic achievement and social behavior. For most children whose progress in school learning causes concern, the problems are related to their experience and learning history rather than to intrinsic intellectual deficits (Kerschner, 2000, 280). While some learning problems are within the student, it is most unlikely that this is the case with the vast majority; environmental factors are much more frequent causes of learning problems (Westwood, 2004, 55). It should be recognized that students with LDs experience various difficulties in the context of their environments. These students experience a significantly different reality in the classroom than their non-disabled peers (e.g. Lago-Dello, 1998; Wenz-Gross & Siperstein, 1998). They may experience more stress, less peer support and poorer adjustment in the classroom. In the classroom, the context is teacher, student and place, including curriculum and materials (Bauer & Sapona, 1991 as cited in Bauer, Keefe, & Shea, 181). The components of the classroom ecology are dynamic, and they may enhance or impede the success of the student with LDs.

Are the learning problems exhibited by those students with SpLD and learning difficulties not similar in nature – at least for teachers, considering the instructional implementations? Are their learning problems not simply located at different points on the same continuum (Kim S, Kim KO, Kim SD, Lee SD, Lim HS, & Han SM, 2001, 33)?

In the real school practice, it is hard to clearly classify 'SpLD' and 'learning difficulty'. At this point, it should be noted that there has been a noticeable trend in practice. There are many problems in dealing with the special education categories, since a lot of disabled children can not be clearly classified. This may be due to the complexity and difficulty in practice to clearly classify disabilities as well as the increasing number of multiply handicapped. Moreover and importantly, whatever the differences, children in both groups are eligible for special education and related services. Conclusively, this chapter consolidates much of the information that

- Learning Difficulty includes LD (SpLD) and there are more significant similarities between learning difficulty and LD than differences in intellectual, academic achievement and social behavior – a broader perspective on LD;
- Students' learning difficulties are related to their experience and learning. Although some learning problems are within the student, environment factors are much more frequent causes. Many such factors in the learning environment are amendable to modification and improvement, whereas deficits within the individual are not so easily changed – more emphasis on environmental factors;
- The classroom context is an important factor that contributes to the achievement of students who have LDs – the importance of factors related to the classroom

and presents the causes contributing to LDs in the environmental (in particular, within school context) and individual contexts.

CAUSES CONTRIBUTING TO LEARNING DISABILITIES

Many factors (can) cause or exacerbate difficulties in children's learning. There are many theories concerning the factors that may lead to LD. It should be mentioned here that the possible causes of LD in this study were based on factors (variables) collated from the survey of Kataoka, Kraayenoord, & Elkins (2004) and were chiefly based on the literature of Westwood (2004).

ENVIRONMENTAL VARIABLES:
INSUFFICIENT OR INADEQUATE TEACHING METHODS

Westwood (2004, 55) argued that the environmental factor over which teachers have most control is the teaching method, and according to him, when it is not matched to students' interests and abilities, learning difficulties will ensue. Similarly, Slavin (1994, 1ff.) suggested that inadequate teaching methods can be a major cause of learning difficulties, particularly students with a lack of 'school readiness' are potentially at risk, since their experiences of frustration and failure trigger a negative attitude towards learning and school (e.g. Slavin, 2006; Slavin & Karweit, 1992; Morris, 2003). Often, insufficient teaching and inappropriate teaching methods exacerbate the learning problem of students with LDs. However, most definitions of LD state that LD is not the direct result of environmental, socio-economic and cultural disadvantages – that is the exclusion clause (for more discussion about the exclusion clause cf. Ch. 7). In addition, Westwood (2004, 57) pointed out that some teaching methods known to be highly successful (such as direct instruction) are not widely used or willingly adopted in schools (e.g. Waldron & McLeskey, 2000, 171ff.).

IRRELEVANT OR UNREALISTIC SCHOOL CURRICULUM

No less important than the teaching methods, the content of curriculum may also contribute to LD. Many, perhaps most, learning difficulties are not caused by cognitive deficits in the student but are due to students not having the necessary prior level of knowledge or skill needed for the task (e.g. Howe, 1999 as cited in Westwood, 2004, 57; see also Roberson, Hamill, & Hewitt). Much of the research on the curriculum for students with learning difficulties has focused on curriculum content, its selection and delivery (e.g. Brennan 1979, 1985; Wilson 1981 as cited in Ireson, Evans, Redmond, & Wedell, 1992, 155). According to Brennan (1985 as cited in Westwood, 2004, 58) the curriculum content selected for students who have learning difficulties should be based on 4Rs. That means, the curriculum should cover topics that feature in the student's life (Real). The knowledge, skills, strategies and values learned through these topics should be useful to the student (Relevant). It should be feasible for the student to attempt the work given his/her age, ability, prior knowledge and motivation (Realistic). Finally, the student should understand that there is value and purpose in engaging in this learning (Rational). However, the general curriculum do not match up to these standards and (as Westwood puts it) so contribute to or exacerbate students' learning problems.

UNSUITABLE CLASSROOM ENVIRONMENT

Several studies have suggested that the physical environment of the classroom may exacerbate learning difficulties (e.g. Alban-Metcalfe & Alban-Metcalfe, 2001; DuPaul & Stonder, 2003). The noise level and multiple sources of distraction can impact students' attention and on-task behavior; factors such as temperature, lighting, stimulating display materials, availability of resources were also assumed to be factors contributing to students' learning problems (Westwood, 2004, 58). In addition, the way children are seated and grouped influences the students' on-task time, motivation and participation. Hasting & Schwieso (1995, 279) suggested that students' on-task behavior can be significantly better when they are seated in row instead of informal groups, since distracting group arrangements (Lyle, 1996, 13ff.) and group work (Jenkins, Antil, Wayne, & Vadasy, 2003, 99ff.) in classroom, such as students being physically arranged for group work with peers seated together around a table and working on different individual assignments, may yield poor concentration, hence poorer academic achievement. Westwood (2004, 59) argued that although it is commonly believed that smaller class cater for better learning, solely reducing the class size does not induce high achievement or lower failure rates, because many other factors such as behavior and quality of teaching are also important.

POOR TEACHER-STUDENT RELATIONSHIP

The teacher-student relationship is essential for students who are at risk or considered to have difficulties. It should be noted that the "salient etiological condition" most often mentioned in the histories of these children is the lack of adequate adult care (Morse, 1994 as cited in Bauer, Keefe, & Shea, 2001, 182). For an optimum learning in the school there needs to be a good rapport between the teacher and the student in the classroom. It should be noted that one of the ways in which some students with learning difficulties impede themselves is by failing to seek help from the teacher even though they need it (Westwood, 2004, 60). In this regard, Ravenette (1968 as cited in 2004, 60) remarked that it is crucial to know if the students like the teacher. If the students do not feel at ease with the teacher, they are even less likely to seek assistance (Altenbaugh, 1988, 52ff.). Particularly in teaching, in situations where relations may be necessarily unequal, teachers must adopt the perspective of the student (e.g. Witherell & Noddings, 1991). By doing so the teacher and student may together build a caring relationship in which the student then responds by fully engaging in the task, since students want teachers to have faith in them and to care about them (Hilty, 1998, 72ff.). For example, in their research on students with emotional and behavioral disorders, Bacon & Bloom (1994, 8) indicated that the teacher-student relationship was of great concern; they argued that teachers' personal qualities should support interaction with students. School and classroom then become a place where teacher and student talk to each other, reason together, and enjoy each other's company (Noddings, 1991, 157ff.). As Santrock (2001, 238) stated, when people are asked what schools are for, a common reply is: to help children learn.

LOW SOCIO-ECONOMIC STATUS BACKGROUND

Several studies over many years have indicated and maintained that students' socio-economic status correlates with their school achievement and school performance (e.g. McLoyd, 1998; Hilty, 1998; OECD, 2001; Chatterji, 2006). There are exceptions: students who successfully adapt despite risk and adversity (Masten, 1994, 3ff.). Most often students from higher socio-economic status backgrounds display higher academic achievement, while students from lower socio-economic status backgrounds tend to show lower academic achievement and more behavioral problems (McLoyd, 1998, 185ff.). Chatterji (2006, 489ff.) argued that parents from lower socio-economic backgrounds lack the funds to give their children early academic experiences, and pointed out that close to 40% of the associations between economic disadvantage and young children's lower academic performance are explained by lower quality home-learning environments. Socio-economic disadvantage particularly extreme poverty is one of the factors over which teachers have little control. Nevertheless, it is important that teachers understand and recognize the impact that a student's background environment has on their ability to learn at school (Westwood, 2004, 60). Teachers should not lower their expectations for these students; instead, they should understand that these students need intensive and continual support in order to reach their potential (McLoyd, 1998, 185ff.). It seems very likely that many students from lower socio-economic background families have less school readiness, and often less parental involvement in student's schoolwork and low interest of parents for their children's education is manifest. Although there are different opinions regarding the effectiveness of early intervention for increasing student's learning aptitude and intelligence (Westwood, 2004, 60), researchers have agreed that early intervention involving parents at schools, and thereby using structured teaching programs, will prevent many of the learning problems that occur in students exposed to ongoing socio-economic disadvantage (Campbell & Ramey, 1994, 684f.). Hence there is a need for comprehensive community services (Soderlund, Bursuck, Polloway, & Foley, 1995, 150) for students with LDs who come from low socio-economic backgrounds. According to Knitzer (1993, 8f.), the unavailability of appropriate support services in schools and the lack of collaboration among professionals in schools and community agencies have placed serious limitations on the application of effective intervention across settings. Eber, Nelson, & Miles (1997, 539ff.) suggested a "school-based wraparound process", which is a needs-driven process for providing support for individual students and their families. The school-based wraparound process is not a program or a type of service, but an approach that involves a commitment to blend services for students, their families and their teachers together. In this process, one integrated plan addresses the needs of the student during and beyond the school day. With regard to students with LDs, this plan is translated into an IEP which includes comprehensive services blended across agencies and addressed by the school besides the needed support and interventions in classrooms (Bauer, Keefe, & Shea, 2001, 161).

INDIVIDUAL VARIABLES:
NEGATIVE SELF-CONCEPT

Many students with LDs have a less positive self-concept (e.g. Bear & Minke, 1996). Many, perhaps most of these students have constructed negative self-concepts based on the responses they have perceived from their teachers, parents and peers (Ravenette, 1999 as cited in Westwood, 2004, 63; see also Peters, Klein, & Shadwick, 1998; Montgomery, 1994). In particular, Bear, Minke, Griffin, & Deemer (1998, 91f.) found that perceived teacher feedback on students with LDs contributed significantly to these students' feeling of self-worth. Moreover, Howe (1999 as cited in Westwood, 2004, 63) pointed out that low self-confidence impacts the student's learning as negatively as an absence of knowledge. Montgomery (1994, 254f.) maintained that teachers tend to underestimate the self-concepts of students with LDs, and pointed out that students with LDs who are educated in special classes tend to have similar self-concepts as the students without LDs, while those educated in regular classes tend to have poorer self-concepts. On the other hand, it was suggested that factors such as socio-economic status, intelligence, achievement and grades are less important for students with LDs regarding their self-concept, while these factors were traditional markers for school success among students without LDs (Hagborg, 1996, 117f.). Furthermore, students with LDs do not differ in their self-concept from their peers without LDs, regarding the non-academic areas such as the social, physical and family areas (Montgomery, 1994, 254f.).

LOW MOTIVATION

Motivation occupies a central role in learning, with reference to the impact that success and failure in the classroom can have on students' motivation to learn (the motivation theory focuses on the individual's reasons for learning and the conditions under which motivation is maximized (Covington & Mueller, 2001, 157f.)). Westwood (2004, 30) argued that teachers often believe that a lack of motivation is the underlying reason for students' difficulties in learning. He pointed out that teachers tend to blame a student's learning difficulty on his/her lack of motivation, and do not consider that the motivation can be significantly shaped and influenced by outside factors. On this concern, Galloway, Rogers, Armstrong, & Leo (1998, 17) argued that motivation can be seen as a product of an interaction between students and the varying situations in which they find themselves at school. Wilson & William (1994, 148f.) explored the academic intrinsic motivation and attitudes of students with LDs. They suggested that students with LDs perceive school environment and academic tasks as two separate factors, and these students' attitudes towards the school environment were more positive than towards academic tasks. In addition, students with LDs were likely to attribute success and failure to external factors such as luck (Pintrich, Anderman, & Klobucar, 1994, 360f.).

EMOTIONAL AND BEHAVIORAL PROBLEMS

Students with emotional and/or behavioral problems tend to have significant difficulties in learning within the school curriculum (e.g. Bauer & Shea, 1998). Emotional and/or behavioral problems can be both a cause and an effect of LD. However, it is often difficult to determine whether the emotional or behavioral problem is the primary underlying cause of a LD/learning difficulty, or is the result of such difficulty (Bauer & Shea, 1998, 5f.). It is suggested that teachers often view students' school failures due to the students' emotional and behavioral problems. It is, however, more likely in many cases that these are negative consequences arising from persistent failure, since bad school experiences contribute to any pre-existing emotional problems (Van Kraayenoord & Elkins, 1998 as cited in Westwood, 2004, 64). On this issue, Westwood (2004, 64) suggested that interventions concerning these students need to be guided by constant personal counseling. In particular, he emphasized that the family must be involved in any intervention to maintain consistent management and support for the student.

POOR ATTENTION

Poor attention for tasks can be a serious potential cause of LD (Westwood, 2004, 68). Students with LDs are generally referred for special education due to low academic achievements, however many of these students are also referred for attention problems (e.g. Kavale & Reese, 1992). Research indicated that students with learning difficulties are frequently found to be weak in controlled attention (Swanson & Saez, 2003, 182f.) or selective attention (Bender, 2000, 74). However, as yet, it may be difficult to determine the nature of attention problems due to the lack of reliable and valid measures (e.g. Mercer, 1997). In this regard, maladaptive learning style has been implicated as a causal factor of LD (e.g. Chan & Dally, 2001; Graham & Harries, 2000). According to Westwood (2004, 78), maladaptive learning style might be defined as an approach to learning that is self-defeating and leads to failure and frustration. He suggested that it is almost impossible to determine whether the inefficient approach to learning displayed by many students with LDs is the cause of the difficulty or simply a natural outcome of persistent failure (e.g. poor attention to tasks, distractibility, impulsive guessing, limited self-monitoring, and lack of self-correction are all features of poor learning style). It should be recognized that, regardless of whether they are the causes or the outcome of learning problems, inefficient approaches to learning need to be modified. In particular, the improvement of students' approaches to learning must be given priority in intervention.

POOR SHORTTERM/LONGTERM MEMORY AND POOR METACOGNITION

Studies have shown that students with LDs have memory problems (short term memory, working memory and long term memory), and most often these memory problems do not improve with age (e.g. O'Shaughnessy & Swanson, 1998; Swanson & Saez, 2003; Ashbaker & Swans, 1996; Swanson, 1994a, 1994b). In their meta-analysis of the literature, O'Shaughnessy & Swanson (1998, 123ff.) argued that students with LDs have weaknesses in immediate recall compared to their peers with comparable intelligence without LDs. It was also found that these students with LDs are less likely to use strategies in order to facilitate memory. With regard to reading performance, Ashbaker & Swans (1996, 106ff.) reported that adolescents with LDs perform more poorly on short-term memory and working-memory tasks than their peers without LDs. Swanson (1994a, 34ff.) maintained that short-term memory and working memory are both important for children and adults with LDs concerning their performance in reading and mathematics. He suggested that students with LDs are more likely to rely on short-term memory, while their peers without LDs use the working memory in order to, for example, recall words in a phrase. Furthermore, Swanson & Saez (2003, 182ff.) indicated that both children and adults with LDs have difficulties not only with their working memory, but also with recalling information from the long-term memory. It should be mentioned that stress and anxiety also impair the ability to recall information (Kaufeldt, 1999 as cited in Westwood, 2004, 70). In his research of working memory and dynamic assessment, Swanson (1994b, 109ff.) maintained that dynamic assessment can better assess the learning potential of students with LDs.

POOR VISUAL OR AUDITORY PERCEPTION

In the early investigation of LD, much attention was given to assessing students' visual-perceptual skills; there was a time in the 1960s and early 1970s when special education teachers considered visual-perceptual problems or deficits in visual-motor development as the causes of students' learning difficulties (Venezky, 1993 as cited in Westwood, 2004, 68). However, these problems are no longer considered as major causes in most cases of general learning difficulties today, and few teachers may use such approaches, since it has been demonstrated that visual perception deficits were implicated in some cases but not evident in all cases of LD (Hallahan & Kauffman, 2003 as cited in Westwood, 2004, 77). On the other hand, interest in auditory perceptual weakness in particular, such as phonological awareness and automatic naming as causes for reading and spelling disability, has become a focus of attention (e.g. Silver & Hagin, 2002 as cited in Westwood, 2004, 77). Lyon, Fletcher, & Barnes (2003, 520f.) suggested that deficiencies in phonological processing may represent the most important causal factor on specific and general reading problems.

3.3.2 TEACHER STANCE

The term 'stance' has been used in many different contexts, but generally it refers to how we position ourselves in a given context. The term 'teacher stance' in this study is based on the literature of Berghoff (1997). 'Stance' depends on a postmodern approach (cf. Ch. 3.2.1) of reality as being situational and interpreted rather than fixed and predefined (Berghoff, 1997, 3). A teacher's stance encompasses teachers' personal postures toward themselves and others as well as their theoretical orientation, instructional and classroom management strategies (McGee, Menolascino, Hobbs, & Menousek, 1987 as cited in Bauer, Keefe, & Shea, 2001, 303). Hence, when teachers take a stance, it aims at shaping and changing the student's perception. This is done in relation to gender, race, sexuality, religion, socio-economic status, ability, ethnicity and – all those other differences (or rather diversities, as mentioned in chapter 1) that affect an individual's quality of life and sense of self (Berghoff, 1996, 11). In sum, teacher stance has a crucial impact on students' perceptions of their teacher, their peers and themselves. Based on extensive research on teachers' classroom practice, it was suggested that a teacher stance towards the curriculum, students and purpose of school is more influential than any other education program in determining what happens in the classroom (Allington, 1996, as cited in Berghoff, 4). How, then, do teachers come to take up a particular stance? By quoting Sumara[6], Berghoff (1996, 5) argued that teachers' knowledge of themselves and their surrounding environment originates from interaction and interpretation of their experiences within their environmental context. Stance is a relational concept. Teachers assign students a position relative to themselves when they assume a stance. Teachers deliver curriculum and education with conscious and unconscious[7] assumptions about 'who' the student is, 'what' the student needs to learn, and how they should support the student in learning (Berghoff, 1996, 8). This relationship between the teacher and the student is a close social relationship wherein the social construction of knowledge and learning become deeply personal (Berghoff, 1996, 10). Moreover, this is a relationship the subtleties of which can shape and misshape lives, passions for learning, and broader social dynamics (Ellsworth, 1997, 6).

At the beginning of this book, we argued that a successful inclusive practice largely depends on special education teachers' stance towards inclusion (e.g. European Agency for Development in Special Needs Education, 2003; Schechtman, Reiter, & Schanin, 1993). Clearly, special education teachers must take up a stance which advocates the inclusion of students with LDs. As mentioned above, teacher's stance has a significant impact on the student within the school context and is more powerful than any other education program. Special education teachers' stance towards LDs is therefore a vital factor for the educational and social inclusion of students with LDs. In this regard, Harris & Graham (1996, 134) suggested a constructive teacher stance. In fact, constructivism does not define a particular (or practical) teaching method. Rather, it is a philosophy about teaching which builds on the earlier work of Piaget, Bruner and Vygotsky. Constructivism basically assumes that the child constructs the knowledge in developmentally appropriate ways within social contexts. Thus, a teacher who takes up a constructive teacher stance may conceive the student wth LD as active, self-regulating learner and also believe that learning is socially situated (cf. Ch. 3.2.1 for social system perspective). A constructive teacher stance assumes that a good learning cannot be directly passed from one teacher to student, but rather has to be constructed anew by each student in his/her own mind as a result of experience and reflection (e.g. Harris & Graham, 1996, 134f.; see also Waite-Stupiansky, 1997 as cited in Westwood, 2004, 22).

---

[6] Sumara (1996, 387): "as human subjects, we are not contained in a context rather, we are simultaneously subject and context".

[7] Felman (1982) as cited in Berghoff, 1996, 11: the unconscious is the third participant in the teacher-student relationship. Although it cannot be accounted for in direct terms, it often shows up as resistance to learning.

Dollard, Christenssen, Colucci, & Epanchin (1996, 1ff.) suggested a constructive classroom management, in which emphasis is laid on facilitative instruction such as caring relationships, dialogue among teachers and students. A teacher who takes up a constructive teacher stance, therefore, will place importance on strategies such as cooperative group work and discussion focused on authentic investigations and problem solving (e.g. Gagon & Collay, 2001; Selley, 1999 as cited in Westwood, 2004, 22).

However, the constructive approach does have its critics when it comes to classroom practices (e.g. Westwood, 1996, 28ff.; Westwood, 1993, 87f.; Greham & Harries, 1994, 275f.; Cobb, 1994, 4). Firstly, for instance, concerning the teacher – there is a lack of specific practical advice or guidance given to teachers which can lead teachers to assume that student engagement always equals learning (Eggen & Kauchak, 2003 as cited in Westwood, 2004, 23). Secondly, concerning the student – the constructive approach to instruction can be effective at particular learning stages, but not necessarily effective at all stages of learning (Westwood, 1996, 28ff.). Some students who do not cope well with unstructured tasks will experience failure when the demands of learning tasks are not clearly communicated to them and when they are not taught adequate learning strategies to use (e.g. Greham & Harries, 1994; Westwood, 1993). On the contrary, direct instruction has often been suggested to be the efficient method by research evidence from work with students with LDs (e.g. Kim, YO, 2007; Kim, YO & Kim SS, 2004; Kim, YO & Jeoun JM, 2003; Kavale & Forness, 2000b; Swanson, 2000a). When dealing with students with LDs, explicit teaching (such as direct instruction) may be needed immediately to assist the student, whereas implicit teaching (such as dialog, cooperative group work and discussion) may be supportive of more mature students (Bauer, Keefe, & Shea, 2001, 306). There are several applications of the constructive continuum of instruction that may be usefully applied (Mercer, Jordan & Miller, 1996, 147f.).

3.3.3 RELEVANT BACKGROUND THEORIES

It has become an accepted idea that teachers' ways of thinking and understanding are vital components of their practice (Nespor, 1987, 317). Poulou & Norwich (2002, 111) stated that teachers' beliefs, thoughts and decisions on educational matters occupy the major part of the psychological context of the teaching process. And therefore, in order to understand, predict and influence what teachers do, the psychological process by which teachers perceive their teaching circumstances must be investigated. Teacher's general attitude toward the student guides the teaching method of choice and the strategy used accordingly (Ainscow, 1998, 18f.). Brophy (1985, 210f.) argued that teachers' beliefs and expectations motivate and control their behavior and their interaction with students in general – and students with difficulties in particular. Basically, we act as we do because of our beliefs, and we judge others by our beliefs about people and the freedoms and constraints on their actions (Bauer, Keefe, & Shea, 2001, 61). What teachers think shapes what they do and vice versa (Reid & Valle 2004, 466f.). On the other hand, Poulou & Norwich (2002, 112) stated that students are very sensitive receivers and responders of teachers' emotional and behavioral discourses. And thus, teaching becomes a circular and continuously interactive process, with complex causal relationships among the events taking place within it. Likewise, Tomilnson (2004, 516f.) referred to school procedures as a *Möbius* strip that perpetuates a never-ending cyclic sequence of practices and consequences contributing to one another. Moreover, it is important to understand that the same (teaching) method implemented by teachers with different attitudes, beliefs and perceptions about their students may lead to vastly different experiences and outcomes for the students (Rhodes, 1972, 573ff.). Thus, if teachers have different perceptions about the student with LD, even the same intervention implemented by them may provide different results regarding the student; personally and materially (e.g. Reid & Valle, 2004; Flook, Repetti, & Ullman, 2005). Particularly, the methods that a teacher employs make a difference not only in terms of what is learned, but also in how it is learned (Bauer, Keefe, & Shea, 2001, 35). The fact that each student will react differently to the same type of situation also should be taken into account.

The following section presents a selective review of social learning theories. Following a review of research on motivation, beliefs, values and goals, focusing on developmental and educational psychology (Eccles, Wigfield, 2002, 109ff.), Weiner's motivation theory, Ajzen's planned behavior theory and Bandura's social cognitive theory (Poulou & Norwich, 2002, 111ff.) were selected for this study.

WEINER'S ATTRIBUTION THEORY OF MOTIVATION

Since Heider (1958[8]) presented his original formulation of attribution theory, many refinements and elaborations have been proposed (e.g. Kelly, 1967; Jones, Kanouse, Kelley, Nisbett, Valins, & Weiner, 1972). Attribution theory has been applied to a diverse set of social psychological issues such as achievement motivation, and how people explain their successes and failures (Shields, 1995, 261; see also Weiner, 1985). Weiner (1979) elaborated Heider's (1958) attribution model by adding the causal dimension of controllability to the ones of locus and stability, and by linking each causal dimension with affective responses (Poulou &

---

[8] Attribution theory has its modern roots in the publication of Fritz Heider's (1958) book 'The psychology of interpersonal relations'. Heider (1958, 89) first described the attribution process as "[...] the linking of an event with its underlying conditions [...]" in addition, Heider (1958, 123) suggested that the attributions are made on the basis of a "[...] naive factor analysis of action".

Norwich, 2002, 113; see also Weiner, 1985[9]; Weiner & Graham, 1989[10]; Weiner, Nierenberg, & Goldstein, 1976). Attribution theory had been based on the assumption that an individual's helping behavior is determined by his/her perception of the cause of the need. However, Weiner further suggested that the perception of cause and helping behavior are not directly linked, rather, they are mediated by affective reactions such as pity or anger (cognition–affect–behavior model[11], e.g. Weiner, 1979, 1980a). Therefore, in order to explain teachers' helping behavior, it is essential to understand teachers' perceptions of why the student is in need of aid, and how their affective reactions are influenced by their causal attributions (Weiner, 1983 as cited in Poulou & Norwich, 2002, 113).

Several studies have indicated that teachers make causal attributions regarding the students' academic achievement (e.g. Clark, 1997; Conway, 1989; Soodak & Podell, 1994). In particular, it has been shown that teachers tend to attribute students' learning failure to individual variables within the student rather than to external factors such as family or teacher factors (e.g. Cheng, 1998; Westwood, 1995; Georgiou, Christou, Stravrinides, & Panaoura, 2002; Medway, 1979; Tollefson & Chen, 1988). Thus, as Westwood (2004, 54) maintained, teachers tend to blame students themselves and this may imply that the contribution of internal factors to student achievement is overestimated and the contribution of situational factor is underestimated. According to Bearne (1996), this 'blame-the-victim perspective' has a negative impact on teachers' classroom practices and expectations they hold for students with difficulties. Attribution for expected outcomes, such as failure in students for whom teachers have low expectations, were more often attributed to internal, stable factors than were unexpected outcomes (e.g. Burger, Cooper, & Good, 1982). Medway (1979) found that teachers attribute students' learning difficulties to ability (67%). Hence teachers mostly regard learning difficulties as consequences of stable and uncontrollable factors, which implies that neither the student nor the teacher can act to change or improve the situation, which leads to continued low expectations of future performance. Such attributions (internal, stable and uncontrollable) may influence teacher-student relationship in classroom. It was found that teachers feel pity for students with difficulties and so are more likely to help and praise them (e.g. Georgiou et al., 2002; Tollefson & Chen, 1988).

---

[9] In terms of locus of control, those who believe they can make choices to affect their environment are considered to have an internal locus of control, while those who believe their environment is controlled by external factors (outside the individual's control) are said to have an external locus of control (Weiner, 1985, 548f.).

[10] Weiner & Graham (1989, 401) attribute causality to three characteristics to evaluate causes for success and failure: (a) internal (ability, effort within the individual) or external (luck, task difficulty); (b) stable (consistent or inconsistent over time) or unstable (temporary, changeable factors), and controllable (control over cause, effort) or uncontrollable (luck).

[11] cf. studies of Covington & Omelich (1984); Tollefson & Chen (1988), Caprara, Pastroelli, & Weiner (1997), which provide empirical validation of this model of teacher helping behavior.

Similarly, Clark (1997) suggested that teachers were less likely to be angry; instead they gave greater rewards and expected further failure from students with LDs. Jordan, Lindsay, & Stanovich (1997) found that teachers who viewed the problem as being inherent in the individual engage less in instructional teacher-student interaction in comparison to teachers who attributed the students' problems with an interaction between learner and environment. It should also be mentioned, however, that there may be cultural differences in the values placed on different causal attributions (e.g. Clark & Artiles 2000; Ho, 2004).

AJZEN AND FISHBEIN'S THEORY OF PLANNED BEHAVIOR

Though Weiner's attribution theory of motivation offered a link between cognitive and affective reactions, which in turn explain behavior, Weiner's model (cognition-affect-behavior model) did not take into consideration the influential role of the social environment and the probability of intentional behavior (Poulou & Norwich, 2002, 114). The way the individual perceives the effect of environmental factors on his/her behavior and whether the individual feels any restrictions from external factors, or becomes subject to social demands may not be clarified in this model. The theory of planned behavior (see Ajzen & Fishbein, 1969, 1977, 2005; Fishbein & Ajzen, 1972; Ajzen, 1991, 2002), derived from the theory of reasoned action (developed by Fishbein & Ajzen, 1975 as cited in Ajzen, 2002, 1), embraces both perceptions of environmental factors and intentions as determinants of behavior. In the theory of planned behavior, human behavior is explained to be guided by three kinds of considerations: beliefs about the likely consequences or other attributes of the behavior (behavioral beliefs), beliefs about the normative expectations of other people (normative beliefs), and beliefs about the presence of factors that may further or hinder performance of the behavior (control beliefs). Behavioral beliefs produce a favorable or unfavorable attitude towards the behavior; normative beliefs result in perceived social pressure or subjective norm; finally, control beliefs give rise to perceived behavioral control, the perceived ease or difficulty of performing the behavior. In combination, attitude towards the behavior, subjective norm and perception of behavioral control lead to the formation of a behavioral intention (Ajzen, 2002, 1). In other words, within a specific situation, individuals ask themselves what will happen if they perform the given behavior, what others will think, and whether they have the ability to or not. The planned behavior theory focuses on behavior intent and postulates that an individual's intention to perform a given behavior is determined by his/her attitudes toward the behavior, subjective norms and perceived behavioral control. It therefore combines two determinants, the one dealing with personal factors and the other reflecting social factors (Poulou & Norwich, 2002, 115). However, it should be also mentioned that, Ajzen & Fishbein (2004, 431) have noted in their publications that the relative importance of attitudes, subjective norms and perceptions of behavioral control for the prediction of intentions is expected to vary from behavior to behavior and from population to population (see Ajzen, 1988, 1991; Ajzen & Fishbein, 1980; Fishbein, 2000; and Fishbein, Triandis et al., 2001 as cited in Ajzen & Fishbein, 2004, 431). The relevance of using the theory of planned behavior to study teachers' stance is evident when considering current educational trends and mandates. Current educational reforms emphasize the effective teaching for all students. These reforms contain standard setting, accountability testing, improvements in instructional materials and focus on evidence-based decision-making (Chard, 2004, 216). Teachers are required to implement evidence-based practices which involve the use of scientifically based research to guide educational decisions regarding teaching approaches, and to establish themselves as highly qualified teachers (e.g. Baglieri & Knopf, 2004). This implies the impact that educational policy has on the teaching practice. One may conclude that teachers' stance towards LDs are also impacted by the environmental demands and constraints due to such educational trends and mandates. With regard to educational trends, there are other environmental demands and constrains which may influence teachers' stance towards LDs. The dominant theme of LD in theory and practice has been that LD is a pathology that resides in the heads of individuals (Dudley-Marling, 2004, 482). In consequence, treatment and remedial efforts have been focused on what goes on in the heads of students with LDs (e.g. Dudley-Marling, 2004; McDermott, Goldberg, Watkins, Stanley, & Glutting, 2006; Mcdermott & Varenne, 1999). Recently, however, there has been a consensus within the field of LD that LD occurs with students who have difficulties at school, and that such difficulties are strongly linked to the school (Dudley-Marling, 2001, 13; Reid & Valle, 2004, 467). This may shed new light on the roles of teachers, as for some students the school and classroom is their most reliable environment, and the teacher is their most responsive adult.

BANDURA'S SOCIAL COGNITIVE THEORY

According to Weiner's model, expectancy of success and failure is the cognitive predictor of behavior, and, designated by the stability causal dimension, it determines the effort spent and the persistence of behavior (Poulou & Norwich, 2002, 114). The controllability dimension is often related to self-efficacy in the literature. Also, it was suggested that Bandura's social cognitive theory seems to have common features with Weiner's model, with reference to the controllability dimension (Eccles & Wigfield, 1985 as cited in Pouloy & Norwich, 114). However, Bandura (1977, 1997) stated that perceived self-efficacy and control refer to different phenomena and must therefore be treated separately. Though Bandura (1982, 122ff.) concurs that behavior is effectively predicted by both perceived self-efficacy and outcome expectancy, Bandura (1977, 191ff.) made distinction between efficacy expectancy and outcome expectancy. Baundura (1977, 193) defined outcome expectancy as "a person's estimate that a given behavior will lead to certain outcomes" whereas efficacy expectancy as "a judgment of how well one can execute courses of action required to deal with prospective situations" (Bandura, 1982, 122). Efficacy expectancy can be seen as the conviction that one can successfully execute the behavior required to produce outcomes. In other words, individuals acknowledge that a given behavior they perform produces certain outcomes (i.e. outcome expectancy). But if they have doubts about their ability to perform the behavior (i.e. low self-efficacy expectancy), then these beliefs they have do influence their behavior. Hence, one may conclude that the degree of self-efficacy an individual has not only determines the effort spent and the persistence of behavior but also determines whether the individual will perform the given behavior (Bandura, 1982, 127,128, "higher levels of perceived self-efficacy correlate to greater levels performance accomplishments"). Using the attribution theory framework and applying it to the achievement domain, Bandura (as cited in Poulou & Norwich, 2002, 114) asserted that self-efficacy is an important determinant for behavior, and is in turn determined by the causal attribution of the outcome (ability, effort or task difficulty). Bandura's emphasis on self-efficacy has implications for students' outcomes based on the level of teacher self-efficacy. In terms of teacher self-efficacy, Tschannen-Moran & Woolfolk-Hoy (2001, 783) defined teacher efficacy as a teacher's "judgment of his/her capabilities to bring about desired outcomes of student engagement and learning, even among those students who may be difficult or unmotivated". In several studies, teacher efficacy has been suggested to be one of the important variables consistently related to positive teaching behavior and student achievement (e.g. Gibson & Dembo, 1984; Enochs, Scharmann, & Riggs, 1995; Woolfolk & Hoy, 1990; see also Ashton & Webb, 1986; and Henson, 2001 as cited in Çakiroglu, Çakiroglu, & Boone, 2005, 31). It was suggested that teachers' behaviors such as persistence at a task, risk-taking, and the use of innovations are related to degrees of efficacy. For instance, teachers with higher level efficacy were more likely to use student-directed instruction, while teachers with lower level efficacy were more likely to use teacher-directed instruction (Ashton & Webb, 1986 as cited in Çakiroglu et al., 2005, 31). In addition, Enochs & Riggs (1990, 694f.) spoke of teachers' belief system. They suggested that there are two types of teacher beliefs relevant to teaching: belief that students' learning is influenced by effective teaching (outcome expectancy beliefs) and belief in one's own teaching ability (self-efficacy belief). Similar to findings of Ashton & Webb above, Riggs (1991 as cited in Çakiroglu et al., 2005, 32) reported that primary school teachers with low science teaching efficacy beliefs avoided science teaching even though their outcome expectancy beliefs regarding teaching generally were high. Also, Ashton & Webb indicated that students generally learn more from teachers with high self-efficacy than those same students would learn from teachers with low self-efficacy. Teacher efficacy is a situation-specific and even subject-specific construct according to Bandura (1986 as cited in Çakiroglu et al., 2005, 32). Tschannen-Moran et al. (1998, 202ff.) suggested that teachers' efficacy judgments are the result of the interaction between a personal judgment of the relative importance of factors that make teaching difficult and a personal assessment of his/her personal teaching competence, with reference to Bandura's social cognitive theory (1997) and Weiner's (1974) internal and external locus of control. Cross-cultural studies have suggested that such teacher efficacy varies among teachers from different countries (particularly between Western and Asian, e.g. Gorrell & Hwang, 1995; Lin & Gorrell 2001; Lin, Gorrell, & Taylor, 2002; Yeung & Watkins, 2000). Teachers in different cultures vary concerning the degree to which they believe themselves to be efficacious in their teaching. Lin & Gorrell (2001, 623f.) and Lin et al. (2002, 37f.) maintained that teacher efficacy may be influenced by the context of their academic programs, by their increasing competence and experience as teachers, and by cultural perspectives in each country, and therefore needs to be carefully examined when applied on teachers in different countries.

3.3.4 RELEVANT STUDIES IN KOREA AND OTHER COUNTRIES

The most important beliefs that teachers have about students are those that deal with the teachers' perceptions of the causes of students' failure, students' learning or behavioral difficulties (e.g. Clark & Peterson, 1986; Georgiou, et al., 2002). Studies on teacher attribution of student's learning or school failure have provided insight into the identification and assessment of students with LDs (Mavropoulou & Padeliadu, 2002, 192). Studies supporting the link between teachers' perceptions and practices have suggested that teachers' perceptions about the causes (hereafter causal perceptions) of student failure have important implications for teacher referral and the methods used for assessment (e.g. Jordan, Kirkaali-Iftar, & Diamond, 1993; Podell & Soodak, 1993; Soodak & Podell, 1994[12]). Teachers' causal perceptions of student's failure have been found to influence the expectancies teachers hold for the students' future academic achievement ("academic success", Clarkson & Leder, 1984, 413) and impact the students' own attributions (Fennema, Peterson, Carpenter, & Lubinski, 1990, 55). Weiner's attribution theory[13] (cf. Ch. 3.3.3) may offer a theoretical framework for this line of investigation ("sin versus sickness", Weiner, 1993, 957). A teacher who attributes the students' learning failure (i.e. academic achievement) to internal, unstable and controllable

---

[12] Soodak & Podell (1994, 44f.) suggested that teachers tend to attribute the students' learning and behavioral difficulties mostly to the students (self-esteem) or students' family (family situation) factors. According to them, teachers' beliefs were related to the interventions used. Teachers who tended to attribute the students' difficulties to family factors used parental involvement, while those who tended to attribute students' difficulties to school factors used teacher interventions.

[13] cf. Ch. 3.3.3: According to Weiner's attribution theory, causal factors of one's success/failure can be classified along three dimensions. These are locus of control (external or internal), stability (stable or unstable) and controllability (controllable or uncontrollable).

factors may think that his/her own contribution (such as teaching method for intervention) may be effective. On the other hand, a teacher who attributes students' learning failure to external, unstable and uncontrollable factors may have a low expectation for his/her own contribution in a successful intervention. Therefore, Mavropoulou & Padeliadu (2002, 192) argued that the role of teachers' causal perceptions about students' learning- and behavioral difficulties in their decision-making process is highly critical. This is why teachers' perceptions of the causes of LD have such vital importance. Several studies have looked into teachers' perceptions of students with LDs. Regarding the causes of LDs, teachers seemed to attribute LD to factors external to the instructional and school setting. Simmons, Kameenui, & Chard (1998, 10) explored teachers' perceptions of factors that influence learning for students with LDs in terms of within-the-learner and outside-the-learner variables. When given 100 points to divide among five different factors, teachers assigned approximately half of the points to internal factors (i.e. "learner based factors" including student academic ability and student motivation), whereas teacher delivery accounted for 25% of the total points, design of instructional materials only for 9% and opportunities to learn for 16% (Simmons et al., 1998, 14). These teachers believed that significant responsibility for learning resides within the students and is determined by the student, the majority felt confident in their teaching practice (for example, they were certain in their ability to modify instructional inadequacies). However, one may conclude that those teachers who believed that student internal factors are more important than their efforts may struggle with a sense of efficacy when teaching students with LDs. Likewise, Clark (1997, 75f.) suggested that teachers tend to consider LD as internal to the child, stable and uncontrollable; rather than as something on which they can have an impact (meaning that LD is centered within the child rather than in the educational environment). According to Clark (1997, 79), it was reasonable to hypothesize from the beginning that most teachers will conceptualize LD in this way, because LD is rooted in the traditional medical model of disability (cf. Ch. 3.2.1). Although some have begun to challenge the medical model as mentioned previously, it remains the dominant model for LD identification. This is also valid when considering the current definition of LD (for example, IDEA's definition of SpLD, cf. Ch. 3.2.3) and its within-the-child orientation. Consistent with earlier findings (e.g. Bender, 1985, 1987; Cardell & Parmar, 1988; Weiner, Graham, & Chandler, 1982; Weiner & Kukla, 1970)[14], Clark (1997, 76) suggested that teachers make causal attributions and thereafter respond to students with LDs in the belief that these students are more likely to fail than students without LDs (that is, high expectation of future failure). Similarly, Carlisle & Chang (1996, 18) concluded that teachers consistently rated students with LDs as having less adequate learning ca-

---

[14] In these studies, students with LDs were rated lower than students without LDs by their teachers.

pability and as being lower in achievement than their peers without LDs. In their research of evaluation of academic capabilities by students with and without LDs and their teachers, two cohorts of students with respectively without LDs were observed for three years. Students and their teachers annually rated their capabilities and efforts in science. When comparing student and teacher ratings, teachers often had higher expectations for students than students had for themselves (Carlisle & Chang, 1996, 18).

COMPARISON BETWEEN WESTERN AND ASIAN TEACHERS' PERCEPTIONS OF THE CAUSES OF LDs

According to Westwood (1995, 19), when asked about the causes of students' difficulties in school learning, within-the-student factors were mentioned by 62% of the interviewed Australian teachers (n=311), while family background or culture were mentioned by 14% (and factors within the curriculum were mentioned by 8%). On the other hand, Japanese teachers and principals believed environmental variables such as parents (i.e. parents' understanding and cooperation) and teacher factors (i.e. classroom management, teaching skills, teachers' professional development and team teaching) were more influential (Project Team on Educational Support for Children Who Experience Learning Difficulties, hereafter Project Team, 2000, as cited in Kataoka, Kraayenood, & Elkins, 2004, 164). Both Japanese principals and teachers perceived the parents and teacher factors to be contributing strongly to students' learning difficulties. However, the principals emphasized the lack of classroom management, whereas the teachers emphasized the lack of a cooperative support system among teachers in schools. Thus, when comparing the findings from two studies, it can be seen that the Australians teachers tend to view the causes of LDs as internal rather than external to the instructional and school setting, as well as related to individual variables; whereas the Japanese teachers tend to see the causes of LDs as external and related to environmental variables. Haynes, Hook, Macaruso, Muta, Hayashi, Kato et al. (2000, 215ff.) compared Japanese and U.S teachers' skill ratings of students with LDs. According to them, using the same set of criteria, when comparing the prevalence rate of students with LDs between US teachers and Japanese teachers, the US teachers identified 4% of their students, whereas Japanese teachers identified 1.5%. When comparing US teachers' and Japanese teachers' evaluations of deficit areas for students with LDs, the significant difference between these teachers was that the US teachers perceived their students' weaknesses to lie in the area of academic skills (such as listening, speaking, reading, writing and study skills) whereas Japanese teachers perceived their students' weaknesses to be in the area of social skills. In addition, Japanese teachers perceived parents' understanding of LDs and social indices as key factors in students' difficulties in learning at school (see also Project Team, 2000; Christensen & Elkins, 1995 as cited in Kataoka et al., 2004, 171.).

Kataoka et al. (2004, 172) recently investigated Japanese teachers' perceptions of the causes of LDs. Teachers' situations and ineffective classroom teaching were seen as important causes of LDs. The factor for which there was most support as a cause of LD was "teachers' situation factor". On the other hand, the factor for which there was least support was "governmental issues factor". While teachers' situation, such as being busy, being under pressure and teacher shortages was perceived to negatively influence the learning of students with LDs, the government's curriculum guidelines, psychological tests and early detection were perceived by Japanese teachers to have little relevance for the cause of LD (Kataoka et al., 2004, 170). Particularly, it was suggested that the discrepancy between teachers' perspective and the official LD criteria may impede teachers' identification of students with LDs (Kataoka et al., 2004, 171). As shown above, some studies have suggested that teachers perceived teacher-school factors and parents factors to be important ("dyspedagogia", Cohen, 1971, 269). Recently, there has been a consensus within the field of LD that LD occurs is strongly linked to school (Dudley-Marling, 2001, 13; Reid & Valle, 2004, 467). These findings may be in contrast to the dominant theme of LD (critics on medical model, cf. Dudley-Marling, 2004; McDermott et al., 2006; Mcdermott & Varenne, 1999). Often, teachers tend to blame students themselves or students' family backgrounds for LDs, rather than to look into the teaching method or teacher-student relationship (Westwood, 2004, 54). Westwood (1997, 1) reported that when teachers were asked to list all the factors they believe caused learning problems in their classrooms, he discovered that 76% of the reasons teachers give for students' learning failure were located within the learner (e.g. below average intelligence, sensory impairment, attention deficits, hyperactivity, short-term memory problems, poor language skills, low level of motivation, behavior problems, laziness), or within the learners' home background and culture (e.g. lack of support, low expectations, poor management, poverty, absence of role models, language other than English) (see also Westwood, 1995). Westwood (1997, 2) contended that while these factors obviously do impact upon a student's ability to learn in school, they are all factors over which teachers have minimum control. On the other hand, the factors over which teachers have most control are those related to teaching method, curriculum content and student-teacher rapport. However, as mentioned above, these variables gained only 14% of the teacher responses in his study. Likewise, Henderson (2002, 50) reported that the teachers' narratives clustered into 3 groups: blaming families, blaming children and explanations that moved beyond blame and focused instead on teaching, he referred to this as the deficit discourse surrounding learning difficulty. Westwood (1997, 2) pointed out that the problem arising from such situation is that while teachers continue to blame the victim for learning difficulties, there is little likelihood that they will examine their own classroom practices or rethink the ways in which they deal with these students (e.g. Soodak & Podell, 1994). He argued that while it is common practice in schools to blame the victim when failure occurs in the learning of basic skills, it is much more useful to teachers for examining their own teaching methods and the suitability of their own curriculum (Westwood, 1997, 2). In this regard, McLaren (1998, 210) argued that the "psychologizing student failure" amounts to blaming it on an individual trait or series of traits and is part of the hidden curriculum that relieves teachers from the need to engage in pedagogical self-scrutiny or in critique of their personal roles within the school, and the school's role within the wider society.

Hence, it is of crucial importance that teachers reflect on their attitudes and beliefs about students with LDs, and rethink their role in the classroom. Teachers have far more positive influence over their students than they may realize. Answering the question what teachers perceive as the main causes of LD, and how these perceptions affect teacher practice may be a good starting point.

Relevant studies in Korea

The following section provides a summary of research on LD in Korea – studies relevant to teachers' perceptions of LD.

Definition and prevalence of LD

In Korea, efforts have been made to reach consensus on how to operationalize the authoritative definition of LD since LD was officially included as a category of special education under the Special Education Promotion Act (SEPA) of 1994 (e.g. Jung DY, 1991; Kim YO, 1992; Park HS, 1992; Kang WY, 1992; Baek WH, 1993; Hwang JW, 1995; Lee SH, 1999; Shin JH, 1999). However, despite the efforts to settle the issue, the definition of LD has become articulated in many different operational definitions and LD identification criteria vary across educational institutions and by researchers as shown below (e.g. SEPA, 1994; KEDI, 1990 as cited in Kim DI, Lee DS, & Shin JH, 2003, 28; MOE & HRD, 2006 as cited in Jung DY, 2007, 186; KISE, 2001).

- SEPA (1994): "pupils with special educational needs identified as learning disabled are pupils with disabilities in specific academic learning areas such as mathematical calculation, speaking, reading, and writing" (cf. KISE, Law Database);
- Korean Educational Development Institute (KEDI, 1990): "LD is a generic term that refers to a heterogeneous group of disorders manifested by significant difficulties in the acquisition and use of listening, speaking, reading, writing, reasoning or mathematical abilities. These disorders are intrinsic to the individual and presumed to be due to perception, perception-motion, and other nervous system dysfunctions. However, the term does not include learning problems that are primarily the result of visual, hearing, or motor disabilities, of mental retardation,

of emotional disturbance, or of cultural, environmental, or economic disadvantages" (Lee NM & Yun JR, 1990 as cited in Kim DI, Lee DS, & Shin JH, 2003, 28);
- MOE & HRD (2006): LD means "the standardized achievement test scores or standardized development test scores are 1.5 standard deviation below the mean within an age or grade group" (Park JY, Jung DY, Kim, J Y, Kim, DS, & Kim, E J, 2006 as cited in Jung DY, 2007, 186);
- Korea Institute for Special Education (KISE): LD is "with an IQ score ($\geq$-2 standard deviation) greater than or equal to -2 standard deviation, and whose basic skill performance in one or more than one area of reading, writing, mathematical reasoning ,problem solving ,calculating performance is 2 grade level lower than or -2 standard deviation below within the same age group. However, those whose learning problems are due to visual, hearing disabilities, or of mental retardation, of emotional disturbance, or of cultural disadvantages are not included". LD is classified into 'reading (learning) disability', 'writing (learning) disability', 'mathematics (learning) disability', and 'multiple learning disability' (KISE, 2001, 187-188).

As a result, the reported prevalence rate of LD ranges from 0.83% to 14% (Kim DI, Lee DS, & Shin JH, 2003, 45; see also Korea Inclusive Education Association, 2006). According to the findings of KISE (1998), the prevalence of LD was 2.46%. They surveyed 5,052 fourth-grade students in 20 primary schools across the nation. On the other hand, the prevalence rate of LD stood at 3.83% when 2,662 third and fourth grade students across the nation were surveyed. The prevalence of LD in primary school in Seoul was reported to be 0.83% (Jung DY, 1985 as cited in Kim DI, Lee DS, & Shin JH, 2003, 45). A review of national researches on prevalence of LD showed that the prevalence rate of LD in primary school was found to range from 4% to 8% in Korea, while the prevalence rate of LD in middle school was found to range from 4% to 14% (Lee SH, 1999, as cited in Korea inclusive education association, 2006, 394). The KISP (2001) recently surveyed 24,864 fourth-grade (9years old) students from 180 primary schools across the nation (for the definition used see above); the prevalence of LD was 1.17% and represented 43.17% of the special education population (Korea inclusive education association, 2006, 395). They consisted of about 20% reading disability, 6% writing disability, 15% mathematics disability, and 59% multiple learning disability. That is, the overall estimated number of students with LDs in Korea was approximately 47,771 of 4,000,000 primary school students (Kim DI, Lee DS, & Shin JH, 2003, 45).

Therefore, it might be difficult to ascertain the real prevalence of LD in Korea. It should be mentioned here that there has been very little relevant research on the prevalence of LD in Korea (Kim DI, Lee DS, & Shin JH, 2003, 45). According to the latest government report, there are 8,447 students with LDs enrolled in schools, which represents 14.5% of the number of students with special educational needs (SEN) enrolled in special education (MOE & HRD, 2005b, 7). Experts, however, assume that there is a large number of students at risk for LDs or who have LDs uncovered – students who have learning difficulties in one or more learning areas, but who are not receiving any support, because they have not been identified as eligible for special education and related services (e.g. Jeong KS & Kim AH, 2006; Park HS & Cho JK, 2004; KISE, 2001). In this regard, researchers have suggested that the obscurity of current definition (Jung DY, 2007, 185) and the oversimplification of criteria (Byun CS, 2007, 56) provoke difficulties in LD identification. Hence, there is an urgent need for a clear formal definition of LD, which serves to be accepted by practitioners and which can provide a framework for LD identification to guide practice.

TEACHERS' PERCEPTIONS OF LDS

During the 2000s, Korean researchers have become more aware of the need to close the gap between theory and practice in the field of LD (Byun CS, 2002b, 298). Studies supporting the link between teachers' perceptions and practices have provided insight to LD identification and definition (e.g. Kim YO & Bong WY, 2004; Kim DI & Lee IH, 2003; Byun CS, 2002a; Park HS & Cho YK, 2004). Recent studies have shown that the assessment process for LDs was often shortened under the prevailing circumstances in regular school settings: many special education teachers used mainly (or even solely) IQ tests and basic skill tests (e.g. KEDI-individual basic learning skills test) for identifying LD. Researchers are alert about the risk of both under- and over-identification of LD. There probably exist students with LDs who receive no special education or related service, whereas those who are identified as having LD is/may in fact not LD students. In this regard, researchers argued that the discrepancy between teachers' perspectives and official criteria for LD may impede teachers' identification of students with LD. Also the lack of assessment tools in the field and the lack of procedural guidelines for practical purposes in the SPEA (as well as the revised version of SPEA) were suggested to contribute to all these problems. For instance, firstly, Kim YO & Bong WY (2004, 85) looked at the definitions and assessment methods of LDs that special education teachers use in primary schools. According to their findings, the assessment processes for LDs were probably not performed by qualified professionals. Most of those special education teachers who conducted LD assessment used the simplified SEPA's definition and did not use various assessment methods. Instead, they tended to shorten the procedure (Kim YO & Bong WY, 2004, 100). There may be several reasons, some of which were shown to be 'lack of teacher self-competence', 'lack of assessment tools' or 'lack of reliance on teacher's observation and decision' (KISE, 2006 as cited in Byun CS 2007, 61). Secondly,

Byun CS (2002a, 260) explored special education teachers' perceptions regarding the use of assessment methods for LDs. He focused on teachers' self-reports: what methods they actually used and found most useful, and their self-perceived levels of competency. Comparing special education teachers' responses about the usefulness of the assessment methods (standardized test, teacher-made test, classroom observation, interview with general education teacher, error analysis of class assignments), it was found that, particularly, special education teachers perceived 'classroom observation' as the most useful method for assessing LDs. Likewise, special education teachers considered themselves 'most competent' in 'classroom observation' while they generally perceived themselves to be 'competent' in all five areas. However, when asked about the frequency of use, the 'most frequently' used methods among them turned out to be 'standardized test' and 'teacher made test' – and not 'classroom observation' (Byun, 2002a, 269). In respect thereof, the difference in special education teachers' responses between perceived usefulness and actual use of assessment methods is noteworthy. The emphasis on standardized tests may be a consequence of the general belief that the standardized test is objective and therefore respectable. This belief is largely fueled by concerns about the psychometric adequacy of the assessment measures and furthermore a perusal of special education textbooks available for university courses indicates an emphasis on the use of standardized measures within the context of subject areas (Lopez-Reyna, 1996, 44). It may be suggested that there is considerable public comfort with formal assessment methods/procedures (Madaus, 1993 as cited in Lopez-Reyna, 1996, 44). Another reason was suggested to be that teachers are being administratively required to gather particular types of assessment data to document the presence of LD. For example the discrepancy component, which has predominated the field of LD, has traditionally been demonstrated through the use of standardized tests (Byun, 2002a, 270). Thirdly, Kim DI & Lee IH (2003, 70) explored both regular teachers' and special education teachers' perceptions about the definition and characteristics of LDs. According to their findings, regular and special education teachers slightly differ in their definitions of LD, while their descriptions of the characteristics of LD were more similar to each other. Kim DI & Lee IH (2003, 75) indicated that special education teachers were more aware of the elements of LD definition such as the 'discrepancy component' and the 'exclusion clause', 'central nervous dysfunction' and 'learning difficulties', whereas most regular teachers were merely aware of 'learning difficulties'. Researchers assumed that this is likely to be a consequence of the different pre-service education curriculums of regular teachers and special education teachers. Hence the need for teacher preparation programs in order to enhance their understanding of LD for regular teachers on both pre-service and in-service level (Kim DI & Lee IH, 2003, 75). In addition, they emphasized the required professional development of special education teachers ('highly qualified teachers') and asserted that special education teachers' implicit knowledge of LD also needs to be enhanced through in-service education (Kim DI & Lee IH, 2003, 75). Finally, it has been claimed that the quality of educational inclusion of students with LDs remains limited to physical inclusion (Jeong KS & Kim AH, 2006, 30).

At present, students with LDs attend classes in the same setting with their nondisabled peers, provided with only some degree of support. As yet, the quality of special education (and related) service in special classrooms and the professional development (proficiency) of special education teachers may vary heavily across schools and districts. It should be mentioned here that education is highly valued by Korean parents who invest considerable resources and effort in providing their children with the best available education opportunities. Thus, much pressure concerning school achievement is exerted on children, and academic success is connected to the family's aspirations of social elevation. Even though special education has been free and compulsory for quite a long time (cf. Ch. 2), Koreans are demanding parents who are very critical and sensitive about the quality of special education service and special education teachers. As an example, according to Jung DY (2007, 187), special classroom in which the parents' satisfaction rate is high are accordingly highly crowded. Were they not, those classes may lose students and would hardly continue to exist. Thus, in order to facilitate instructional inclusion for students with LDs and achieve fundamentally aimed social inclusion (that is, inclusive quality education), many questions remain to be answered in the near future. Issues in educational assessment on how special education service are determined by students' diverse needs; and how students with LDs can be accepted as full members of the classroom, so that they have their own place in the classroom and will be included in all class activities. In addition, in comparison to primary school level, there is a serious gap in special education and related services for students with LDs on the secondary school level (Jung DY, 2007, 188), accompanied by a lack of research on this field.

An argument is made for an alternative perspective which carry implications for Korea and beneficially impact the Korean public school practice (for example, see KMK, the German concept of LD cf. Ch. 3.2.3, for further discussion about the German and US concept of LD cf. Ch. 7.1). However, solely adopting definition concepts from other countries or changing assessment formats is not likely to bring about meaningful reform in LD education. One must consider that current educational trends and mandates such as SEPA, which guide teachers the way to define and identify LD, influence Korean special education teachers' perceptions of LDs (Ch. 3.3.3). As Soodak (2000, 276) puts is: perceptions about students' learning failure should reflect "a more holistic view whereby teachers and schools accept greater responsibility for student performance".

Part III.

Research Design and Methodology

4

METHODS

4.1 PARTICIPANTS

4.1.1 POPULATION AND DISTRIBUTION

The population in this study was 3,413 special education teachers working at special classes in regular primary schools in Korea (MOE & HRD, 2005b). Table 4.1 lists the numbers of Korean special education teachers sorted by their qualification and education offices. According to the MOE & HRD, there are a total of 16 city provincial education offices and 181 county education offices in Korea[1] (Figure 4.1; Figure 4.2). The numbers regarding the distribution of special education teachers in regular primary schools are drawn from the basis of the distribution range from the MOE & HRD.

Capital and Urban area: in the capital of Korea (Seoul), there is one metropolitan office of education that includes 11 district education offices. In total, 528 special education teachers were working in the primary schools subordinated to these offices. Most of them have a certified special education teacher, whereas there are few general education teachers with both general education and special education teacher certificates. Moreover, there are 6 metropolitan city offices of education, 1 in each of the 6 metropolitan cities (Gwangyeoksi). These offices include 20 district education offices. The majority is in all cases made up of special education teachers, however there are also a few general education teachers with both certificates, or with additional in-service education in the area of special education.

Suburban and Rural area: there are 9 provincial offices of education in each province (Do). These offices include 150 district education offices in all. Although most of the teachers are special education teachers, compared to Capital (Seoul)

---

[1] The nation is divided into 16 administrative units: capital city, six metropolitan cities, and nine provinces (MOE & HRD, 2007b, 7). Regarding the administrative units, there are three administrative tiers in South Korea. The highest tier includes seven independent Metropolitan cities and nine provinces (Do). The metropolitan cities are urban areas with a population of over one million (e.g. Seoul, the capital of South Korea, is the largest urban center, having 10 million residents). The nine provinces (Do) are subdivided into cities (Si) and counties (Gun). A city (Si) has a population of more than 50,000 and a Gun consists of one town (Eup) and five to ten villages (Myeon) (KOIS, 2007a).

and other metropolitan cities, there are more cases of general education teachers with both certificates or with additional in-service education in suburban and rural areas.

Table 4.1 Distribution of Korean special education teachers by their qualification and education offices

Office of Education			
Metropolitan Office of Education (1)		*Regional Office of Education*	
Seoul	Metropolitan Office of Education	11	District Office of Education
Metropolitan Office of Education (6)			
Busan	Metropolitan City Office of Education	6	District office of Education
Daegu	Metropolitan City Office of Education	4	District office of Education
Incheon	Metropolitan City Office of Education	4	District office of Education
Gwangju	Metropolitan City Office of Education	2	District office of Education
Daejeon	Metropolitan Office of Education	2	District office of Education
Ulsan	Metropolitan City Office of Education	2	District office of Education
Provincial Office of Education (9)			
Gyeonggi-do	Office of Education	25	District office of Education
Gangwon-do	Office of Education	17	District office of Education
Chungcheongbuk-do	Office of Education	11	District office of Education
Chungcheongnam-do	Office of Education	15	District office of Education
Jeollabuk-do	Office of Education	14	District office of Education
Jeollanam-do	Office of Education	22	District office of Education
Gyeongsangbuk-do	Office of Education	23	District office of Education
Gyeongsangnam-do	Office of Education	20	District office of Education
Jeju-do(Island)	Office of Education	3	District office of Education

Resource: Ministry of Education and Human Resources Development (2005b)

4.1.2 SAMPLING

Stratified random sampling[2] was used in this survey in order to ensure that it will be able to represent not only the overall population, but also subgroups of the population (particularly small minority groups such as special education teachers from suburban or rural areas).

---

[2] The population was divided into non-overlapping groups (i.e. strata, school districts according to education offices); N1, N2, N3, ... Ni, such that $N1 + N2 + N3 + \ldots + Ni = N$. A simple random sampling was then done of $f = n/N$ in each strata.

4.1 Participants

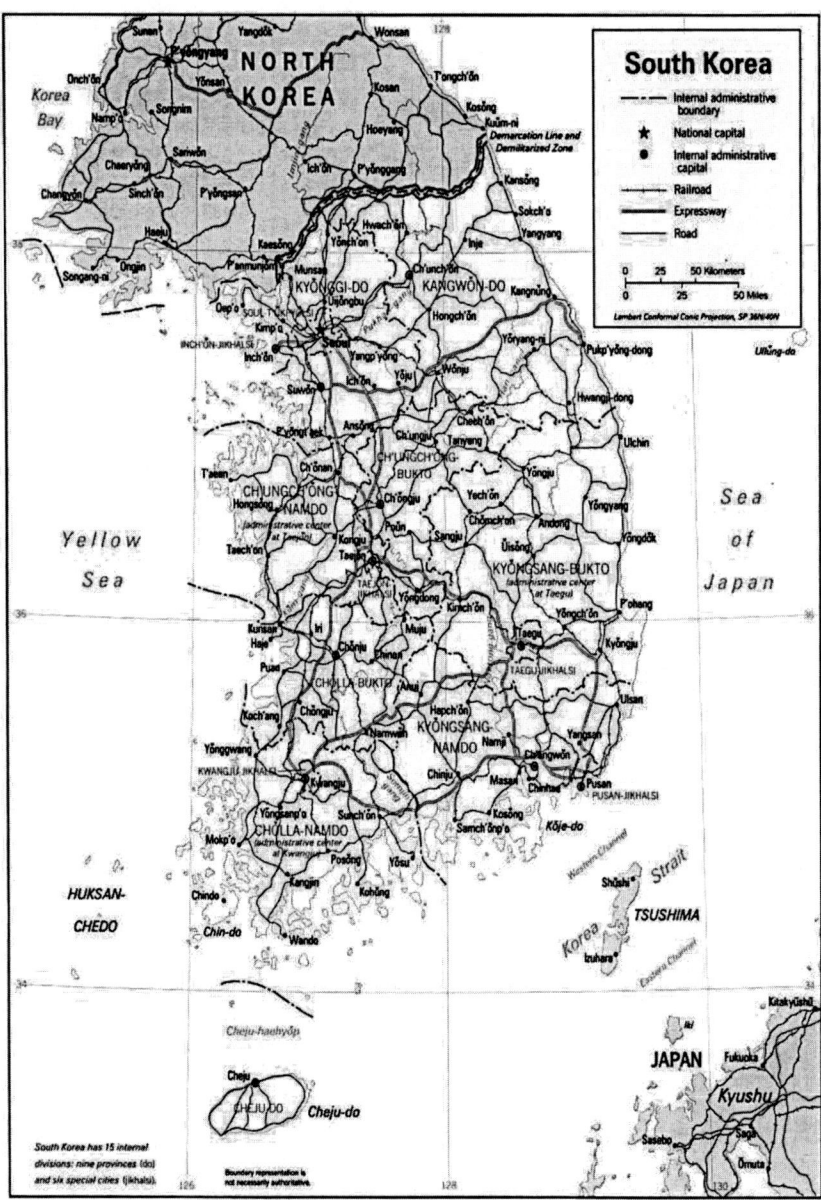

Figure 4.1   Administrative divisions of South Korea

Table 4.1 cont.

Special teachers by certifications (N)				
Special Teacher	Special + Regular teacher	Regular teacher + Inservice		Total
		Over 60h	Under 60h	
517	11	0	0	528
207	116	6	1	330
123	33	0	0	156
161	21	1	0	183
59	10	11	5	85
67	7	0	0	74
43	2	2	0	47
606	6	1	0	613
133	21	21	19	194
76	8	4	5	93
210	11	7	6	234
39	78	17	11	145
76	102	23	0	201
187	39	21	13	260
137	51	25	22	235
7	23	5	0	35
				3413

First, the population (n= 3,413) was divided into subgroups; that is, education offices and their district offices (Table 4.1; Figure 4.2); on the basis of the distribution range from the offices of education by MOE & HRD and on the assumption that the strata of offices of education are stratified by socioeconomic status and the population of each region and population of the area. Second, simple random sampling was applied to each subgroup with a sampling fraction of 15 percent (%). In total, 512 special education teachers were randomly selected from primary schools nationwide (Table 4.2).

With reference to the valid email address confirmation, it turned out that 487 special education teachers were contacted. Concerning the conducted methods of data analysis, the aim of the study was to obtain above 50% of the responses. Since the first return rate was assumed to be under 50%, further samples (n=100) were asked via an additional mailing to respond to the questionnaire (Table 4.2). In this case, participants were randomly sampled from the metropolitan office of education in the capital (Seoul) and the provincial office of education in the provinces (Gyeonggi), for the reason that these two education offices possessed the largest size and range of areas (urban, suburban and rural areas) regarding the participants (Table 4.1; Figure 4.2).

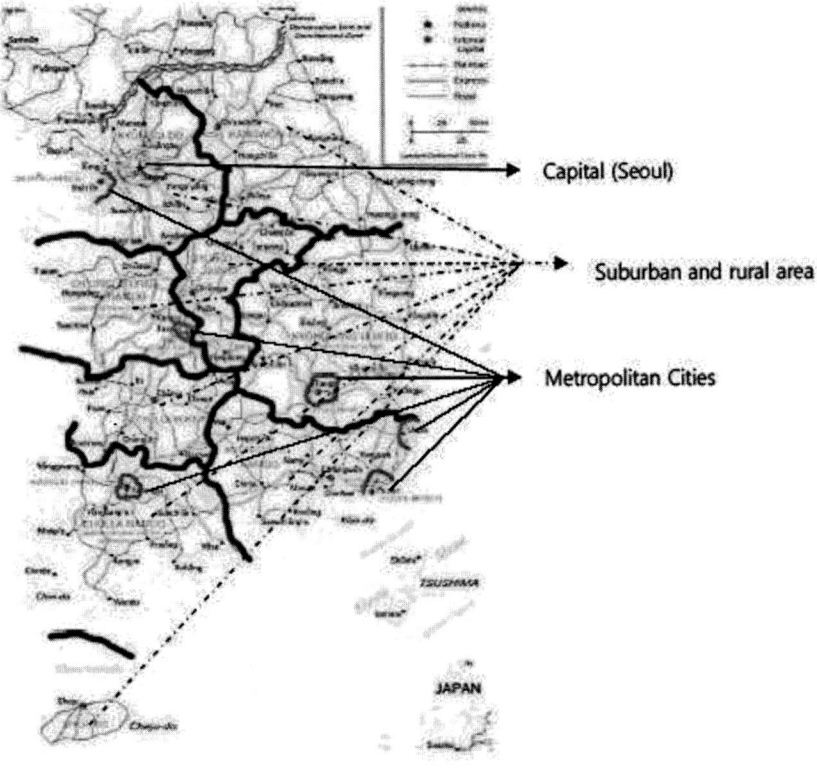

Figure 4.2   Educational offices in South Korea under the MOE & HRD

Table 4.2 Distribution of samples by their education offices and number of e-mails sent to samples

Regional location	Education office	Special teacher N	Samples N
Capital	Seoul	528	79
Metropolitan city	Busan	330	50
	Daegu	156	23
	Inchon	183	28
	Gwangju	85	13
	Daejeoun	74	11
	Ulsan	47	7
Province	Gyeonggi	613	92
	Gangwon	194	29
	Chungbuk	93	14
	Chungnam	234	35
	Jeounbuk	145	22
	Jeounnam	201	30
	Gyeoungbuk	260	39
	Gyeoungnam	235	35
	Jeju Island	35	5
Total		3413	512
Additional mailing Capital and Province	Seoul and Gyeonggi		100

Table 4.3   Description of sample (Respondents)

	Survey Items	Frequency	Percent (%)
School Location: Provincial Office of Education	Seoul	110	34.7
	Busan	12	3.8
	Daegu	7	2.2
	Incheon	18	5.7
	Gwangju	4	1.3
	Daejeon	3	0.9
	Ulsan	1	0.3
	Gyeounggi	122	38.5
	Gangwon	7	2.2
	Chungbuk	6	1.9
	Chungnam	17	5.4
	Jeonbuk	1	0.3
	Jeonnam	2	0.6
	Gyeongbuk	4	1.3
	Gyeongnam	3	0.9
School Location: Regional Location	Seoul	110	34.7
	Urban	46	14.5
	Suburban	130	41.0
	Rural	31	9.8
Grade Levels taught	Lower grades level	188	59.3
	Higher grades level	129	40.7
Qualification	Special education teacher certification	317	100.0
Years of Teaching Experience	Over 3 under 5 years	212	66.9
	Over 5 under 10 years	103	32.5
	Over 10 years	2	0.6
Students with LD taught	From 2 to 4 LD student	133	42.0
	Over 5 LD student	184	58.0
Pre-service Training	Yes	313	98.7
	No	4	1.3
In-service Training	Yes	8	2.5
	No	309	97.5
Total		317	100.0

4.1.3 CHARACTERISTICS

A total of 317 Korean special education teachers from primary schools responded to the survey; 240 of the returns were fully completed (cf. Ch. 4.3 for partly completed returns). A description of the sample (respondents) is given in Table 4.3.

– Qualification
  All of the respondents reported having a certified special education teacher.
– Grade levels taught
  The respondents included 188 (59.3%) lower grade level (i.e. 1st-3rd grade level) and 129 (40.7%) higher grade level (i.e. 4th-6th grade level) special education teachers.
– Years of teaching experience
  Among the respondents, 212 (66.9%) special education teachers stated having over 3 to under 5 years of teaching experience, whereas 103 (32.5%) stated having over 5 to under 10 years, and 2 (0.6%) stated having over 10 years of teaching experience.
– Numbers of students with LD taught
  133 (42%) respondents reported they taught from 2 to 4 students with LD whereas 184 (58%) declared teaching more than 5 students with LD.
– Teacher education
  Almost all of the respondents (313, 98.7%) reported they had taken a course on LD at universities (pre-service education). Conversely, 97.5% (309) of the respondents answered they did not participate in any kind of training on LD (in-service education).
– Regional characteristics
  The majority within the respondents (110, 34.7%) were special education teachers from Seoul, the capital of Korea, and 122 (38.5%) were from Gyeounggi. Regarding the regional location of schools by their education offices, 130 (41%) of the special education teachers were from suburban areas and 31 (9.8%) were from rural areas, whereas 46 (14.5%) were from urban areas.

4.2 MATERIALS

4.2.1 DEVELOPMENT OF QUESTIONNAIRE

On development of the questionnaire, research questions and corresponding hypotheses (Table 4.11) were considered, and items drawn from the literature on LD regarding special education teachers' perceptions were generated:
– LD assessment
  The use of assessment methods for students with LDs and teachers' self-confidence in using them were based on items from the survey of Lopez-Reyna, Bay & Patrikakou (1996, 46-48), which was applied to Korean special education teachers by Byun CS (2002a, 264). In the present study, 10 items from the survey were adopted; a further 8 items were added by the researcher based on other literature, for example from NICHCY (1997, 7-12, 18-21) and Shin HK & Jung JY (2002, 247f.).

– Causes of LD
The causes of LD, or rather causal factors which may contribute to LD (hereafter causal factors of LD), were based on items from the survey of Kataoka, Kraayenoord, & Elkins (2004, 174,175) and chiefly on the literature of Westwood (2004, 54-60, 63-65, 67-68, 75-78). The items were theoretically divided into two major categories; that is, individual and environmental variables referring to Hooper, Montgomery, Swartz, Reed, Sandler, Levine, Waston, & Wasileski (1994, 385).

– LD definition
The definition of LD (definition component of LD) was based on literature reviews and surveys from Korea (e.g. Kim YO & Bong WY, 2004; Jung DY, 2005; Shin JH, 2005; Kim JK, 2005; Park HS, 1992; Kim YO, 1992; Kim DI, Lee DS, & Shin JH, 2003) and also from other countries (e.g. Reschly & Hosp, 2004[3]; Kim SA & Sung JG, 2005[4]; Yang MH & Landrum, 2005[5]). Finally, the researcher designed a set of questions.

4.2.1.1 DIMENSIONALITY

The purpose of this procedure was to examine the dimensionality of the causal factors of LD perceived by special education teachers, which refer to the previously mentioned literature. Factor analysis was performed in order to examine if there were distinct dimensions, whether the response patterns of participants suggest that certain items were indicators of similar components, while other items were indicators of other components.

For the extraction method, the Principle Components Analysis (PCA) was chosen (number of factors= 4). This method seeks to extract independent components which explain the maximal amount of variance of items. The reason for choosing the method was to ensure that specific items, which theoretically hypothesized to describe distinct dimensions; that is, individual and environmental variables do not mix each other. For the Rotation method, Varimax rotation was chosen. This method facilitates the interpretation of the component structure by maximizing the variance on the components (e.g. Backhaus, Erichson, Plinke, & Weiber, 1994). The results stem from the sample of the final study (n =317). It should also be mentioned that a pilot study was conducted in advance. However, due to its small sample size (n=30) this study was not taken into consideration regarding the psychometric properties, although the dimensionality was similar to that found in the final study.

---

[3] Reschly & Hosp (2004, 197) analyzed the common components of state definition of LD regarding the "conceptual definition" and "classification criteria" of LD.

[4] Kim & Sung (2005, 59-61) suggested some aspects of LD definitions in Germany which carry implications for Korea.

[5] Yang MH & Landrum (2005, 107) discussed the LD definition; identification in reauthorized IDEA 2004.

4.2.1.2 ITEM REVISION

Finally, items 2.4, 3.1, 3.3, and 3.6 were excluded (cf. Table B 4.1; Table B 4.2; Table B 4.3, Appendix B).

EXCLUSION OF ITEM 3.1 AND 2.4

Item 3.1 'unsuitable curriculum' loaded substantially negative (-0.560) on component 3. With respect to the fact that other items were loading positively on component 3, which describes the student's "cognitive ability" factor, and also because it did not match with other items concerning the content, item 3.1 'unsuitable curriculum' was deleted.

Item 2.4 'phonological language disorder' loaded substantially negative (-0.659) on component 4. However, regarding other items loading positively on component 4, and regarding the two highly loading items which describe the student's "family" factor, and since its content did not match the other items, item 2.4 'phonological language disorder' was deleted.

EXCLUSION OF ITEM 3.6 AND 3.3

In addition, item 3.6 'inadequate physical classroom environment' (0.449) and item 3.3 'lack of text book materials' (0.471) were deleted, because they did not match with the other highly loading items regarding the content which describe the student's "family" factor. An additional reason is that the absolute values were less than 0.50, much lower than other comparable values.

4.2.1.3 CAUSAL FACTORS OF LEARNING DISABILITIES

The Principle Components Analysis (PCA) over final item set is presented in Table 4.4 (suppressed absolute values less than 0.50) (cf. Table B 4.3 for suppressed absolute values less than 0.40). According to the test, as shown in Table 4.4, it may be suggested that the "causal factors of LD" regarding the items of individual and environmental variables do not mix with each other. Overall, the test indicated four components, which were labeled according to the items loading highly on them:

1 component = "teacher-school" factor	(teacher related school items [6])
2 component = student's "personality" factor	(personality items [7])

---

[6] Items (n=8) labeled as "teacher-school" factor: 'inappropriate assessment method', 'lack of regular-special teacher cooperation', 'poor student-teacher relationship', 'regular teachers' lack of understanding of LD', 'inappropriate teaching method', 'special teachers' lack of professional knowledge of LD', 'inadequate social classroom environment', and 'lack of special teacher-parents cooperation'.

[7] Items (n=5) labeled as student's "personality" factor: 'poor self confidence', 'lack of pre-knowledge', 'poor motivation', 'poor learning style', and 'emotional- behavioral problems'.

4.2 MATERIALS

3 component = student's "cognitive ability" factor (cognitive items [8])
4 component = student's "family" factor (family items [9])

In addition, as shown in Table 4.5, the total percentage (%) explained by variance was 66.98%. The sums of squared loadings (Eigenvalues) after rotation were as follows.

Table 4.4 Factor analysis – Rotated Component Matrix(a)

Rotated Component Matrix(a)		Component			
		1	2	3	4
3.4	inappropriate assessment method	0.839			
3.5	poor student teacher relationship	0.808			
3.11	regular teachers' lack of understanding of LD	0.801			
3.8	lack of regular-special teacher cooperation	0.797			
3.2	inappropriate teaching method	0.776			
3.7	inadequate social classroom environment	0.737			
3.10	special teachers' lack of professional knowledge of LD	0.702			
3.9	lack of special teacher-parents cooperation	0.618			
2.9	poor self confidence		0.886		
2.7	lack of pre-knowledge		0.838		
2.8	poor motivation		0.809		
2.10	poor learning style		0.625		
2.6	emotional behavioral problems		0.578		
2.2	memory problem			0.739	
2.5	neurological impairment			0.700	
2.3	perceptual disorder			0.689	
2.1	attention problem			0.530	
3.13	unsupportive parent				0.877
3.12	poor economic home background				0.750

Extraction Method: Principal Component Analysis.
Rotation Method: Varimax with Kaiser Normalization.
a Rotation converged in 6 iterations.

---

[8] Items (n=4) labeled as student's "cognitive ability" factor: 'memory problem', 'neurological impairment', 'perceptual disorder', and 'attention problem'.
[9] Items (n=2) labeled as student's "family" factor: 'unsupportive parent' and 'poor economic home background'.

Table 4.5   Total Variance Explained

Total Variance Explained			
	Rotation Sums of Squared Loadings		
component	Total	% of Variance	Cumulative %
1 teacher-school items	5.010	26.369	26.369
2 personality items	3.440	18.106	44.474
3 cognitive items	2.348	12.357	56.831
4 family items	1.929	10.151	66.982
Extraction Method: Principal Component Analysis.			

4.2.1.4 Reliability

The reliability of the causal factors of LD was tested. Analysis of internal consistency (Cronbach's Alpha) for each component's item set ("teacher-school" factor, "personality" factor, "cognitive ability" factor) was tested. Regarding the "family" factor, the Spearman correlation was conducted instead of Cronbach's Alpha due to the number of items (n=2). The presented results stem from the final study (n=317). The reliability tested in the pilot study was similar to that found in the final study, but, as previously mentioned, the sample size of the pilot study were too small to obtain solid results.

The item's total statistics are reported as follows:

1 component = "teacher-school" factor items,
$\qquad$ Cronbach's Alpha= 0.902 (Table 4.6)
2 component = "personality" factor items,
$\qquad$ Cronbach's Alpha = 0.843 (Table 4.7)
3 component = "cognitive" factor items,
$\qquad$ Cronbach's Alpha= 0.648 (Table 4.8)
4 component = "family" factor items,
$\qquad$ Spearmans' roh= 0.734** (Table 4.9)

Due to the exploratory nature of the analysis -for instance, the purpose of this study was not to develop a measurement tool- these reliabilities were considered acceptable. Hence, to some degree, there is empirical support for the assumption of distinct dimensions within the causal factors of LD perceived by special education teachers.

4.2 MATERIALS

Table 4.6   Item-Total Statistics – Teacher related school items

Reliability Statistics Cronbach's Alpha 0.902 Item-Total Statistics					
		Scale Mean if Item Deleted	Scale Variance If Item Deleted	Corrected Item- Total Correlation	Cronbach's Alpha if Item Deleted
3.4	inappropriate assessment method	26.262	17.226	0.825	0.878
3.5	poor student teacher relationship	26.470	17.161	0.762	0.883
3.11	regular teachers' lack of understanding of LD	26.183	17.618	0.795	0.882
3.8	lack of regular-special teacher cooperation	26.511	16.953	0.748	0.884
3.2	inappropriate teaching method	26.240	17.480	0.756	0.884
3.7	inadequate social classroom environment	26.205	18.145	0.694	0.890
3.10	special teachers' lack of professional knowledge of LD	26.650	16.450	0.642	0.899
3.9	lack of special teacher-parents cooperation	26.164	19.296	0.403	0.914

N of Items 8

Table 4.7   Item-Total Statistics – Student's personality items

Reliability Statistics Cronbach's Alpha 0.843 Item-Total Statistics					
		Scale Mean if Item Deleted	Scale Variance If Item Deleted	Corrected Item- Total Correlation	Cronbach's Alpha if Item Deleted
2.9	poor self confidence	15.388	7.827	0.844	0.754
2.7	lack of preknowledge	15.356	7.895	0.734	0.788
2.8	poor motivation	15.659	7.991	0.694	0.801
2.10	poor learning style	15.259	9.572	0.524	0.844
2.6	emotional behavioral problems	15.082	11.101	0.517	0.850

N of Items 5

Table 4.8   Item-Total Statistics – Student's cognitive items

Reliability Statistics Cronbach's Alpha 0.648 Item-Total Statistics					
				N of Items 4	
		Scale Mean if Item Deleted	Scale Variance If Item Deleted	Corrected Item- Total Correlation	Cronbach's Alpha if Item Deleted
2.2	memory problem	12.082	1.348	0.566	0.530
2.5	neurological impairment	12.353	0.976	0.414	0.629
2.3	perceptual disorder	12.189	1.186	0.467	0.553
2.1	attention problem	12.000	1.392	0.369	0.620

Table 4.9   Correlations as indicator of component 4 (Student's family items) homogeneity

Correlations				
				3.12 poor economic home background
Spearman's rho	3.13 unsupportive parent	Correlation Coefficient		0.734**
		Sig. (2-tailed)		0.000
		N		317
**. Correlation is significant at the 0.01 level (2-tailed).				

4.2.2 Procedure of Conducting Regression

4.2.2.1 Logistic Regression

The binary logistic regression enter model was conducted in order to test the hypotheses (cf. Table 4.11). It was assumed that the LD definitions by special education teachers vary according to their perceptions of the causal factors of LD. The hypotheses corresponding to research question 1 (Do special education teachers' definitions of LD differ due to their perceptions of causal factors of LD, and their demographic background?) was that 'the likelihood that the LD definition is utilized by special education teachers is related to both their perceived causal factors of LD and demographic background'. Thus, the binary logistic regression enter model was conducted in order to examine how much variation of the dependent variables (LD definition components) can be explained by the independent variables (causal factors of LD). The underlying model assumes that the variation of the dependent variables can be predicted by a linear combination of theoretically expected causal factors of LD (variables). This linear combination is used as an exponential term in order to estimate the relevant probabilities. The whole model is a logistic instead of a linear one, as the probability of the dependent variable to happen can reach from zero to one.

INDEPENDENT VARIABLES

– Factor scores
The independent variables were the factor scores regarding the components computed by regression method (computation of factor scores of the causal factors of LD, i.e. "teacher-school", student's "personality", student's "cognitive ability" and student's "family" factor by regression method).
– Demographic backgrounds
Independent variables were special education teachers' demographic background (cf. Table 4.3: sample description). Due to the distribution and variance, items such as special education teachers' 'regional location of school', 'years of teaching experience', and 'numbers of students with LDs taught' were recoded into dichotomous variables.

DEPENDENT VARIABLES

– Definition of LD
Dependent variables were special education teachers' responses on utilized definition components of LD. In order to recode the dependent variables into dichotomous variables, a median split was applied, coded by 0 and 1. Special education teachers were divided into two groups according to their responses on using the definition components; the groups were coded by 0 and 1. It has to be noted that there were four definition components which reported some variance. Furthermore, two types of responses were dominant (undecided; agree).

4.2.2.2 LINEAR REGRESSION

The linear regression analysis model was conducted to test the hypothesis (Table 4.11). It was assumed that the assessment methods used by special education teachers vary with regard to their perception of the causal factors of LD.

EVALUATION OF ASSUMPTION FOR MULTIPLE LINEAR REGRESSION

– Ratio of cases to independent variables: according to Tabachnick and Fidell (2001), the number of cases for a test of the overall model has to be equal to or higher than (50+8* number of predictors), which is 82 for this analysis (four predictors; factor 1-'factor2- factor3- factor4-). The number of cases for a test of single predictors has to be equal to or higher than (104+ number of predictors), which is 108 for this analysis. With an N of at least 236 these conditions are fulfilled.
– Homoscedasticity (equality of residual variances; practically important for time series analysis); Possibility: Goldfeld/Quandt-test.

- Multicollinearity (predictors are linearly dependent on each other): for this analysis there is intrinsically no concern of multicollinearity because the tested predictors are factor scores stemming from PCA (principal component analysis). This method produces linearly independent factors.
- Autocorrelation of residuals (practically important for time series analysis) tested in each analysis (cf. Tables Durbin-Watson test).
- Linearity: because the regression analysis in this research is more exploratory in nature than strictly testing a model, the linearity is assumed and not explicitly tested. Therefore, no linearizing transformations (e.g. logarithmic transformations) are done.
- Multinormality of involved variables: multinormality is not explicitly tested. According to Tabachnick and Fidell (2007), only few empirical data sets fulfill this assumption. Nonetheless, multiple linear regression is practically used, because the method is quite robust against the violation of this assumption.

INDEPENDENT VARIABLES
- Factor scores
  Independent variables were the factor scores regarding the components computed by regression method (computation of factor scores of the causal factors of LD i.e. "teacher-school", "personality", "cognitive", and "family" factors by regression method).

DEPENDENT VARIABLES
- Assessment methods
  The dependent variables were theoretically summarized by computing their mean and due to the interval scale level, linear regression was conducted. Since these items did obviously not have the purpose of indicating latent components of factors, but were descriptive in nature, the researcher attempted to test the content validity [10].

4.2.3 VALIDITY

Two special education teachers with and without a Master's degree were asked to review the items of LD assessment methods, whether it covers the range that they would expect. In addition, they were asked to modify the questions clearer and easier for them to understand. For instance, they pointed out that terms such as 'dynamic assessment' and 'learning style assessment' were unfamiliar to special education teachers and may therefore lead to ambiguous responses. Consequently, the researcher decided to include examples in the questionnaire.

---

[10] "The content validity is based on the extent to which a measurement reflects the specific intended domain of content" (Carmines & Zeller, 1991, 20).

4.2.4 PILOT STUDY

A pilot study was carried out during the months of December 2004 and January 2005. Participants were privately contacted by phone, and those who agreed to fill in the questionnaire were sent e-mails with hyperlinks of the website as well as ID and password for log-in. Thereafter, an additional phone call prompting was done by the researcher.

In the pilot study, the entire process of the web-survey was tested regarding participants' log-in to the website, monitoring of the time record, numbers in order to avoid duplication of responses, and finally saving their responses simultaneously and anonymously in data files. The pilot study was aimed at confirming the effectiveness of the procedure and examining statistical analysis. Thus factor analysis and reliabilities (Cronbach's alpha) were tested in the pilot study. However, this was not reported in consequence of its small sample size (n=30), although the results were similar to those gathered in the final study. At last the questionnaire was simplified, using the data from the pilot study. Mainly, the survey was replenished regarding its technical part with respect to its online functionality. The bias resulting from it being a web survey was minimized through the pilot study:

(a) the responses were basically set to be saved per page/part. In order to avoid drop-outs after collecting the data, each page/part of the questionnaire was ensured to be completed before jumping to the next page. For instance, if a participant skipped some questions or tried to jump to the next page without filling in the present page, she or he was prompt with a message 'please complete these questions to go to the next page' showing the remaining questions. This enabled the researcher to collect selectively and obtain efficiently useful data;

(b) responses were saved automatically and anonymously by code name in data files. It enabled the researcher to get an overview of return rates during the survey and save time in coding the data as well as to work effectively with the SPSS program;

(c) upon return of the data file, the ID and password given to the participant was blocked to avoid duplications.

4.2.5 DESCRIPTION OF SCALES AND QUESTIONNAIRE CONSTRUCTION

The questionnaire designed by the researcher and used in the study consisted of four parts (Table 4.10). In this questionnaire, 5-point rating scales with verbal marks were used (1 = strongly disagree; 5 = strongly agree, 1 = not at all; 5 = very often)[11].

---

[11] A score around the value of '1' indicates 'strongly disagree', '2' indicates 'disagree', '3' indicates 'undecided', '4' indicates 'agree' and '5' indicates 'strongly agree' with regard to the items which constitute the scale.

Table 4.10 Overview of questionnaire structure

Part	Question/items	Sub items	items
Teacher demographic background	School location	Location of 'Office of Education'	1
		Regional location of schools	1
	Teacher variables	Grade levels taught	1
		Qualifications	1
		Years of teaching experience	1
		Numbers of students with LDs taught	1
		Pre-service education of LD area	1
		In-service education of LD area	1
		Subtotal	8
Definition of LD	Definition components	Subtotal	7
Causes of LD	Causal factors	Individual variables	10
		Environmental variables	13
		Subtotal	23
LD assessment process	Assessment methods	utilized for gathering information on the student	10
	Self-competences	Self competences in using the methods	8
	Collaborations	Situation when interpreting the assessment data	9
		Subtotal	27
		Total number of items in questionnaire	65

4.3 Procedure

In the period of data collection for the final study during the months of June and July 2005, 487 e-mails were sent to special education teachers. 3 weeks later, a second mailing (n=100) was carried out in June 2005. The e-mails sent to special education teachers contained hyperlinks of the web site, on which the online-questionnaire was posted. The e-mails also informed about ID and password for log-in, briefly repeated information about the survey notifying that the responses were saved anonymously. In addition, the researcher contacted special education teachers by phone in order to inform them about the e-mail and to personally ask them to visit the web site.

Partly completed returns

In the final study, the researcher received 317 responses of special education teachers in total, 240 of which were fully completed, and the rest partly completed. Concerning the uncompleted returns, as previously mentioned, responses were set to be saved automatically per pages in data files due to the nature of the web survey. Therefore, the researcher was able to receive each completed page of the questionnaire. That is, for example, if a respondent completed the questionnaire as far as part 2 and stopped during part 3, the researcher received the data of questionnaire parts 1 and 2. The researcher finally determined not to exclude these uncompleted subjects, in order to gather as much information as possible. Hence all valid cases, as reported in Table 4.3, were taken into consideration for the analysis.

4.4 Research Design and Data Analysis

An overview of research design and data analysis is illustrated in Figure 4.3 and Figure 4.4.

A. Factor analysis (principle components analysis, varimax rotation) was performed in order to examine the dimensionality regarding the causal factors of LD which refer to the literature as well as to how they are perceived by the special education teachers. The analysis was aimed at examining if there were distinct dimensions, and more specifically to see whether the response patterns of the special education teachers suggest that certain items were indicators of similar components, while other items were indicators of different components. The reason for choosing this method was to ensure that specific items, which theoretically hypothesized to describe distinct dimensions, do not mix with each other.
The reliability was tested as follows: (a) analysis of internal consistency (Cronbach's Alpha) for each component item set (1, 2, 3 components) was tested, and (b) regarding the fourth component, due to the number of items (n=2), the Spearman correlation was conducted instead of Cronbach's Alpha.

B. The logistic regression model (Figure 4.4) was fitted to the data in order to test the hypothesis correspondingly to research question 1 (Table 4.11). The dependent variable was special education teachers' definition of LD, the independent variable were their causal factors of LD. Independent variables were the factor scores regarding the components computed by regression method (Figure 4.3). The whole model is a logistic instead of a linear one, because the probability of the dependent variable to happen can reach from zero to one.
In addition, the Spearman correlation was performed to test the correlation between particular definition components and items (Figure 4.4): (a) 'basic psychological processes disorder' and the student's "cognitive" factor, (b) the ex-

clusion clause ('it is not the direct result of environmental, cultural, economic disadvantage') and student's "family" factor were tested.

C. The linear regression analysis model (Figure 4.4) was conducted to test the hypothesis corresponding to research question 2 (Table 4.11). Evaluation of assumption for multiple linear regression was carried out. Independent variables were the factor scores regarding the components computed by the regression method, and dependent variables were the special education teachers' assessment methods.

In addition, the items regarding the interviews (Figure 4.3) were theoretically summarized by computing their means. Thus, the method 'interviews' represents the interview with parent, regular teacher and the student with LD in the analysis hereafter. Moreover, the items regarding the curriculum based assessment (CBA), dynamic assessment (test-train/intervention-retest) and learning style assessment were also theoretically summarized by computing their means. Thus, here the methods 'alternative assessment' represents these methods mentioned above.

D. The Spearman correlation was conducted to examine if special education teachers' self-competence in using the assessment method is significant and correlates with their frequency of use (research question 3). In addition, descriptive statistics were used in order to analyze the collaboration situation during the LD assessment process.

Table 4.11 Research questions and corresponding hypotheses

Research question 1:	Do special education teachers' definitions of LD differ due to their perceptions of the causes of LD and their demographic background?
Hypothesis 1.1	The likelihood that the definition component *normal or above average intelligence* is utilized by special education teachers is related to both their perceived causal factor of LD and demographic background.
Hypothesis 1.2	The likelihood that the definition component *disorder in basic psychological processes* is utilized by special education teachers is related to both their perceived causal factor of LD and demographic background.
Hypothesis 1.3	The likelihood that the definition component *it is not the direct result of environmental, cultural, economic disadvantages (exclusion clause)* is utilized by special education teachers is related to both their perceived causal factor of LD and demographic background.

Hypothesis 1.4	The likelihood that the definition component *central nervous system dysfunction* is utilized by special education teachers is related to both their perceived causal factor of LD and demographic background.
Research question 2:	Do special education teachers' assessment methods used for the assessment of students with LDs differ due to their perceptions of the causes of LD?
Hypothesis 2.1	Special education teachers' use of *interviews* to gather students' information in the LD assessment is related to their perceived causal factors of LD.
Hypothesis 2.2	Special education teachers' use of *standardized tests* to gather students' information in the LD assessment is related to their perceived causal factors of LD.
Hypothesis 2.3	Special education teachers' *observation in regular classroom* to gather students' information in the LD assessment is related to their perceived causal factors of LD.
Hypothesis 2.4	Special education teachers' use of *error patterns analysis in students' work* to gather students' information in the LD assessment is related to their perceived causal factors of LD.
Hypothesis 2.5	Special education teachers' use of *alternative assessment methods* such as Curriculum Based Assessment, dynamic assessment (test-train/intervention-retest) and learning style assessment to gather students' information in the LD assessment is related to their perceived causal factors of LD.
Research question 3:	Do special education teachers' self-competences in assessing students with LDs differ in their frequency of use of assessment methods?
Hypothesis	Are there any relationships between special education teachers' *self-competence* in using the assessment methods and the frequency of using the method?

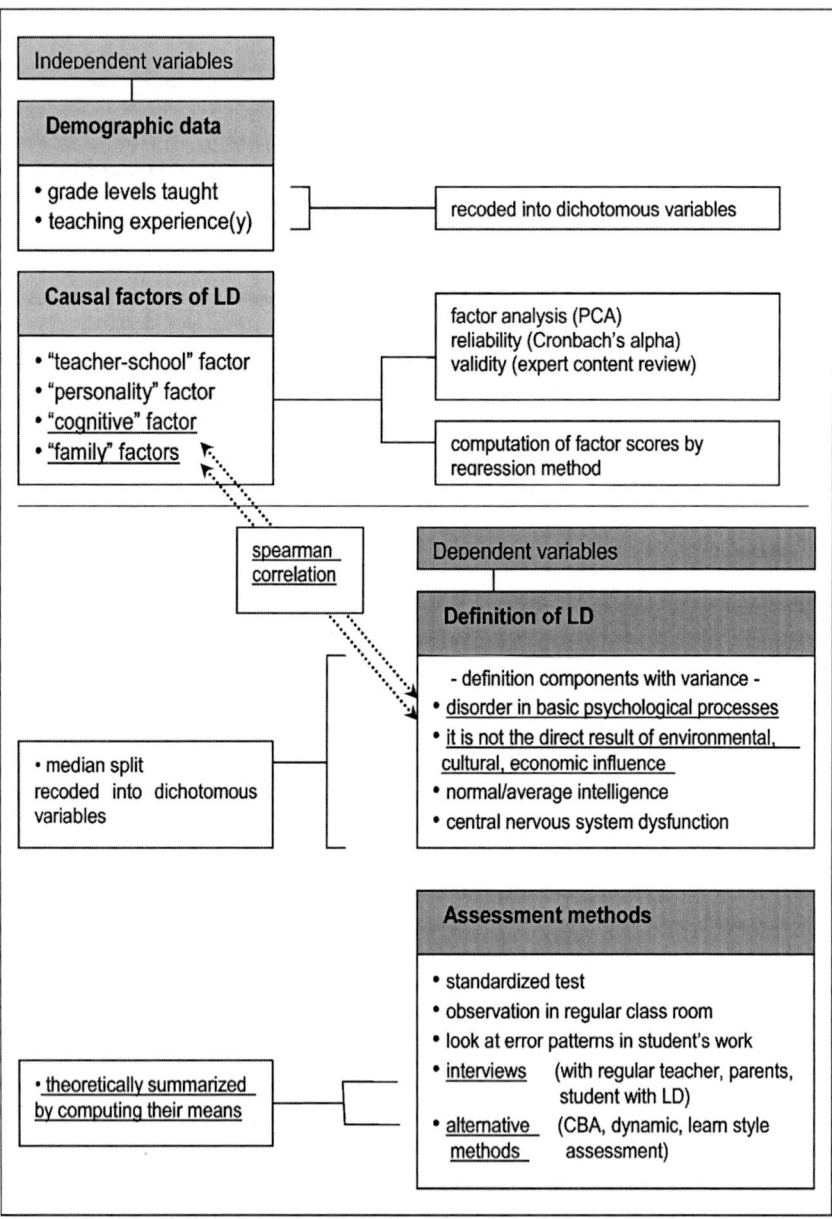

Figure 4.3   Research design

4.4 Research Design and Data Analysis

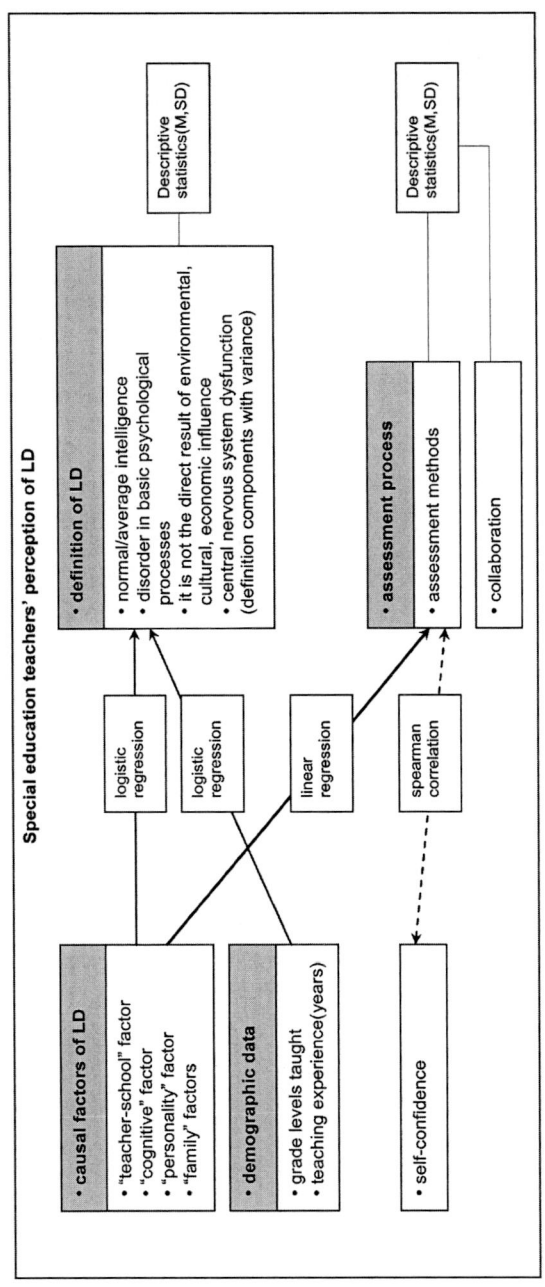

Figure 4.4   Data analysis

Part IV.

Research Results

5

RESULTS

It is important to note that the 'causal factors of LD' perceived by Korean special education teachers were discussed in the previous chapter. There was empirical support for the assumption of distinct dimensions within the causal factors of LD as follows: student's "cognitive (ability)", "personality", "family" and "teacher-school" factors. The focus of this study was to examine the relationship between these causal factors of LD and teachers' self-reported assessments method and definitions of LD. The data were obtained from 240 special education teachers working in special classes at (regular) primary schools. These data were gleaned by an online questionnaire (5-point rating scale with verbal marks) which was conducted for this study.

5.1 RESEARCH QUESTION 1 AND HYPOTHESES

Research Question 1: Do special education teachers' definitions of LD differ due to their perceptions of the causes of LD and their demographic background?

The hypothesis posed to the data was that 'the likelihood that special education teachers use the definition is related to their perceived causal factors of LD and their demographic data'. The *binary logistic regression enter model* was fitted to the data to test the hypothesis: the relationship between the LD definition components special education teachers reported to use and both their perceived causal factors of LD and their demographic data (their grade levels taught and teaching years of experience, for detail cf. Ch. 4). Generally most Korean special education teachers reported utilizing all the seven given components of LD definition (for means >4, Table B 5.11, Appendix B). Nevertheless, according to the descriptive statistics, there were some responses reporting 'undecided' to employ components as follows: '*normal or above average intelligence* (intelligence component)' (mean= 4.81), '*basic psychological processes disorder* (process disorder component)' (mean= 4.56), '*central nervous system dysfunction* (CNS dysfunction component)' (mean= 4.66) and '*it is not the direct result of environmental, cultural, economic disadvantages* (exclusion clause)' (mean= 4.39). In consequence, these four components of LD definition were assumed to predict differences in other variables concerning the following hypotheses and analyses, whereas every single special education teacher reported including *'academic learning problem'*, *'discrepancy between intellectual and academic achievement'*, and *'it is not the direct result of other handicapping conditions'* in their definitions of LD.

5.1.1 Hypothesis 1.1

The likelihood that the component *normal or average intelligence* is utilized by special education teachers is related to both their perceived causal factor of LD and demographic background.

Out of 317 respondents, 30 (9.5%) were 'undecided' whereas 287 (90.5%) reported including the component *'normal or average intelligence'* in their definition of LD. According to the model, the log of the odds of the LD definition component (*normal or average intelligence*) being utilized by special education teachers was negatively related to both causal factors "teacher-school" and "personality" which prove as significant predictors ($p < 0.05$, teacher school factor B= -0.9414, S.E= 0.3473, Wald= 7.3473, df= 1, p= 0.0067, Exp(B) odds ratio= 0.3901, personality factor B= -0.4837, S.E= 0.2765, Wald= 3.0602, df=1, p= 0.0802, Exp(B) odds ratio= 0.6165; Table B 5.1, Appendix B).

Table 5.1 Predicted logit of normal or above average intelligence

$P = 1/1+e^{-z}$ $Z = a+bn(xn)$
Predicted logit of (*normal or average intelligence*)= Z
Z= 18.8075 −(0.9414)* "teacher-school" −(0.4837)* "personality"

For the increase of each score of response (strongly disagree=1; strongly agree=5) on "teacher-school" and "personality" as responsible for LD, the odds of the LD definition component *'normal or above average intelligence'* being utilized decrease from 1.0 to 0.3901 and 1.0 to 0.6165 (for odds ratio, Table B 5.1, Appendix B). That is, given the same score of response on "teacher-school", a special education teacher who responded with 'strongly agree' on "personality" was 0.6165 times (61.6%) less likely to utilize the LD definition component *'normal or above average intelligence'* than one who responded with 'agree'. For the opposite case, it may be inferred that for a given response (e.g. agree) on "personality", the probability of the LD definition component *'normal or above average intelligence'* being utilized is 0.3901 times (39%) lower for a respondent who rated 'strongly agree' on "teacher-school" than that of a respondent who rated 'agree'. In addition, 15.6% of the variance was accounted for (Nagelkerke R Square= 0.1564; Table B 5.1, Appendix B). The data show that special education teachers who consider teacher related aspects in school and students' personality as important factors that influence LD are less likely to apply the intelligence component *'normal or above average intelligence'* in their definition of LD.

5.1.2 HYPOTHESIS 1.2

The likelihood that the component *disorder in basic psychological processes* is utilized by special education teachers is related to both their perceived causal factor of LD and demographic background.

It has to be noted that the correlation between the LD definition component *'basic psychological processes disorder'* and the causal factor "cognitive" (four items: students' attention problem, memory problem, perceptual disorder and neurological impairment, cf. Factor analysis and Cronbach's alpha) was positive and significant (Spearman correlation 0.147, $p < 0.01$, $n = 317$) in a small effect size (as the numerical value of correlation can be interpreted as the numerical value of effect size). Nevertheless, it has to be taken into account that many other factors (such as emotional, social factors which were not determined in this survey) influence the causal attribution to "cognitive" factors (e.g. Clark, 1997). Therefore an effect size of 0.147 can be regarded as meaningful. Thus, it may be assured that special education teachers' responses to the particular term *'basic psychological processes'* correspond with the items as follows: students' attention problem, memory problem, perceptual disorder and neurological impairment. In other words, it may be suggested that special education teachers who respond to utilize the *'disorder in basic psychological processes'* in their definition of LD also perceive these cognitive factors as relevant and vice versa (that is, special education teachers who were 'undecided' about applying the LD definition component *'basic psychological processes'* indicated less emphasis on cognitive factors). Out of 317 respondents, 70 (22.1%) were undecided whereas 247 (77.9%) reported including *'basic psychological processes disorder'* in their definition of LD. The result indicated four significant predictors: "personality" and "family" factors and special education teachers' grade levels and years of teaching experience ($p < 0.05$, personality factor B= -0.4918, S.E= 0.1878, Wald= 6.8577, df= 1, p= 0.0088, Exp(B) odds ratio= 0.6115, family factor B= 0.7537, S.E= 0.1594, Wald= 22.3495, df= 1, p= 0.0000, Exp(B) odds ratio= 2.1250, grade levels taught B= -0.8651, S.E= 0.3656, Wald= 5.5990, df= 1, p= 0.0180, Exp(B) odds ratio= 0.4210, years of teaching experience B= 0.8599, S.E= 0.4188, Wald= 4.2160, df= 1, p= 0.0400, Exp(B) odds ratio= 2.3630; Table B 5.2, Appendix B).

Table 5.2 Predicted logit of disorder in basic psychological processes

Predicted logit of (*disorder in basic psychological processes*) = Z
Z = 19.9372 −(0.4918)* "personality" +(0.7537)* "family" −(0.8651)* grade levels taught +(0.8599)* teaching years

According to the model, the log of the odds of the LD definition component (*disorder in basic psychological processes*) being utilized by special education teachers was negatively related to the causal factor "personality" and to demographic data grade levels, whereas positively related to the causal factor "family" and to demographic data years of teaching experience. 28.9% of the variance was accounted for (for Nagelkerke R Square= 0.28972, Table B 5.2, Appendix B). When the scores of responses on other predictors were held as a constant (e.g. given the response 'agree' on both "personality" and "family"), special education teachers with higher grade levels (i.e. 4th-6th grade) are 0.8651 times (86.5%) less likely to utilize the LD definition component *'basic psychological processes disorder'* than those with lower grade levels (i.e. 1th-3th grade). Special education teachers who have longer years of teaching experience (i.e. over 5 but under 10 years) are 0.8599 times (85.9%) more likely to apply *'basic psychological processes disorder'* in their definition than those with fewer years of teaching experience (i.e. over 3 but under 5 years) (for odds ratio, Table B 5.2, Appendix B).

5.1.3 HYPOTHESIS 1.3

The likelihood that the component *'it is not the direct result of environmental, cultural, economic disadvantages'*) is utilized by special education teachers is related to both their perceived causal factor of LD and demographic background.

It has to be noted that the correlation between the causal factor "family" and this component (i.e. exclusion clause) was negative and significant, although in a small effect size (Spearman correlation: -0.226, $p< 0.01$, $n= 317$). Special education teachers who were 'undecided' to include the exclusion clause in their definitions of LD systematically tended to perceive the "family" factor as the main cause of LD and vice versa (that is, special education teachers who responded applying the exclusion clause in their definition of LD, they tended to perceive the "family" factor as the main cause of LD to a lesser extent. It may be suggested that special education teachers perceive what they (responded to) utilize (regarding the exclusion clause and the "family" factor).

Out of 317 respondents, 97 (30.6%) were undecided whereas 220 (60.4%) reported utilizing the component *'it is not the direct result of environmental, cultural, economic disadvantage'*. The result showed that "teacher school", "personality" and "family" proved as significant predictors, accounting for 31.6% of the variance ($p< 0.05$, teacher school factor B= 0.4221, S.E= 0.1512, Wald= 7.7958, df= 1, p= 0.0052, Exp(B) odds ratio= 1.5251, personality factor B= -1.1508, S.E= 0.1904, Wald= 36.5276, df= 1, p= 0.0000, Exp(B) odds ratio= 0.3164, family factor B= -0.4810, S.E= 0.1612, Wald= 8.9007, df= 1, p= 0.0029, Exp(B) odds ratio= 0.6182, Nagelkerke R Square= 0.3166; Table B 5.3, Appendix B). According to the model, the log of the odds of the component "exclusion clause" being utilized by special education teachers was positively related to "teacher school" whereas negatively related to "personality" and "family".

5.1 RESEARCH QUESTION 1 AND HYPOTHESES

Table 5.3   Predicted logit of exclusion clause

Predicted logit of (exclusion clause) = Z
Z = -19.1065 +(0.4221)* "teacher school" −(1.1508)* "personality"
    −(0.4810)* "family"

For the increase of each score of response (strongly disagree=1; strongly agree=5) on "teacher-school", the odds of the component of LD definition *'it is not the direct result of environmental, cultural, economic influence'* being utilized increase from 0 to 1.5251 (Odds ratio; Table B 5.3). That means, when all other predictors are held constant, a special education teacher who responds with 'strongly agree' on "teacher school" is 1.525 times (152.51%) more likely to utilize the LD definition component *'it is not the direct result of environmental, cultural, economic influence'* than one who responds with 'agree'. For the opposite case, it may be inferred that for a given response on "teacher-school", the probability of the component being utilized is 0.3164 times (31.64%) and 0.6182 times (61.82%) lower for a respondent who rated 'strongly agree' on "personality" and "family" than that of a respondent who rated 'agree' (for odds ratio, Table B 5.3, Appendix B).

5.1.4 HYPOTHESIS 1.4

The likelihood that the component *central nervous system dysfunction* is utilized by special education teachers is related to both their perceived causal factor of LD and demographic background.

Out of 317 respondents, 54 (17%) were undecided whereas 263 (83%) reported utilizing the LD definition component *'central nervous system dysfunction'* in their definition of LD. The result indicated three significant predictors; "teacher-school", "cognitive" and "family" ($p< 0.05$, teacher-school factor B= -0.9710, S.E= 0.3524, Wald= 7.5925, df= 1, p= 0.0059, Exp(B) odds ratio= 0.3787, cognitive factor B= 1.2161, S.E= 0.2767, Wald= 19.3148, df= 1, p= 0.0000, Exp(B) odds ratio= 3.3741, family factor B= 0.5231, S.E= 0.2029, Wald= 6.6492, df= 1, p= 0.0099, Exp(B) odds ratio= 1.6873; Table B 5.4, Appendix B).

According to the model shown in Table 5.4, the log of the odds of the component (*"central nervous system dysfunction"*) being utilized by special education teachers was negatively related to "teacher-school" whereas positively related to both "cognitive" and "family"; accounting for 35.4% of the dependent variable variation (for Nagelkerke R Square= 0.354853; Table B 5.4, Appendix B).

Table 5.4   Predicted logit of central nervous system dysfunction

Predicted logit of (*central nervous system dysfunction*) = Z Z =16.2444 −(0.9710)* "teacher school" +(1.2161)* "cognitive"   +(0.5231)* "family"

5.2 Research Question 2 and Hypotheses

Research Question 2: Do special education teachers' assessment methods used in LD assessment differ due to their perceptions of the causes of LD?

The *linear regression analysis model* was applied to test the hypothesis: the relationship between the assessment methods used in the assessment process for LD and causal factors of LD perceived by special education teachers. The hypothesis was that 'the likelihood that the assessment method is used by special education teachers is related to their perceived causal factor of LD'. According to the descriptive statistics, generally most special education teachers reported (not at all=1; very often=5) nearly often or normally utilizing the assessment methods (for means> 3, Table B 5.12, Appendix B) as follows: *standardized test* (mean=3.84), *observation in regular classroom* (mean=3.09), *interview with regular teacher* (mean=3.89), *interview with parent* (mean=3.23), *interview with LD student* (mean=3.61), *look for patterns of errors in students' work* (mean=3.10). Dissimilarly, special education teachers reported 'not often' or even 'not at all' utilizing methods such as *curriculum based assessment* (mean=2.89),*learning style assessment* (mean=1.83) and *dynamic assessment (test-train/intervention-retest)* (mean= 1.10).

5.2.1 Hypothesis 2.1

Special education teachers' use of *interviews* to gather students' information in the LD assessment is related to their perceived causal factors of LD.

Out of 240 respondents, 197 (62.1%) reported that they 'often' *interview regular teachers* in order to gather information on students with LD, 26 (8.2%) rated 'normal' whereas only 4 (1.3%) reported 'not often'. Regarding the *interview with parent*, 33 (10.4%) reported 'not often' while 129 (40.7%) and 69 (21.8%) rated 'normal' and 'often', even 9 (2.8%) responded with 'very often' to *interview with parent*. Similarly, 40 (12%) rated 'not often' to *interview with LD student* whereas 180 (56.8%) and 17 (5.45%) responded with 'often' and 'normal', there were 3 (0.9%) who rated 'very often'. The items regarding the interviews i.e. *interview with parent, interview with regular teacher* and *interview with LD student* were theoretically summarized by computing their means. Hence the method *'interviews'* here represents the interview with parent, regular teacher and student with

LD. As shown in Table 5.5, there were two significant predictors positively predicting the use of *interviews* by special education teachers; "personality" and "family" as responsible for LD; 11.7% of the variance was accounted for (p< 0.05, Adjusted R Square= 0.117, personality factor B= 0.085, S.E= 0.027, std. Beta = 0.201, t= 3.093, p= 0.002, family factor B= 0.084, S.E= 0.028, std. Beta = 0.206, t= 3.004, p= 0.003; Table B 5.7, Appendix B). Their impact on the dependent variable can be labeled as being of the same strength (for std. Beta, Table B 5.7, Appendix B). The autocorrelation of residuals is acceptable as for it is from 1.5 to 2.5 (e.g. Backhaus, Erichson, Plinke, & Weiber, 2003) although it is not given directly (for Durbin Watson test= 1.556, Table B 5.7, Appendix B). The Anova test for the overall model supported the assumption that the model significantly predicts the dependent variables (for F=8.783, df= 4, p< 0.001, 0.05, Table B 5.7, Appendix B) although the Beta confident intervals of the two significant predictors show a large range and therefore the estimation of coefficient may not be highly exact, it is assured that the intervals do not include zero (Table B 5.7, Appendix B).

Table 5.5   Predicted logit of interviews

Predicted logit of (*Interviews*) = Z
Z = 3.583 +(0.085)* "personality" +(0.084)* "family"

For each score of response increase on "personality" and "family", the odds of (*interviews*) being used increase from 0 to 0.085 and from 0 to 0.084 (for un std. Beta, Table B 5.7, Appendix B). Given the same score of response on "personality" (e.g. agree), a special education teacher who responded with 'strongly agree' on "family" is 0.084 times (8%) more likely to use the *interviews* than one who responded with 'agree', as well as the "personality" (0.085 times, 8%).

5.2.2 Hypothesis 2.2

Special education teachers' use of *standardized tests* to gather students' information in the LD assessment is related to their perceived causal factors of LD.

Out of 240 respondents, 39 (12.3%) reported 'not often' using the *standardized test* whereas 161 (50.8%) and 40 (12.6%) reported 'often' and 'very often' using it in the LD assessment in order to gather information on the student with LD. According to the model, as shown in Table 5.6, the log of the odds of *"standardized test"* being used by special education teachers in the LD assessment was negatively correlated with "personality" (B= -0.283, S.E= 0.052, std. Beta = -0.310, t= -5.426, p= 0.000), but positively correlated with both "cognitive" (B= 0.242, S.E= 0.071, std. Beta = 0.198, t= 3.406, p= 0.001) and "family" (B= 0.328, S.E= 0.053, std. Beta= 0.372, t= 6.191, p= 0.000) (Table B 5.5, Appendix B).

Table 5.6   Predicted logit of standardized test

Predicted logit of (*Standardized test*) = Z
Z = 3.810 −(0.283)* "personality" +(0.242)* "cognitive" +(0.328)* "family"

Thus, special education teachers who tend to perceive the student's "personality" factor as the main cause of LD, used *standardized tests* less often. On the contrary, those who tend to perceive students' "cognitive" and "family" factors as the main cause of LD, used standardized tests more often. 30.8% of the variance was accounted for (for Model summary, Adjusted R Square= 0.308, Table B 5.5, Appendix B). In addition, "family" appeared to be the strongest predictor followed by the student's "personality" with a slight difference regarding the impact on the use of standardized tests. The "cognitive" appeared to be the weakest among the three predictors. (for std. Beta, Table B 5.5, Appendix B). The data showed that the more the student's "personality" (was perceived by special education teachers as the main cause of LD), the lesser (28.3%) the standardized tests (were used by them), when the score of other predictors (i.e. "cognitive" and "family") was held constant. It may be suggested that the more the "family" (was perceived by special education teachers as the main cause of LD), the more (32.8%) standardized tests (were used by them), given the same score of response on students' "personality" and "cognitive" aspects.

5.2.3 Hypothesis 2.3

Special education teachers' *observation in regular classroom* to gather students' information in the LD assessment is related to their perceived causal factors of LD.

Out of 240 respondents, 115 (36.3%) responded with 'not often' to do *observation in regular classroom*, whereas 37 (11.7%) and 40 (12.6%) rated 'normal' and 'often', and 48 (15.1%) rated 'very often'. As shown in Table 5.7, "teacher-school" and "cognitive" were negatively predicting *observation in regular classroom* whereas "personality" was positively predicting. 13.0% of the variance was accounted for (teacher-school factor B= -0.559, S.E= 0.106, std. Beta = -0.357, t= -5.295, p= 0.000, cognitive factor B= -0.291, S.E= 0.108, std. Beta = -0.176, t= -2.702, p= 0.007, personality factor B= 0.182, S.E= 0.079, std. Beta = 0.148, t= 2.309, p= 0.022, Adjusted R Square= 0.130; Table B 5.6, Appendix B). *Observation in regular classroom* was highly predictive by "teacher school" (for std. Beta, Table B 5.6, Appendix B). The main variable of *observation in regular classroom* was to what extent special education teachers perceive the "teacher school" factor as the main cause of LD. For the increase of each score of response (strongly disagree= 1; strongly agree= 5) on "teacher school" and "cognitive", the odds of *observation in regular classroom* being used by special education teachers decrease from 1.0 to 0.559 (55.9%) and 1.0 to 0.291 (29.1%) (for un std. Beta, Table B 5.6, Appendix B).

Table 5.7 Predicted logit of observation in regular classroom

Predicted logit of (*observation in regular classroom*) = Z
Z = 3.102 −(0.559)* "teacher school" +(0.182)* "personality" −(0.291)*"cognitive"

Although less predictive, when other predictors were held as constant, the model shows that special education teachers who tend to perceive the students' "personality" factor as the main cause of LD, performed *observation in regular classroom* more often.

5.2.4 Hypothesis 2.4

Special education teachers' use of *error pattern analysis* ('*look at error patterns in students' work*) in order to gather students' information in the LD assessment is related to their perceived causal factors of LD.

Out of 240 respondents, 68 (21.5%) answered 'not often' to *look at patterns of errors in students' work*. There were even 4 (1.3%) who responded with 'not at all'. 69 (21.8%) and 99 (31.2%) responded with 'normal' and 'often' to check*students' error patterns*.

Table 5.8 Predicted logit of error pattern analysis

Predicted logit of (*error pattern analysis*) = Z
Z = 3.181 +(0.186)* "personality" +(0.450)* "cognitive" +(0.125)* "family"

According to the model shown in Table 5.8, the students' "personality", "cognitive" and "family" proved as significant predictors positively predicting the method *error pattern analysis in students' work*. 25.3% of the variance was accounted for ($p < 0.05$, Adjusted R Square= 0.253, personality factor B= 0.186, S.E= 0.053, std. Beta= 0.209, t= 3.528, p=0.001, cognitive factor B= 0.450, S.E= 0.072, std. Beta= 0.377, t= 6.239, p= 0.000, family factor B= 0.125, S.E= 0.054, std. Beta= 0.146, t= 2.334, p= 0.020; Table B 5.8, Appendix B). It was highly predictive of "cognitive", the strongest predictor, followed by "personality" and "family" in order of their strength. When other predictors (i.e. "personality" and "family") were held constant, it may be suggested that the more "cognitive" factor (was perceived by special education teachers as the main cause of LD), the more often (45%) the *error patterns analysis* (was used by them).

5.2.5 Hypothesis 2.5

Special education teachers' use of alternative assessment methods such as *curriculum based assessment (CBA), dynamic assessment (test-train/intervention-retest)* and *learning style assessment* to gather students' information in the LD assessment is related to their perceived causal factors of LD.

The items regarding the *CBA, dynamic assessment (test-train/intervention-retest) and learning style assessment* were theoretically summarized by computing their means. Thus, the *alternative assessment methods* here represent these methods mentioned above. Out of 240 respondents, 111 (35%) reported 'not often' using *CBA* while 45 (14.2%) and 84 (26.5%) 'normally' and 'often'. Regarding the *dynamic assessment (test-train/intervention-retest)*, 219 (69.1%) reported 'not at all' using the method whereas 20 (6.3%) reported 'not often' and only 1 (0.3%) rated 'often'. Similarly, 111 (35%) answered 'not at all' to use the *learning style assessment* and 82 (25.9%) 'not often', 25 (7.9%) and 22 (6.9%) rated that they use this method 'normally' and 'often'.

According to the model, as shown in Table 5.9, the student's "personality" and "family" proved as significant predictors negatively predicting the use of *alternative assessment methods* whereas the "cognitive" was positively predicting the use of *alternative assessment methods* ($p < 0.05$, personality factor B= -0.251, S.E= 0.033, std. Beta = -0.437, t= -7.522, p= 0.000, family factor B= -0.130, S.E= 0.034, std. Beta = -0.234, t= -3.831, p= 0.000 cognitive factor, B= 0.318, S.E= 0.046, std. Beta = 0.411, t= 6.969, p= 0.000; Table 4.5, Appendix B). The model summary shows that the resulting regression model predicts 28.5% of the variance of the dependent variable (for Adjusted R Square= 0.285; Table B 5.9, Appendix B).

Table 5.9   Predicted logit of alternative assessment methods

Predicted logit of (*alternative assessment methods*) = Z Z = 1.973 −(0.251)* "personality" +(0.318)* "cognitive"   −(0.130)* "family"

Special education teachers' use of the *alternative assessment methods* was highly predictive of both "personality" and "cognitive" although the "personality" was slightly stronger than the "cognitive" and therefore, the strongest predictor. For the increase of each score of response (strongly disagree=1; strongly agree=5) on "personality" and "cognitive", the odds of *alternative assessment methods* being used by special education teachers decrease from 1.0 to 0.251 (25.1%) and increase from 0.0 to 0.130 (13.0%) (un std. Beta, Table B5.9, Appendix B).

5.3 RESEARCH QUESTION 3 AND HYPOTHESIS

Research Question 3: Do special education teachers' self-competences to use assessment methods differ in their frequency of use?

5.3.1 HYPOTHESIS

Are there any relationships between special education teachers' *self-competence* to use a particular assessment method and their frequency of use?

The results show that the following assessment methods were proved to be significant and positively correlating with special education teachers' *self-competence* (Spearman correlation, $p < 0.01, 0.05$; Table B 5.13, Appendix B): interview with regular teachers, (Spearman's roh= 0.213), error patterns analysis in students' work (Spearman's roh= 0.301), regular and special education teacher team approach (Spearman's roh= 0.278), CBA (Spearman's roh= 0.224), dynamic assessment (test-train/intervention-retest) (Spearman's roh= 0.366, alternative methods Spearman's roh= 0.129). Hence, special education teachers who generally rated themselves to be competent systematically reported more often to interview with regular teachers and more often to look at patterns of errors in students' work. Likewise, those who felt themselves competent rated more often to use regular and special education teacher team approach, CBA, dynamic assessment (test-train/intervention-retest) and vice versa (that is, those who ascribed themselves little competent were less often using the methods above).

5.3.2 DESCRIPTIVE STATISTICS: COLLABORATION SITUATION

The collaboration situation when interpreting the assessment results of students with LDs in regular (primary) school setting was reported from the special education teachers' perspective (Table B 5.14, Appendix B). In general, most special education teachers reported that they 'often' discuss assessment results with parents, related to a possible family situation that may contribute to students' academic problems (mean=4.35), and also that they 'often' check assessment results which appear to be contradictory (mean=3.94). Special education teachers rated nearly 'often' to discuss with regular teachers about the classroom environment (mean= 3.63), however 'not often' regarding the teaching method (mean= 2.32), general curriculum modification (mean= 1.78) and assessment method (mean= 1.73). Similarly, special education teachers rated 'not often' or lesser than 'not often' to discuss with their principal about the results of work on students' academic problems (mean= 1.80) or likewise with other special educational personnel on students' problems. According to special education teachers, they have 'not often' or even 'not at all' (mean=1.71, min.= 1, max.= 2) joint meetings which are prepared in the form of a written report or an oral presentation.

Part V.

Discussion and Conclusion

6

RESEARCH FINDINGS AND DISCUSSION

In section 6.1 and 6.2, this chapter accumulates the findings that have emerged from the quantitative analysis in the previous chapter. By summarizing the important findings, section 6.3 discusses the relationships between the current findings and those of earlier studies relevant to teachers' perception of LD and teachers' attribution of student learning failure. Further discussion and conclusions regarding major research issues in the field of LD is contained in Chapter 7.

6.1 SUMMARY OF FINDINGS

The main purpose of this study was to explore the relationship (for regression cf. Ch. 4.2.2) between what special education teachers perceive as the main causes of LD and the ways in which they assess students with LDs and define LD (Figure 4.4). The findings suggested that special education teachers' use of assessment methods and definitions of LD differed according to what they perceived as the main causes of LD (Table 6.1). This section focuses on what factors (and considerations) regarding the causes of LD – perceived by special education teachers – were given priority in these decisions. As previously mentioned, there was empirical support for the assumption of distinct dimensions within the causal factors of LD (for preparation of the causal factors cf. Ch. 4.2.1.3, Table 4.4). Four causal factors of LD were determined throughout this study: student's "cognitive ability", "personality", "teacher-school" and "family" factors. See also section 6.3 for an in-depth discussion of the causal factors of LD with regard to the previous findings.

Table 6.1   Overview of findings

Teacher-school factor
Special education teachers who tended to perceive the "teacher-school factor" as the main cause of LD
– were less likely to include 'normal or above average intelligence' (intelligence component) and 'central nervous system dysfunction' (CNS dysfunction) in their definition of LD;
– were more likely to apply the exclusion clause ('it is not the direct results of environmental, cultural, economic influences') on LD;
– performed observation in regular classroom less often when assessing students with LDs.

Student's personality factor
Special education teachers who tended to perceive the student's "personality factor" as the main cause of LD
– and the higher the grade levels taught (i.e. 4th-6th grade), were less likely to include the intelligence component and 'disorder in basic psychological processes' (process disorder) in their definition of LD;
– were less likely to apply the exclusion clause on LD;
– used interviews [1], observation in regular class room and error pattern analyses in students' work more often;
– used standardized tests and alternative assessment methods [2] less often.

Student's cognitive ability factor
Special education teachers who tended to perceive the student's "cognitive (ability) factor" as the main cause of LD
– were more likely to include CNS dysfunction in their definition of LD;
– used alternative assessment methods, standardized tests and error pattern analyses in students' work more often.

---

[1]   cf. Ch. 5: The items regarding the interviews were theoretically summarized by computing their means. The interview methods here represent the interviews with regular teacher, parent and student with LD.
[2]   cf. Ch. 5: The items regarding the alternative items were theoretically summarized by computing their means. The alternative (assessment) methods represent CBA, dynamic assessment and learning style assessment.

6.1 SUMMARY OF FINDINGS

Family factor
Special education teachers who tended to perceive the student's "family factor" as the main cause of LD
– were less likely to apply the exclusion clause on LD;
– were more likely to include CNS dysfunction in their definition of LD;
– and the longer their years of teaching experience (i.e. over 5 but under 10 years), were more likely to include process disorder in their definition of LD;
– used interviews, standardized tests and error pattern analyses in students' work more often.

Table 6.2 Summary of findings

Definition components of LD		Causal factors of LD	Assessment methods	
Less	Intelligence	*Teacher-school factors*	Less	Regular classroom observation
More	Exclusion clause			
Less	CNS dysfunction			
Less	Intelligence	*Personality factors*	Less	Standardized tests
Less	Exclusion clause		More	Regular classroom observation
Less	Process disorder		More	Interviews *[with regular teacher, parent, student with LD]*
			More	Error patterns analysis
			Less	Alternative method *[CBA, Dynamic, Learning style assessment]*
More	CNS dysfunction	*Cognitive factors*	More	Standardized tests
			Less	Regular classroom observation
			More	Error patterns analysis
			More	Alternative method
Less	Exclusion clause	*Family factors*	More	Standardized tests
More	CNS dysfunction		More	Interviews
More	Process disorder		More	Error patterns analysis
			Less	Alternative method

Table 6.3   Descriptive summary of findings

Assessment methods
– In order to gather information on students with LDs and their performance, Korean special education teachers in regular primary schools generally preferred to use standardized tests, interviews with regular teachers and the students with LD.
– In comparison, interviews with parents were reported to be used only occasionally.
– Regular classroom observation and error pattern analyses of students' work were also reported to be used occasionally.
– Alternative assessment such as CBA, which is generally time consuming and requires professional collaboration with regular teachers, were reported to be rarely used, whereas dynamic assessment (test-train/intervention-retest) and learning style assessment were used considerably less frequently (for more detail cf. Ch. 5).

Definition of LD
– There appeared to be general consensus among Korean special education teachers that 'having LD' exhibits (a) academic learning problems, (b) discrepancy between intellectual ability and academic achievement and that (c) LD is not the direct result of other handicapping conditions.
– On the other hand, there were some disagreements among them as to whether 'LD' should include the intelligence component (i.e. normal or above average intelligence) or the 'exclusion clause', and also whether LDs exhibit CNS dysfunction or basic psychological process disorder.

Self-competence
– Particularly those who used less dynamic assessment, CBA, interviews with regular teachers and error pattern analyses of students' work appeared to have 'low self-competence' in using these and vice versa.

Collaboration situation
– Special education teachers demonstrated that collaboration had not been run successfully. Particularly, when they were asked about the collaboration situation in interpreting the students' assessment results, the answer often suggested insufficient collaboration with regular teachers concerning the accommodation/modification of the general curriculum, instruction and evaluation.
– Instead, special education teachers seemed to tend to cope with the parents alone or to settle the matter by themselves when dealing with students' assessment results.
– Discussion with principals or other personnel on students' problems were rarely carried out, as were joint meetings in any form (written report or oral presentation).

6.2 COMPARISON WITH FINDINGS FROM PREVIOUS STUDIES

What causes some students to experience difficulties in learning at school? The reasons why children fail are complex, as there are many factors that cause or exacerbate problems in learning (Westwood, 2004, 53; see also Daly, Martens, & Dool, 1997). Accordingly, there are many theories concerning the factors that may lead to LDs. Which factors do teachers perceive as the main causes of LD? The focal point of this study was the examination of Korean special education teachers' perception of the causes of LD. The current literature on attribution theory (cf. Ch. 3) provides adequate evidence to suggest that teachers' beliefs and perceptions of the causes of students' success and failure are important, since these influence students (own attributions, e.g. motivation) through teacher behavior (e.g. Fennema et al., 1990). In fact, it is rare that a single cause can explain why the student fails to learn, as many different factors contribute to a learning problem: there are factors within the student or the student's background, within the learning environment or the teaching approach, and such related to the teacher-student relationship (Westwood, 2000, 26f.).

It should be mentioned that there was empirical support for the assumption of distinct dimensions within the causal factors of LD (cf. Ch. 4.2.1.3, Table 4.4), and, accordingly, the factors that possibly cause LD were confined to the data provided by special education teachers in this study. The causal factors of LD, divided into four distinct aspects (student's "cognitive ability", "personality", "teacher-school" and "family") basically fall into two major categories; that is, individual and environmental variables[3] which should be taken into account throughout the academic

---

[3] cf. Hooper et al. (1994, 384): Endogenous variables (e.g. personality, genetics, social-emotional

achievement assessment of students with LDs (Hooper et al., 1994, 383f.). Moreover, the analysis of the results indicated that the causal factors of LD perceived by Korean special education teachers were similar to factors mentioned as important in other studies on teachers' perception of LD (e.g. Kataoka et al., 2004; Project Team, 2000 as cited in Kataoka et al., 2004) and teacher attribution for student failure (e.g. Georgiou et al., 2002; Brand, Hayden, & Brophy, 1975; Tollefson et al., 1990). For example, Georgiou et al. (2002, 586) suggested that factors such as "child ability", "child effort", "teacher effect" and "family characteristics" constitute teachers' attributions of student school failure and influence teachers' behavior towards low-achieving students.

The causal factor for which there was most support as contributing to LD by Korean special education teachers was the "teacher-school factor"[4] (teacher-related aspects at school). This finding is consistent with the existing research of Kataoka et al. (2004, 170f.). They examined educators' perceptions of the causes of LD and concluded that both principals and teachers perceived that "teachers' situations" were a cause of LD. They argued that the teachers' situation associated with teaching meant that students had greater difficulty with learning; thus limitations in the effectiveness of classroom teaching were seen as important causes of LD. Similarly, in a survey about teachers' perceptions of teaching students with LDs (Project Team, 2000 as cited in Kataoka et al. 2004, 164), the most important needs teachers perceived for teaching students with LDs were "teaching skills, teachers' professional development, classroom management, team teaching, a cooperative system in school, and parents' understanding/ cooperation". Thus, similar to the current findings, although the Japanese definition of LD[5] (Kataoka et al., 2004, 171) referred to factors within the individual, Japanese teachers often considered teaching skills one of the main causes of LD. Korean special education teachers did likewise, from which can be inferred that they assume heavy responsibilities for academic progress at school for students with LDs. In this context, it should be mentioned that, in Korea, education is highly valued by parents, who invest considerable resources and efforts in providing their children with the best education opportunities. Much pressure on school achievement is exerted on children, and academic success is connected to the social elevation aspirations of the

---

characteristics, neuropsychological functions), exogenous variables (e.g. family, school, teacher characteristics, classroom environment, socio-economic status) and instrument variables (e.g. reliability, validity).

[4] The teacher-school factor mainly explained the aspects concerning teaching method, assessment method, special education teacher-regular teacher cooperation, special education teacher-parent cooperation, special education teachers' professional knowledge, regular teachers' understanding of LD, social/physical classroom environment, teacher-student relationship (cf. Ch. 3).

[5] The definition of LD used in Japan excludes environmental factors (e.g. familial or social aspects) as possible causes of students' difficulties (Committee on Guidance/Education Planning for Children with Learning Disabilities, 1999 as cited in Kataoka et al. 2004, 171f.).

family. In this framework, Korean teachers focus relatively strongly on the transmission of knowledge, and their main purpose is to lead their students to high academic performance. Moreover, the renewed emphasis on educational policy in Korea (highly qualified teachers) has enforced the enhancement of special education service through the improvement of teaching and the quality of school instruction; hence the professional development of special education teachers (MOE & HRD, 2006a). Within these situations, concerning the social and political influences on education in Korea, special education teachers are required to endorse the role and responsibility of inclusion facilitators [6] in regular schools. Special education teachers would have to think that they should be able to provide appropriate education for students with LDs and thereby achieve successful inclusion. Successful inclusion of students with LDs largely depends on special education teachers' perceptions of LD, on their views on differences in classrooms and on their willingness to handle these differences effectively (European Agency for Development in Special Needs Education, 2003). On the other hand, cross-cultural comparisons suggested that different societies emphasize factors as parameters of achievement differently, for instance concerning ability and effort, as, in an educational setting, ability and effort are two major internal sources (Georgiou et al., 2002, 583). Results of Westwood (1995) and other previous studies (e.g. Clark, 1997; Simmons, Kameenui, & Chard, 1998; Cheng, 1998, see also Dunbar, 1988; Allington, 1991a, 1993; Allington & McGill-Franzen, 1989) differ somewhat from current findings. For instance, Westwood (1995, 19f.) reported that Australian teachers maintained by 62% that the causes of LD lay within the students, while family background or culture were maintained by 14% and factors within the curriculum by 8% of the sample. Likewise, Simmons et al. (1998, 6ff.) found that teachers consider internal variables as the primary (50%) factor contributing to LD, compared to other variables such as the quality of instructional materials (9%) or teacher delivery (25%). Moreover, in a cross-nation study of teacher attributions of LD, Clark & Artiles (2000, 77f.) found that teachers tend to consider LD as internal and uncontrollable rather than as something on which they can have an impact. According to Clark (1997, 69f.), the locus of causality refers to whether the teacher perceives a cause as occurring within the student (internal) or in the student's surroundings (external). Referring to Weiner [7] (1985, 548ff.) (cf. Ch. 3), the "teacher-school factor" and the "family

---

[6] Ferguson, Meyer, Jeanchild, Juniper, & Zingo (1992): inclusion facilitator is who serves as an adaptor who develop and suggest accommodation, and a collaborator who work closely with other teachers and personnel both inside and outside the school (as cited in Bauer, Keefe, & Shea, 2001, 342).

[7] Cf. Weiner's theory of attributions (1985): causal factors accounting for one's success or failure can be classified along three dimensions; that is, locus of control (external versus internal), stability (stable versus unstable), and controllability (controllable versus uncontrollable). Teachers' attributions of student's learning failure can be internal or external in terms of its locus, stable or unstable in terms of its stability over time, and controllable or uncontrollable by the acting individual (teach-

factor" are external in terms of its locus. The first is unstable and controllable, while the second is stable and uncontrollable in terms of its stability over time and by the acting individual (e.g. teacher). Hence, those who were inclined to perceive external variables as the main causes of LD may preferably attribute an external locus of control to LD, whereas those who were inclined to perceive individual variables as main causes of LD might be considered to have an internal locus of control.

When teachers believe that they have some control over the students' learning, they consequently feel more responsible to make sure that the student learns (Guskey, 1982, 70f.). Moreover, when teachers believe that the problem is beyond the student's control, they are more likely to instruct, advise, socialize and seek help (Brophy, 1985, 175ff.). The environmental factor over which teachers have most control is the teaching method, whereas teachers have little control over students' socio-economic background, such as poverty (Westwood, 2004, 55). It was therefore assumed that special education teachers who tended towards the "teacher-school" factor expressed more commitment or willingness to help the student than others who tended towards the "family", "cognitive ability" and "personality" factors. This is stringent because special education teachers who perceived students' learning failure as uncontrollable were supposed to attribute students' achievement to their own teaching performance and to be more willing to take responsibility for students' learning failure than if the causes of failure were believed to be controllable. As described in Table 6.1 and 6.2, special education teachers who tended towards the "teacher-school factor" were more likely to apply the exclusion clause and were less likely to include the intelligence component and CNS dysfunction in their definition of LD. This implies that they seemed inclined to restrict (or exclude) the influence of students' socio-economic background or cognitive factors such as intelligence and CNS dysfunction as causes of LD. They did not blame the 'victim'. Instead, they may believe that some causes of LD were linked to teacher-related aspects in school. In contrast, for instance, those who tended towards the 'family factor' seemed to perceive 'having LD' as a negative consequence of environmental and social influences. They assumed that LD is linked to neurological matters which may stem from parents (and are thus genetic), but may also be exacerbated by socio-economic disadvantages. While there have recently been some assumptions about genetic influences on LD (e.g. Grigorenko, 2001; Lyon, Fletcher, & Barnes, 2003), several studies over a number of years have argued that many students from families with lower socio-economic background display lower academic achievement and more behavioral problems at school (e.g. McLoyd, 1998; Ormrod, 2003) (for more details refer to Ch. 3).

---

ers) in terms of its controllability.

However, regarding their assessment practice, Korean special education teachers who tended towards the 'teacher-school factor' appeared not to use various assessment methods; particularly, they used 'regular classroom observation' less frequently compared to other teacher groups in the survey. (Whereas others appeared to use assessment methods depending on the perceptions they held about LD, the former did not indicate any assessment pattern – except that they carried out less regular classroom observation). This contrasts the fact that 'regular classroom observation' is an integral part of assessment in regular school settings, and was one of the methods reported to be used occasionally by special education teachers according to the descriptive statistics (Table 6.3). Issues related to Korean special education teachers' assessment practice and definition of LD will be further discussed in Chapter 7. The results also revealed that these teachers mentioned above were not one of the groups who described themselves as 'competent' in using the assessment methods they reported. Other groups of special education teachers had, at any rate, three assessment methods for which they felt competent, and consequently used them more frequently. This seems not entirely unrelated to the collaboration situation in regular school settings (as described in Table 6.3 below), in which special education teachers demonstrated that there is often insufficient collaboration with regular teachers. Korean special education teachers' perception of LD, and therewith their behavior towards students with LDs, are influenced by environmental demands and constraints [8] within the educational domain [9] concerning the current educational tendencies, policies and mandates. It may be suggested that social demands are an external factor which increases or limits the controllability of the environment and thus influences the degree of effort, self-motivation and assumption of responsibility a teacher assumes within the classroom. In Chapter 3, it was mentioned that each of the social learning theories of Weiner, Ajzen & Fishbein and Bandura conveys the message that an individual's perception is influenced by personal experience and her or his environment. The present study assumes that, referring to Bandura's social cognitive theory, individuals (special education teachers) respond to their environment based on their concept of themselves, through the use of their cognitive processes and their perceived causes of behavior. Moreover, it might be concluded that, according to Weiner's attribution theory, teachers' beliefs, perceptions and expectations motivate and control their behavior. Hence special education teachers' controllability of their environment may enhance their perceived abilities and may have an impact on their perception of students with LDs. The perceived behavior control of teachers becomes the link between an individual's perception of how the task will have to be performed and

---

[8] e.g. Ajzen & Fishbein, 1980; Ajzen, 1996; Chatzisarantis & Biddle, 1998; see also Allington, 1986, 1991b.

[9] e.g. Norwich & Rovoli, 1993; Norwich, 1994.

the social pressure to perform. In addition, the degree of teachers' perception of their own effectiveness (e.g. self-competence in using the assessment methods, cf. Ch. 5) is not only likely to affect how much effort they will expend and how long they will persist in facing obstacles and aversive circumstances, but is also likely to determine whether they will even initiate the coping behavior. In addition, it has been underlined that people with high control construct more effective action plans and exerts sustained effort in their enactment (Skinner, 1995, 72). Such a level of internal control can serve as a basis to develop awareness in special education teachers, who will thus be more willing and confident to examine how the teacher-school factor may contribute to LD.

Conclusively, Korean special education teachers in regular school settings need to be encouraged and supported by all available means, particularly to work effectively as collaborators who take their leadership role seriously and work closely with regular teachers and other personnel. This need was supported by the findings which indicated the following most significant points: (a) even though the teacher related school aspect was the factor supported most strongly (cf. Ch. 5) as contributing to LD among Korean special education teachers, those who perceived the teacher-school factor as a main cause of LD contradictorily appeared to use least assessment methods; (b) Korean special education teachers demonstrated an overall insufficient collaboration in the assessment of LD, particularly concerning the collaboration with regular teachers, both in collecting information on students and in interpreting the assessment data; (c) alternative assessment methods which are time-consuming and require professional collaboration were very rarely used in special education teachers' assessment practice, which may be associated with these teachers' self-competence.

7

CONCLUSION AND PRACTICAL IMPLICATION

Just like every child has a right to a good education, every teacher has a right to a good education.

In the previous chapter, we discussed the research findings and findings from previous studies. The survey confirmed findings from previous studies that teachers' causal perception of LD are linked with their assessment practice and affect the way they define LD. In this chapter, we argue that there are many questions about the concept of LD that remain unanswered, and by describing the major findings of this study, we focuses on current issues that need to be addressed. The results of this study revealed three major issues:

(a) The need to rethink the Korean concept of LD within a broader perspective. Particularly, this chapter presents a brief discussion of the German and the US concept of LD (in KMK and IDEA)[1] which may carry implications for Korea;
(b) the urgent need for a clear formal definition of LD, which serves to be accepted by practitioners and which can provide a framework for LD assessment to guide practice;
(c) the need for reform in special education teacher preparation programs, particularly the need for a national framework of standards of quality and effectiveness for teacher preparation at both the pre-service and the in-service level.

Finally, this chapter contains limitations and suggestions for further research.

---

[1] Ch. 3.1.2.3: cf. ICD-10 (International Statistical Classification of Diseases and Related Health Problems. Tenth Revision), Recommendations of KMK (*Empfehlungen zur sonderpädagogischen Förderung in den Schulen der Bundesrepublik Deutschland von der Ständigen Konferenz der Kultusminister der Länder*) in Germany, and IDEA (Individuals with Disabilities Education Act) in U.S.

7.1 Rethinking the Korean Concept of Learning Disability: The Need for a Broader Perspective

Learning disabilities research and practice in Korea, and especially its implementation of inclusive practices and teacher education, have a relatively short history compared to other disability categories such as hearing or visual impairments (cf. Ch. 2). During the past 15 years, the field of LD in Korea has progressed rapidly in the context of inclusive education[2]. Still, while the quantitative growth remains impressive, the quality of education remains a major concern. The most urgent problem in Korea is that there is no commonly accepted operational definition of LD and no unified scheme for identifying which children are eligible for special education service in the category of LD. This issue is not new, and it has plagued the Korean field of LD since LD was as a category of special education defined in the law (cf. Ch. 2). Hence there is a need for consensus on a formal definition of LD that meets the criteria of significance and meaningfulness[3], which are indispensable for a valid operational definition.

GERMAN (KMK) AND US (IDEA) CONCEPTS OF LD

At this point, rethinking the Korean concept of LD is of great importance, considering that many researchers have as yet mainly introduced and cited the IDEA (US) definition of LD in Korea (Kang JG, Kim JH, & Foley, 2004, 293). As previously outlined in chapter 3, the German (KMK) and US (IDEA) concepts of LD and their definition and identification contexts display some major differences which may allow for inferences regarding the Korean construction of LD. The KMK focuses on individuals' ecological aspects of learning (*"Unter Lernen soll vor allem eine selbstständige und entwicklungsfördernde Auseinandersetzung des Kindes und Jugendlichen mit seiner Umwelt verstanden werden"*, Schlichting & Schulz, 2000, 317) and the living environment (*"Kind-Umfeld-Analyse/Diagnose"*,

---

[2] cf. Ch.2.3.2.2: Until now, special education was free and compulsory in primary and middle schools, while it was free in kindergartens and high schools. As from May 26th, 2008, it became compulsory in Kindergarten and high school, too. Special education is provided in one or a combination of the following forms across school levels: regular classroom at regular school, special classroom at regular school, special school (cf. IDSEA Ch. 3, Article 17). Most of the students with LD are taught in special classrooms. Special classrooms run on either full-time or part-time basis, and the special educational service is provided by special education teachers.
[3] Significance: authoritative marker of the concept, meaningfulness: rational and logical marker of the concept (Bergmann, 1961, 41f.)

Bundschuh, 2005[4], 324) within the scope of SNE[5]. While the definition of LD in IDEA is referred to as SpLD, which articulates the presence of disorder in basic psychological processes and adds other included disorders (e.g. perceptual disabilities) and declares the exclusion clause[6] at the same time. The crucial aspect which supposedly holds implications for Korea and distinguishes Germany from the US and Korea is that Germany turned to focus more on the students' learning process and learning environment from an instructional perspective, rather than to sort and identify deficiencies within the student. The *Deutscher Bildungsrat* (1973) (as cited in Eberwein, 1997, 16) suggested to consider the causes of LD to not only be arising from the student personally, but to also be associated to the school situation, the school curriculum and the interaction of teachers and peers. Nevertheless, it should be mentioned that there was also a time when the classic definition of LD in earlier German theory (Hofsäss, 1993, 119, see also, Opp, 1994; Werning & Luetje-klose, 2003) – which was similar to the US concept of SpLD – was criticized for its tendency to define LD objectively, and to identify specific characteristics of individuals without considering the individual interaction in an environmental and social context. Referring to the current assessment system in Germany, the regular teacher generally enrolls the student suspected to have LD for the relevant special school for LD (*Sonder-/Förderschule für Lernbehinderte*) at the end of the school year (Prücher & Langenfeldt, 2002, 401). During the period called *Diagnostikwoche* (diagnostic week), the assessment process is undertaken by the special education teacher as well as the *Diagnostiklehrer* (expert teacher) of the special school for LD. Unlike Korea[7], the student suspected of having LD can be assessed within a small group of other pupils of the same age with comparable difficulties in special schools for LD (*Schulen für Lernbehinderte, Förderschulen* or *Förderschule zur Lernföderung*) and/or within the class in which special education service and relevant support will be provided (at regular/special schools).

---

[4] "*Die Kind-Umfeld-Analyse grenzt sich ab von einer einseitig kind-zentrierten Diagnostik, die auf der Grundlage von Testverfahren, ergänzt durch mehr oder weniger beiläufige Beobachtungen, in einem abschließenden Gutachten die Fähigkeiten und Unfähigkeiten festhält, die ein Kind in Bezug auf die Anforderungen der Schule mitbringt. Die Kind-Umfeld-Analyse (Kind-Umfeld-Diagnose) versteht sich dem gegenüber als wesentlich breiterer Ansatz*" (Bundschuh, 2005, 324-325).

[5] cf. Ch. 3: Special Needs Education means specific support for disabled pupils. With regard to Germany, since the school year 1999/2000, all Länder agreed on a joint definition of SNE. The area of responsibility of SNE in Germany with respect to all organizational aspects refers to special needs within the context of disability exclusively.

[6] cf. Ch. 3: The IDEA definition of SpLD includes an exclusion clause, stating that "such term (SpLD) does not include a learning problem that is primarily the result of visual, hearing, or motor disabilities, of mental retardation, of emotional disturbance, or of environmental cultural, or economic disadvantage" (Public Law 108-446 Status TITLE 1/A/602/30).

[7] cf. Ch. 2: i.e. besides the Special Education Support Center (according to the revision of the SEPA which will take effect on May 26th, 2008) or, as previously mentioned, mainly implemented by special education teachers in the regular school settings as before.

This is called *probeweise Unterrichtung* – the student is assessed during the instruction process, according to his/her individual circumstances. This is supposed to be undertaken for a maximum of two weeks or, with the parents' consent, up to a maximum of twelve weeks (Sächsisches Staatsministerium für Kultus, 2005, 47). In Germany, special education teachers primarily hold responsible for the assessment process, as they provide the expert opinion (in a written report) i.e. the *Sonder-/Förderpädagogisches Gutachten*, on the student's educational placement either in regular school or in a special school for LD (Sächsisches Staatsministerium für Kultus, 2005, 115, see also "*Pädagogische-psychologische Gutachten*", Hofsäss, 1993, 172, Bundschuh, 2005). On the other hand, in Korea, the identification decisions have been stipulated by SEPA[8] (Ch. 2. Article 10) to be made by the local committee on special education (or otherwise the national committee on special education under the MOE & HRD), a (so-called) multidisciplinary team similar to those in the US[9]. A number of recent studies have shown (similar to the results of this study) that teacher collaboration and shared decision-making in IEP development for students with SNE and team decision-making in special education placement have proven to be rather inconsistent in some aspects (Cho KS & Hwang IK, 201; see also Kang KS et al., 2000). Similarly, a number of US studies revealed that placement teams (multidisciplinary teams) seldom meet the criteria of effective functionality, and the team members reported they were often unsatisfied with each other (e.g. Yoshida, Fenton, Maxwell, & Kaufman, 1978; Fenton, Yoshida, Maxwell, & Kaufman, 1979). Few teachers endorsed the view that current methods for assessing students with LDs were effective, and most felt that improvements should be put in place (NCLD, 2002). Many of the teachers (and also parents) were negative about the current assessment system (Fletcher, Coulter, Reschly, & Vaughn, 2004, 307).

Across countries, the most fundamental problem the LD field faces remains the definition, i.e. reaching a consensus on and operationalizing the definition of LD. Thus, choosing the appropriate definition and criteria for LD eligibility is one of the most commonly debated tasks in the field of special education (e.g. Kavale et al., 2005; Proctor & Prevatt, 2003). But, most importantly, it should not be forgotten that each country has its own cultural background and values based on its unique social, economic and political context. The level of economic development and growth differs from country to country, and these standards impact the decision

---

[8] It should be mentioned that, according to the revision which will take effect on May 26th, 2008 (cf. Ch. 2.3.2.2 and Table 2.2 for the current SEPA and revised version "IDSEA"), the Special Education Support Center will conduct the assessment process of students with SEN. The Statement on Educational Support, implemented by a Special Education Support Center, should be comprised of special education, vocational education and special education related services.

[9] In 1977, the federal register stated that each public agency shall insure that the placement decision is made by a group of persons (Epps, Ysseldyke, & McGue, 1984, 99).

on disability categories, as disability has been diversely defined within particular societies and in any given social context (e.g. Bogdan & Taylor, 1998; Richardson, 1997; Burch & Sutherland, 2005; Oliver, 1989, 1986, 1993; Oliver & Zarb, 1989; Finkelstein, 1993, Swain, 1993). LD is no less socially constructed than other disabilities (e.g. Klotz, 2004; Bogdan & Taylor, 1989; Taylor & Bogdan, 1989). Hence, the national context should be taken into sufficient (appreciative) consideration when deciding 'what LD is'.

The findings from this study indicated the need for a clear operational definition of LD, which will be accepted by teachers (meaning that it will have to include means of practically feasible and useful implementation) and will provide a framework for LD assessment. Particularly, the provision of a formal eligibility guideline, which can serve as practical guide for special education teachers to implement effective assessment (for example, stipulate the procedural guidelines for collaboration in regular school settings) would serve as a good starting point. The following section approaches this issue by discussing the findings of this study and addressing some of the practical considerations that need to be focused on in the Korean context.

WHAT KOREAN SPECIAL EDUCATION TEACHERS THINK WHO STUDENTS WITH LDS ARE AND TO WHAT EXTENT THEY AGREE ON THE MAJOR COMPONENT OF THE CURRENT DEFINITION OF LD

The findings of this study indicated some controversial tendencies among special education teachers towards the exclusion clause [10], which may lead to a reconsideration of the current Korean definition of LD that mostly adopted the SpLD definition from the US. Even though more than one half of the survey respondents reported to be using the exclusion clause for defining LD, a rather alarming percentage (30.6%) indicated that they were rather undecided on whether to use it or not (cf. Ch. 5). The exclusion clause is the most controversial aspect of the current definition of LD (Bauer et al., 2001, 49). Most definitions [11] of LD, particularly the SpLD definitions from the US, have described the exclusion clause, meaning that they exclude children from the LD category whose learning difficulties may primarily be related to environmental, cultural or socio-economic disadvantages. However, these very conditions can place some children at a significant risk for LDs. As mentioned in chapter 1, this study posits that the child's environment (including such as social, cultural and economic factors and each combination of them) can influence the child's development (and even the brain function, as it

---

[10] In the survey, special education teachers were asked about two types of exclusion clause: LD is not the direct result (1) of other handicapping conditions such as visual, hearing, or motor disabilities, of mental retardation, or of emotional disturbance; (2) of environmental, cultural or socio-economic disadvantages". This chapter discusses the latter (2) exclusion clause (cf. Ch. 6, Ch. 5).

[11] cf. IDEA, 1997, 13; Kirk, 1962, 263; Bateman, 1965, 220; NACHC, 1968, 3; LDA, 1986, 15

develops through the interaction of the brain and the environment, including instruction) and thereby affect the child's learning. Particularly, we emphasize the influence of the child's socio-economic background and teachers' instruction and teaching methods. Poor socio-economic conditions are related to a number of factors, all of which can place children at risk for weaker neurological development and for secondary learning difficulties such as cognitive, linguistic and academic deficits (Lyon, Fletcher, Shaywitz, Shaywitz, Torgesen, Wood, Schulte, & Olson, 2001, 268). In fact, several studies over many years have suggested that students' SES background is strongly related to their school achievements (e.g. Cox, 2000; Hilty, 1998; OECD, 2001; McLoyd, 1998; Ormrod, 2003). When looking into practice at schools, many students with LDs come from disadvantaged SES backgrounds or vice versa. The point is that it is important that teachers understand the impact that the student's environment has on her/his ability to learn at school. Only then may teachers recognize (or appreciate) that these students sometimes need more intensive support (including differentiated teaching) over a longer period of time than their peers in order to scoop their potential. This would avoid teachers' low expectation and negative attribution towards these students from disadvantaged backgrounds, which have often been reported in recent studies, and might enhance the teacher internal locus of control; teachers with an internal locus of control are under less stress and more successful in teaching (cf. Ch. 6). The socio-economic disadvantages, particularly extreme poverty, are among the factors over which teachers have little control whereas the environmental factor over which teachers have most control is the teaching method (i.e. instruction). Although there are many students who learn well despite poor learning environments, there are also less fortunate others, some of which are most likely not to catch up with their peers. One exclusion criterion for LD that is particularly difficult to reconcile is the student's instructional history. All definitions of LD exclude children from consideration if their learning difficulties are primarily the result of inadequate instruction. Of all the different assumptions in the concepts of LD, this one is the least examined, yet perhaps the most important (Lyon et al., 2001[12], 268). However, it is clear that a good teacher-student relationship[13] is essential to good learning and, in turn, good teaching (e.g. Batten, Marland, & Khamis, 1993; Hilty, 1998), since the teacher and the student are involved with each other both as

---

[12] Lyon et al. (2001, 268) pointed out that some would interpret this exclusion feature to indicate that children who profit from instruction do not have a biologically based LD. However, according to them, functional imaging studies suggest that in the area of reading this is not so. Instruction may be necessary to establish the neural networks that support reading.

[13] For example, it was argued that one of the ways in which some students with learning problems impede themselves is by failing to seek help from the teacher even though they need it (Altenbaugh, 1998, 52f.). Thus, there needs to be good rapport between teacher and student. It is especially meaningful to question and find out if the student (with learning difficulties) likes the teacher (Ravenette, 1968 as cited in Westwood, 2004, 60).

actors and reactors during the instruction. Therefore, it is essential that teacher and student develop an awareness of each other's perspective, and that teachers reflect on their own beliefs and practices. Studies arguing that insufficient instruction (or inadequate teaching methods) is one of the main causes of LD (e.g. Slavin, 1994; Cohen, 1971, 269, "Dyspedagogia" as a cause for LD) have also supported this insight. In fact, such environmental factors are hard to pinpoint. Several studies have described the extreme difficulty of finding out if students' learning difficulties are a result of their socio-economic disadvantages (e.g. Stein & Merell, 1992; Costerbader & Buntaine, 1999) or a result of other factors (such as behavioral disorders, e.g. Lovitt, 1975; Engelmann, 1977; or a lack of motivation and social skills, e.g. Pavri & Luftig, 2001 [14]). In sum, the issue of socio-economic factors as causes for LD cannot be ignored (Macmillan & Siperstein, 2002, 22). Also, inadequate instruction/teaching methods as an environmental factor should not be exclusionary (Lyon et al., 2001, 282). As Lyon et al. (2001, 268) put it: "[...] many of the conditions excluded as potential influences on LD are themselves factors in impeding the development of cognitive and linguistic skills that lead to the academic deficits frequently observed in LD." Many children and their families could benefit from special education and related services by taking into account those environmental factors, particularly the SES background and instruction/teaching methods. To achieve this will require a reconsideration of the current definitions of LD.

THE NEED FOR A BROADER PERSPECTIVE ON LD

Differentiation between LDs (i.e. 'SpLD') and 'learning difficulties' has always been problematic (Gresham, 2002, 5). As reviewed in chapter 3, the similarities and differences between these two groups have been debated for years among experts and practitioners (e.g. Epps, Ysseldyke, & McGue, 1984; Fuchs, Fuchs, Mathes, & Lipsey, 2002; Kavale, Fuchs, & Scruggs, 1994; Ysseldyke, Algozzine, Shinn, & McGue, 1982). The facts are that, firstly, it is hard to clearly classify 'SpLD' and 'learning difficulty' in real school practice (for example, as mentioned above, the extreme difficulty to determine environmental factors). Secondly, whatever the differences, children in both groups are eligible for special education and related services [15]. Some practical questions may occur here. Are the learning problems exhibited by those students with SpLD and learning difficulties not similar in nature – at least for teachers, considering the instructional implementations? Are

---

[14] For instance, in 1987, the Interagency Committee on Learning Disabilities proposed a modification of the LD definition so as to include social skill deficits as a primary LD (Pavri & Luftig, 2001, 8f.). With respect to this, particularly socio-economic and cultural factors may accelerate these problems (McLoughlin, 1985, 277ff.).

[15] Referring to Shaywitz et al. (1992), using a variety of child-, teacher- and parent-based measures, they found more similarities than differences between SpLD and learning difficulty (low achievers without severe discrepancy) groups, suggesting that both groups could be considered eligible for special education service.

their learning problems not simply located at different points on the same continuum (Kim S, Kim KO, Kim SD, Lee SD, Lim HS, & Han SM, 2001, 33)? Based on the information provided by Korean special education teachers in the study, one may conclude that Korean special education teachers' assumptions about LD fit the concept of 'learning difficulty' rather than that of SpLD. Regardless of the causes of LD (SpLD or learning difficulty), implementation of their assessment method was nearly the same. At this point, it should be mentioned that, recently, there has been a consensus within the field of LD that LD occur with students who have difficulties at school, and that such difficulties are intensively linked to the school itself (e.g. Dudley-Marling, 2001; Reid & Valle, 2004) – that is, the school situation, the school curriculum and the interaction of teachers and peers (e.g. Eberwein, 1997). For most children whose progress in school learning causes concern, the problems are related to their experience and learning history rather than to intrinsic intellectual deficits (Kerschner, 2000, 280). While some learning problems are within the student, it is most unlikely that this is the case with the vast majority; environmental factors are much more frequent causes of learning problems (Westwood, 2004, 55). For the case of inadequate instruction and cultural/socio-economic factors (environmental factors), Lyon et al. (2001, 279) argued that it may just be these factors that lead to inadequacies in neural and cognitive development and place children at significant risk for LDs. Hence, one may conclude that the key aspect of a definition of LD is difficulties in school. As previously mentioned, this study clearly points out that, regardless of the causes of LD (regardless of whether LD is caused by individual and/or environmental factors, and regardless of the presence of IQ-achievement discrepancy), children who are in need should get the support of special education and related services they deserve – and they should receive it at the earliest possible time. Only early intervention would minimize the number of older students identified as having LD and those who remain learning disabled up to secondary school. These students will require more intensive and long-term intervention, and, even then, some of them may not (ever) catch up with their peers. Prevention and early intervention is more effective than educational treatment afterwards or any other remedial intervention service.

Along with the quantitative growth, now Korea is promoting high quality education for students with LDs. Despite the efforts made from all sides, it is often claimed that the inclusion of LD students thus far remains in the sphere of physical inclusion. Now the Korean special education community seems to be aware that merely placing students with LDs in regular classrooms is not a sufficient measure to allow for their educational and social inclusion and notices that other forms of support need to be put in place to facilitate their acceptance by and their belonging to the whole class. It is time to more tightly link policy, research and practice in

LD education. However, before we adopt a concept or policy from another country, it is essential that we fully understand the current status (i.e. the strengths and weaknesses) of inclusive education in Korea. In conclusion, we may argue that it is reasonable to assume that the feasible durable solution is to seek for a broader perspective of LD adaptable for practice, to embrace students with 'learning difficulties' and to provide them with special education and related services respectively.

7.2 THE NEED FOR REFORM IN SPECIAL EDUCATION TEACHER PREPARATION PROGRAMS

It is hard to understand how a professional could successfully identify, assess, teach and evaluate or generally improve the life of a student with LD, without first having a clear idea of the nature of LD (Hammill, 1990, 74).

Korean special education teachers in regular school settings need to be encouraged and supported by all available means, particularly to work effectively as collaborators. This need was supported by the findings, similarly to previous studies (cf. Ch. 6). However, in order to take the leadership role among regular teachers and fulfill their role as inclusion facilitators, special education teachers first need to develop high professional competency in the area of special education. In addition, they should have an instructional knowledge base that focuses on intensive intervention and assessment. In other words, in order to be able to implement intensive interventions in inclusive settings and feel self-competent in doing so, special education teachers need to develop content expertise in reading, writing and mathematics besides their special education area. This need was supported by the findings which indicated that special education teachers rarely use various alternative assessment methods for LD, and this, besides the insufficient collaboration situation, appeared to be associated with their self-competence. Similar to previous studies, the findings indicated that there is a risk on the part of special education teachers to reduce the assessment process by neglecting some relevant assessment methods, which generally take up more time and require collaboration with regular teachers. It might be easier to call it a failure on the part of special education teachers, as many previous studies concluded. However, considering the results, we have come to the conclusion that the reason may not be that they do not value particular assessment methods or do not feel competent to use them (for more detail information see chapter 5). Instead, we have come to pay (more) attention to understand the special education teachers' current status in regular school, the school climate and collaboration situation. The results thus indicated that Korean special education teachers prefer to use assessment methods they can implement themselves independently or to work with parents rather than with regular teachers. For instance, even those who felt highly self-competent in and often used various alternative assessment methods appeared to avoid methods which involved collaboration with regular teachers – particularly regular classroom observation and interviews with regular teachers. Observing the student with LD where she or he mainly operates – in the regular classroom – is particularly important for providing inclusive practice, because regular classroom observation provides initial information not only about the student's academic performance, but also about the student's communication, social skills or behavior that contribute to, or detract from, learning and overall attitude. All these pieces of information are important elements for teachers in understanding the "student's construction, particularly in regard to those who are at risk of educational failure due to their learning- and behavioral difficulties" (Hofsäss, 1999, 156). The reason is that these students often become entangled in a vicious circle created by the weight of expectation from their environment (*Erwartungsdruck durch das Umfeld*), their own pressure to perform (*eigene Leistungsdruck*) and experience psychosocial as well as emotional consequences (e.g. Betz & Breuninger, 1982, see also Breuninger & Betz, 1996, Betz & Breuninger, 1998). Unfortunately, special education teachers tend to avoid regular classroom observation. As mentioned above, the reason may not be that they consider regular classroom observation less important or have less self-competence to do it [16] – their hesitation may more likely be attributed to other barriers. Thus, the reluctance to use it is more likely to result from other barriers than solely the special education teachers' perception, such as limited collaboration and school climate, social and educational atmosphere of the school which is related to regular teachers' perception. For example, previous studies revealed that although teachers often feel that their lack of teaching skills is the reason why students fail in learning, mostly such teachers do not discuss their difficulties with certain teaching methods with others, but try to solve issues by themselves, falling prone to their limited knowledge (Noutomi, 1998 as cited in Kataoka et al., 2004, 171). By now, it is commonly known that although regular teachers generally believe that special education teachers are a valuable resource, communication or collaboration about planning instruction often remain infrequent (Schumm et al., 1995, 335f.).

The point is that despite the increasing demands posed upon special education teachers due to inclusion policy and promotion, their status and working conditions in many regular schools make it difficult to promote inclusion. In order to achieve inclusive quality education, policies must address special education teachers' status, welfare and professional development. There is not only a severe spe-

---

[16] cf. Ch. 5: considering that those who perceived the classroom as the most reliable environment for the student used less regular classroom observation; those who had a high self-competence in using alternative assessment methods and reported their frequent usage also avoided regular classroom observation and did not report about interviews with regular teachers.

cial education teacher shortage, especially in suburban and rural areas in Korea, but also a lack of adequately educated teachers regarding LD education. Assessment itself may (temporarily) help teachers to measure student performance; but teachers need to understand the value of (good) assessment practices and, as mentioned above, to develop professional competency and content expertise in order to implement high intensive intervention and assessment for LD. Adequate special education teacher preparation at both pre-service and in-service level is essential in this regard. Clearly, special education teachers deserve a good education which will lead to more effective teaching and, thus, more effective learning on the part of students.

IN-SERVICE EDUCATION

As is evident from the survey results, in-service education in the area of LD seemed to be sporadic or non-existent in many cases. Even though more than half of the respondents reported they taught over 5 students with LDs, merely 2.5% of them claimed to have participated in LD-related training (for description of sample, see chapter 4). Although not examined in this study, measures of in-service education programs for LD education have frequently been regarded as ineffective by teachers, as the content did not focus on specific subjects and instructional strategies to teach them (DeSimone & Parmar, 2006, 108, see also Brownell & Pajares, 1999). This, however, would be necessary for practicing special education teachers, because the curriculum for pre-service education in many universities focuses on the special education area rather than the general education curriculum. It may be assumed that the reason why the participation in the in-service training was so low might be that relatively few courses of adequate quality to serve this purpose were offered. A recent study stated that special education teachers consider the trainings as ineffective and poorly planned; especially the lack of motivation and the insufficient equipment/instructional materials were found to serve as obstacles to effective training (Kwak, Paik, Jeon, Lee, & Lee 2002, 40). Suggestions to improve the conditions and opportunities of special education teachers' in-service education in Korea have been maintained for years. Primarily, special education teachers themselves demand the development of teacher preparation programs and the expansion of teacher training institutes (e.g. Kwak et al., 2002). In this regard, taking into account the findings, an in-service education program that focuses on content expertise in reading, writing and mathematics and that delivers instructional knowledge for the intervention and assessment for LD is essential. To start with, training programs need to address age-appropriate strategies for primary school age students with LDs, dealing with their reading, writing, speaking and mathematical calculation, which are actual instructional modifications. It is also necessary to provide information on how to make curriculum modifications and accommodation (e.g. CBM and IEP) by means of prioritization and integration of topics, since curriculum modification and the ways in which the curriculum is delivered are essential for providing an IEP.

PRE-SERVICE EDUCATION

Contrary to in-service education, perhaps the positive and consoling thing was that almost all within the respondents had taken courses in the area of LD during their pre-service education. Nevertheless, considering the findings of this study (cf. Ch. 5), it could not be assumed that their pre-service education programs have equipped them with the necessary professional competencies, qualifications and skills to face the challenges of inclusive education for students with LDs. It might be assumed that special education teachers would have knowledge of the idea of problem solving and constructivist/holistic frameworks regarding their causal perception and definition of LD; yet in practice it seemed rather infeasible. The survey showed that there are areas of the program that can be improved, particularly concerning the special education teachers' role serving as adaptors and collaborators – special education teachers should be able to integrate and align content and instruction across grade levels as well as throughout the entire primary school years, and they should be capable of collaborating with regular teachers. As McLaughlin (1999, 13) puts it: "[…] a firm understanding on the part of special education teachers of what constitutes the general curriculum" is essential. It should not be forgotten that the ultimate purpose of LD assessment is to develop an IEP and an instructional plan for the students with LDs. The relevant professional development must begin on pre-service level in the form of compulsory courses across the major subject, since teachers with a more intensive and specific professional development are better prepared for the challenge (Brownell and Pajares, 1999, 154f.). There is value in preparing special education teachers so they have effective instructional skills and can differentiate instruction for most diverse learners.

Conclusively, Korea's special education teacher pre-service education needs to be restructured within the framework of the national standard curriculum. Korea does not yet have a nationwide standard for special education teachers' pre-service education; the universities' curricula vary concerning number and credit of compulsory courses (e.g. Cho IS, Yeo KE, Park HM, & Lee HG, 2005; Kim DI & Lee TS, 2003). Hence, a national level standard for special teachers' education programs needs to be established; instruction across subject areas (e.g. mathematics) relevant to the general curriculum needs to be particularly strengthened, and duration and content of the practical training courses (i.e. *Praktikum/Referendariat*) should be increased. These are important concerns that must be considered as Korea is constantly working towards updating and improving its special education preparation program.

7.3 LIMITATIONS OF THE STUDY

This study has certain limitations which need to be addressed. The main limitations that pose difficulties in generalizing the study's findings are as follows: firstly, it was difficult to obtain an equal representation of respondents from all geographic regions. The majority of respondents were recruited from Seoul, the capital, and the surrounding Gyeonggi-do province area. The sample population of Korean special education teachers may not truly represent an adequate percentage of teachers serving students with LDs in the metropolitan area and province. Secondly, data is based on teachers' self-reports. It solely reflects special education teachers' perceptions. Special education teachers' actual behavior in practice (e.g. assessment processes) was not examined, and aspects such as regular teachers' views were not taken into account in the present study. Additionally, as mentioned above, other factors besides the attributes listed on the questionnaire may have influenced special education teachers' responses directly and indirectly. Thirdly, the rating instrument asked the respondents to rate the predetermined attributes. Although items were drawn from the literature and several previous works of research, the disadvantages of closed-ended questions should be considered, since they may have restricted respondents to a predetermined set of responses. There may have been other attributes that special education teachers would have chosen (e.g. students' social factors as causes of LD). Fourthly, since the questionnaire used in this study is new, repeated use of the instrument when conducting further research should provide additional statistical reliability and validity. Overall, these limitations suggest a need for caution when interpreting and generalizing the results of this study.

7.4 SUGGESTIONS FOR FURTHER RESEARCH

This study used quantitative research methods to measure teachers' perceptions and practices. The present data does not rule out the teacher's response towards the student with LD during the assessment process and the reason why some of the respondents in the survey reported to very rarely use a particular assessment method. Through qualitative research methods, using participant observation in measuring teachers' assessment practice and semi-structured interviews in exploring teachers' causal perceptions of LD might allow us to portray more accurately the relationship between teachers' perceptions and their behavior towards students with LDs. In order to provide a picture of special education teachers' stance towards LDs which is nearer to completion, further research efforts should be directed towards investigating special education teachers' expectations towards students with LDs and the effects their expectations have on their implementation of assessment methods and students' achievements. Also, investigating how special education teachers perceive and describe LD might shed light on the reasons why some of the respondents were undecided about using a particular definition component of LD (e.g. the exclusion clause). The usage of content analysis and interview methods might allow us to answer the questions which have emerged from the present study's findings. More importantly, it should be examined whether these descriptions from special education teachers are valid descriptions of the students observed or the typical difficulties of any student with LD (manifesting teachers' implicit theories on LD). This is a crucial issue, as it is strongly related to the assessment of LD and ultimately relates to the special education services provided for these students. More research needs to be conducted with regard to the reliability of expert opinions (*Gutachten*, written by special education teachers) in the assessment of LD. As previously mentioned, as from May 26th, 2008 the Special Education Support Center conducts the assessment process of students with SEN, in consequence of the revision of SEPA. An important topic that needs to be investigated within the context therefore is to look into the Statement on Educational Support of students with LDs implemented by these centers. Finally, another issue worth looking at in further research is to investigate how special education teachers can be trained at both pre-service and in-service level to give an appropriate description of a student with LD.

REFERENCES

Adelman, H.S. (1971). The not so specific learning disability population. Exceptional Children, 37, 528-533.

Ahrbeck, B., Bleidick, U. & Schuck, K.D. (1997). Pädagogisch-psychologische Modelle der inneren und äußeren Differenzierung für lernbehinderte Schüler. In F.E. Weinert, (Ed.), Enzyklopädie der Psychologie. Themenbereich D. Praxisgebiete. Serie I. Pädagogische Psychologie, Band III: Psychologie des Unterrichts und der Schule (pp. 739-769). Göttingen: Hogrefe.

Ainscow, M. (1998). Would it work in theory? Arguments for practitioner research and theorizing in the special needs field. In C. Clark, A. Dyson & A. Millward, (Eds.), Theorizing special education. London: Routledge.

Ajzen, I. (1991). The theory of planned behavior. Organizational Behavior and Human Decision Processes, 50, 179-211.

Ajzen, I. (1996). The directive influence of attitudes on behavior. In P.M. Gollwitzer & J.A. Bargh, (Eds.), The psychology of action: Linking cognition and motivation to behavior (pp. 385-403). New York: Guilford Press.

Ajzen, I. (2002). Perceived behavioral control, self-efficacy, locus of control, and the theory of planned behavior. Journal of Applied Social Psychology, 32, 1-20.

Ajzen, I. & Fishbein, M. (1969). The prediction of behavioral intentions in a choice situation. Journal of Experimental Social Psychology, 5, 400-416.

Ajzen, I. & Fishbein, M. (1977). Attitude-behavior relations: A theoretical analysis and review of empirical research. Psychological Bulletin, 84, 888-918.

Ajzen, I. & Fishbein, M. (1980). Understanding attitudes and predicting social behavior. Englewood Cliffs, NJ: Prentice Hall.

Ajzen, I. & Fishbein, M. (2004). Questions raised by a reasoned action approach: Comment on Ogden (2003). Health Psychology, 23, 431-434.

Ajzen, I. & Fishbein, M. (2005). The influence of attitudes on behavior. In D. Albarracin, B.T. Johnson & M.P. Zanna, (Eds.), The handbook of attitudes (pp. 173-221). Mahwah, NJ: Erlbaum.

Alban-Metcalfe, J. & Alban-Metcalfe, J. (2001). Managing attention deficit-hyperactivity disorder in the inclusive classroom. London: Fulton.

Albrecht, G.L. & Levy, J.A. (1982). Constructing disabilities as social problems. In G.L. Albrecht, (Ed.), Cross-national rehabilitation policies: A sociological perspective (pp. 11-33). London: Sage.

Algozzine, B., Ysseldyke, J.E. & McGue, M. (1995). Differentiating low-achieving students: Thoughts on setting the record straight. Learning Disabilities Research, 10, 140-144.

Algozzine, R., Serna, L. & Patton, J.R. (2001). Childhood behavior disorders: Applied research and educational practices (2nd ed.). Austin, TX: Pro-Ed.

Allington, R.L. (1986). Policy constraints and effective compensatory reading instruction: A review. In J. Hoffman, (Ed.), Effective teaching of reading: Research and practice (pp. 261-289). Newark, DE: International Reading Association.

Allington, R.L. (1991a). The legacy of 'slow it down and make it more concrete'. In J. Zutell, & S. McCormick, (Eds.), Learner factors/teacher factors: Issues in literacy research and instruction (pp. 19-30). Chicago: National Reading Conference.

Allington, R.L. (1991b). How policy and regulation influence instruction for at-risk learners: Or why poor readers rarely comprehend well and probably never will. In L. Idol, & B.F. Jones, (Eds.), Educational values and cognitive instruction: Implications for reform (pp. 277-299). Hillsdale, NJ: Lawrence Erlbaum.

Allington, R.L. (1993). Reducing the Risk: Integrated Language Arts in Restructured Elementary Schools. Report Series 1.9. Albany, NY: National Research Center on Literature Teaching and Learning.

Allington, R. & McGill-Franzen, A. (1989). School response to reading failure: Chapter 1 and special education students in grades 2, 4, & 8. Elementary School Journal, 89, 529-542.

Altenbaugh, R.J. (1998). Some teachers are ignorant? Teachers and teaching through urban school leavers' eyes. In B. Franklin, (Ed.), When children don't learn (pp. 52-71). NY: Teachers College Press.

Al-Yagon, M., & Mikulincer, M. (2004). Patterns of close relationships and socio-emotional and academic adjustment among school-age children with learning disability. Learning Disabilities Research & Practice, 19, 12-19.

Anderson, P.L. & Meier-Hedde, R. (2001). Early case reports of dyslexia in the United States and Europe. Journal of Learning Disabilities, 34, 9-21.

Andrews, J.E., Carnine, D.W., Coutinho, M.J., Edgar, E.B., Forness, S.R., Fuchs, L.S., et al. (2000). Bridging the special education divide. Remedial and Special Education, 21, 258-260, 267.

Ashbaker, M.H. & Swans, H.L. (1996). Short-term memory and working memory operation and their contribution to reading in adolescents with and without learning disabilities. Learning Disabilities Research and Practice, 11 (4), 106-213.

Audette, B. & Algozzine, B. (1997). Re-inventing government? Let's re-invent special education. Journal of Learning Disabilities, 30 (4), 378-383.

Avissar, G. (2005). Perspectives of teacher training for special education in the 21st century. Teacher Education and School Reform and Development. Israeli German Symposium, 1-5.

Avramidis E., Bayliss P. & Burden R. (2000). A survey of mainstream teachers' attitudes towards the inclusion of children with special educational needs in the ordinary school in one Local Educational Authority, Educational Psychology, 20 (2),193-213.

Avramidis E., Bayliss P. & Burden R. (2002). Inclusion in action: an in-depth case study of an effective inclusive secondary school in the south-west of England. International Journal of Inclusive Education, 6 (2), 143-163.

Baacke, D. (1980). Der sozialökologische Ansatz zur Beschreibung und Erklärung des Verhaltens Jugendlicher. In Deutsche Jugend, 11, 493.

Babad, E. (1993). Pygmalion: 25 years after interpersonal expectations in the classroom. In P.D. Blanck, (Ed.), Interpersonal expectations: Theory, research, and applications. Studies in emotion and social interaction (pp. 125-153). NY: Cambridge University Press.

Bacon, E.H. & Bloom, L.A. (1994). Don't ratl' the kids. Journal of Emotional and Behavioral Problems, 3 (1), 8-10.

Baek, W.H. (1993). Validity of the concept of LD and the need for a reconceptualization of learning disability. Korean Journal of Education Research, 31 (1), 139-157.

Baglieri, S. & Knopf, J.H. (2004). Normalizing difference in inclusive teaching. Journal of Learning Disabilities, 37 (6), 525-530.

Bailet, L.L. (2001). Development and disorders of spelling in the beginning school years. In A.M. Bain, L.L. Bailet, & L.C. Moats, (Eds.), Writing language disorders: Theory into practice (2nd edn). Austin, TX: Pro-Ed.

Balgo, R. (2002). Sonderpädagogik im historischen und akuellen Kontext. In R. Werning, R. Balgo, W. Palmowski & M. Sassenroth, (Eds.), Sonderpädagogik. Lernen, Verhalten, Sprache, Bewegung und Wahrnehmung (pp. 15-128). München, Wien: R. Oldenbourg.

Ballard, K. (1993). Disability, family, whanau, and society. Palmerston North: Dunmore.

Bandura, A. (1977). Self-efficacy: Toward a unifying theory of behavioral change. Psychological Review, 84 (2), 191-215.

Bandura, A. (1982). Self-efficacy mechanism in human agency. American Psychologist, 37 (2), 122-147.

Bandura, A. (1997). Self-efficacy: the exercise of control. NY: W.H. Freeman & Company.

Barnett, D.W., Bauer, A.M., Barnhouse, L., Ehrhardt, K.E., Lentz, F.E., Macmann,

G. & Stollar, S. (1997). Ecological foundations of early intervention: Planned activities and strategic sampling. Journal of Special Education 30, 471-490.

Batten, M., Marland, P. & Khamis, M. (1993). Knowing how to teach well. Melbourne: Australian Council for Educational Research.

Bauer, A.M. & Shea, T.M. (1998). Learners with emotional and behavioural disorders: an introduction. Upper Saddle River, N.J: Merrill Prentice Hall.

Bauer, A.M., Keefe, C.H. & Shea, T.M. (2001). Students with learning disabilities or emotional/behavioral disorders. Columbus, OH: Merrill Publishing, Prentice Hall.

Bauwens, J., Hourcade, J.J. & Friend, M. (1989). Cooperative teaching: A model for general and special education integration. Remedial and Special Education, 10 (2), 17-22.

Bear, G.G. & Minke, K.M. (1996). Positive bias in maintenance of self-worth among children with LD. Learning Disability Quarterly, 19, 23-32.

Bear, G.G., Minke, K.M., Griffin, S.M. & Deemer, S.A., (1998). Achievement-related perceptions of children with learning disabilities and normal achievement: group and developmental differences. Journal of Learning Disabilities 31, 91-104.

Beaver, W. (2004). Can No Child Left Behind work? American Secondary Education, 32 (2), 1-18.

Beck, I., Duee, W. & Wieland, H. (1996). Normailisierung: Behindertenpädagogische und sozialpolitische Perspektiven eines Reformkonzeptes. Heidelberg: Winter.

Begemann, E. (1979). Erziehungs- und Sozialisationsbedingungen des lernbehinderten Kindes in der Familie. In Dennerlein, H., Schramm, K. (Eds.), Handbuch der Behindertenpädagogik (1th edn.) (pp. 450-465). München: Kösel.

Begemann, E. (1996). Miß-Deutungen der Sprache von "Lernbehinderten". In Eberwein, H. (Eds.) Handbuch Lernen und Lern-Behinderungen (pp. 135-156). Weinheim: Beltz.

Belschner, W., Hoffmann, M., Schott, F. & Schulze, Ch. (1976). Verhaltenstherapie in Erziehung und Unterricht (4th ed.). Stuttgart: Kohlhammer.

Belsky, J. (1980). Child maltreatment: an ecological integration. American Psychologist, 35, 320-335.

Belusa, A., Eberwein, H., & Michaelis, E. (1992). Probleme des Lernens und Deutungsmuster – Ergebnisse einer Befragung an Schulen für Lernbehinderte in Berlin. Behindertenpädagogik, 31(2), 162-170.

Bender, W. (1985). Differences between learning disabled and non-learning disabled children in temperament and behavior. Learning Disability Quarterly, 8 (10), 11-18.

Bender, W. (1987). Behavioral indicators of temperament and personality of the inactive learner. Journal of Learning Disabilities, 20 (5), 301-305.
Bender, W.N. (2000). Learning disabilities: Characteristics, identification, and teaching strategies (5th ed.). Boston: Allyn & Bacon.
Benkmann, K.H. (1989). Pädagogische Erklärungs und Handlungsanätze bei Verhaltensstörungen in der Schule. In H. Goetze & H. Neukäter, (Eds.), Pädagogik bei Verhaltensstörungen. Handbuch der Sonderpädagogik (6th ed.) (pp. 71-119). Berlin: Marhold.
Benkmann, R. (2003). Bedingungen und Prozesse bei Beeinträchtigungen des Lernens – – Die Perspektive des soyialen Konstruktivismus. In Leonhardt, A. & Wember, F.B., (Eds.), Grundfragen der Sonderpädagogik: Bildung- Erziehung-Behinderung (pp. 441-464). Weinheim, Basel: Beltz.
Berghoff, B. (1997). Stance and Teacher Education: Understanding the relational nature of teaching. Revised version of a paper presented at the National Reading Conference, Scottsdale, AZ, December 6, 1997 (ERIC Document Reproduction Service No. ED 424218).
Bergmann, G. (1961). Sense and nonsense in operation. In P.G. Frank (Ed.), The validation of scientific theories (pp. 45-56). NY: Collier.
Berkowitz, P.H. & Rothman, E.P. (1967).Public education for disturbed children in New York city. Springfeld, IL: C. C. Thomas.
Berninger, V.W. & Richards, T.L. (2002). Brain literacy for educators and psychologists. NY: Elsevier Science.
Beschel, E. (1980). Geschichte. In G.O. Kanter & O. Speck, (Eds.), Handbuch der Sonderpädagogik. Pädagogik der Lernbehinderten (Vol. IV) (pp. 113-147). Berlin: Marhold.
Betz, D. & Breuninger, H. (1982). Teufelskreis Lernstörungen. Analyse und Therapie einer schulischen Störung. München: Urban & Schwarzenberg.
Betz, D. & Breuninger, H. (1998). Teufelskreis Lernstörungen. Theoretische Grundlegung und Standardprogramm (5.edn.), Weinheim:Psychologie Verlags Union.
Black, A.H. (1977). Comments on 'Learned helplessness: Theory and evidence' by Maier
and Seligman. Journal of Experimental Psychology, 106, 41-43.
Blanton, L.P., Blanton, W.E. & Cross, L.S. (1994). An exploratory study on how general and special education teachers think and make instructional decisions about students with special needs. Teacher Education and Special Education, 17, 62-74.
Bleidick, U. (1968). Über Lernbehinderung. In Zeitschrift für Heilpädagogik, 19 (9), 449-464.
Bleidick, U. (1985). Historische Theorien: Heilpädagogik, Sonderpädagogik, Päd-

agogik der Behinderten. In U. Bleidick, (Ed.), Theorie der Behindertenpädagogik. Berlin: Marhold-V.

Bleidick, U. (2000a). Medizinisches Modell. In J. Borchert, (Ed.), Handbuch der Sonderpädagogischen Psychologie (pp. 183-188). Göttinggen: Hogrefe.

Bleidick, U. (2000b). Interaktionstheorie. In J. Borchert, (Ed.), Handbuch der Sonderpädagogischen Psychologie (pp. 189-199). Goettinggen: Hogrefe.

Bleidick, U. (2000c). Systemtheoretische Ableitung. In J. Borchert, (Ed.), Handbuch der Sonderpädagogischen Psychologie (pp. 200-208). Goettinggen: Hogrefe.

Bleidick, U., Rath, W. & Schuck, D. (1995). Die Empfehlungen der Kultusministerkonferenz zur sonderpädagogischen Förderung in den Schulen der Bundesrepublik Deutschland. In Zeitschrift für Heilpädagogik, 41, 247-264.

Bogdan, R. & Taylor, S.J. (1989). Relationships with severely disabled people: The social construction of humanness. Social Problems, 36 (2), 135-148.

Bogdan, R. & Taylor, S.J. (1998). The social construction of humanness: Relationships with people with severe retardation. In S.J. Taylor & R. Bogdan, (Eds.), Introduction to qualitative research methods: A guidebook and resource (pp. 242–258). NY: John Wiley & Sons.

Borsay, A. (1986). Personal trouble or public issue? Towards a model of policy for people with physical and mental disabilities. Disability, Handicap & Society, 1 (2), 179-195.

Brackett, J. & McPherson, A. (1996). Learning disabilities diagnosis in postsecondary students: A comparison of discrepancy-based diagnostic models. In N. Gregg, C. Hoy & A. F. Gay, (Eds.), Adults with learning disabilities: Theoretical and practical perspectives (pp. 68-84). NY: Guilford Press.

Brandt, L., Hayden, M. & Brophy, J. (1975). Teachers' attitudes and ascription of causality. Journal of Educational Psychology, 67, 677-682.

Brantlinger, E.A. (2004). Confounding the needs and confronting the norms: An extension of Reid and Valle's essay. Journal of Learning Disabilities, 37 (6), 490-499.

Brendtro, L.K. & Van Bockern, S. (1994). Courage for the discouraged: A psychoeducational approach to troubled and troubling children. Focus on Exceptional Children, 26 (8), 1-14, 16.

Breuninger, H. & Betz, D. (1996). Jedes Kind kann schreiben lernen. Ein Ratgeber für Lese-Rechtschreib-Schwäche (6. Auflage). Weinheim: Beltz Grüne Reihe.

Brinkerhoff, L.C., Shaw, S.F. & McGuire, J.M. (1992). Promoting access, accommodations, and independence for college students with learning disabilities. Journal of Learning Disabilities, 25, 417-429.

Bronfenbrenner, U. (1978). Ansätze zu einer experimentellen Ökologie menschlicher Entwicklung. In R. Oerter, (Ed.), Entwicklung als lebenslanger Prozeß. Hamburg: Hoffmann & Campe.

Bronfenbrenner, U. (1979). The ecology of human development: experiments by nature and design. Cambridge, Massachusetts, London: Harvard university press.

Bronfenbrenner, U. (1989). Die Ökologie der menschlichen Entwicklung. Frankfurt am Main: Fischer Taschenbuchverlag.

Brophy, J. (1985). Teachers' expectations, motives, and goals for working with problem students. In C. Ames & R. Ames, (Eds.), Research on motivation in education: The classroom milieu, (vol. 2, pp. 175-213). NY: Academic Press.

Brownell, M.T. & Pajares, F. (1999). Teacher efficacy and perceived success in mainstreaming students with learning and behavior problems. Teacher Education and Special Education, 22, 154-164.

Bryan, T., Pearl, R., Donahue, M., Bryan, J. & Pflaum, S. (1983). The Chicago institute for the study of learning disabilities. Exceptional Education Quarterly, 4 (1), 1–22.

Bundesministerium der Justiz (http://www.gesetze-im-internet.de/gg/index.html). (08.07.2006).

Bundschuh, K. (2005). Einführung in die sonderpädagogische Diagnostik (6th edn.). München: Ernst Reinhardt.

Burch, S. & Sutherland, I. (2006). Who's not yet here? American disability history. Radical History Review, 94, 127-147.

Burger, J., Cooper, H. & Good, T. (1982) Teacher attributions of student performance: effects of outcome. Personality and Social Psychology Bulletin, 8 (4), 685-690.

Byun, C.S. (2002a). Study on special class teachers' perspectives of using assessment procedures for children with learning disabilities. Journal of Emotional Disturbances & Learning Disabilities, 17 (3), 257-275.

Byun, C.S. (2002b). Direction of LD practice and research in Korea. Communication Disorders, 25 (2), 289-300.

Byun, C.S. (2007). The actual condition of the filed study on learning disabilities in Korea. Journal of Special Education & Rehabilitation Science, 46 (1), 55-71.

Çakiroglu, J., Çakiroglu, E. & Boone, W.J. (2005). Pre-service teacher self-efficacy beliefs regarding science teaching: a comparison of pre-service teachers in Turkey and the USA. Science Educator, 14 (1),31-40.

Campbell, F. & Ramey, C.T. (1994). Effects on early intervention on intellectual and academic achievement: a follow up study of children from low income families. Child Development, 65, 684-698.

Campione, J.C. & Brown, A.L. (1987). Linking dynamic assessment with school achievement. In C.S. Lidz, (Ed.), Dynamic assessment: An interactional approach to evaluating learning potential (pp. 82-115). New York: Guilford.

Cappa, S.F., Moro, A., Perani, D. & Piattelli-Palmarini, M. (2000). Broca's aphasia, Broca's area, and syntax: A complex relationship. Behavioral and Brain Sciences, 23, 27-37, Cambridge University Press.

Caprara, G., Pastroelli, C. & Weiner, B. (1997).Linkages between causal ascriptions emotion and behavior, International Journal of Behavioral Development, 20, 153-162.

Cardell, C.D. & Parmar, R.S. (1988). Teacher perceptions of temperament characteristics of children classified as learning disabled. Journal of Learning Disabilities, 21 (8), 497-502.

Carlisle, J.F. & Chang, V. (1996). Evaluation of academic capabilities in science by students with and without learning disabilities and their teachers. The Journal of Special Education, 30 (1), 18-34.

Carmines, E.G. & Zeller, R.A. (1991). Reliability and validity assessment. Newbury Park, CA: Sage.

Carnine, D. (1997). Instructional design in mathematics for students with learning disabilities. Journal of Learning Disabilities, 30, 130–141.

Chan, L.K.S. & Dally, K. (2001). Learning disabilities and literacy and numeracy development. Australian Journal of Learning Disabilities, 6 (1), 12-19.

Chard, D.J. (2004). Maintaining the relationship between science and special education. Journal of Learning Disabilities, 37 (3), 213-217.

Chatterji, M. (2006). African American children were less likely to be enrolled in preprimary education relative to Whites and were more likely to be below modal grade for their age in school. Journal of Educational Psychology, 98 (3), 489-507.

Chatzisarantis, N. & Biddle, S. (1998). Functional significance of psychological variables that are included in the theory of planned behaviour. A self-determination theory approach to the study of intentions. European Journal of Social Psychology, 28, 303-322.

Cheng, P. (1998). Primary school teachers' perceptions and understanding of learning difficulties. In D.W. Chan, (ed.), Helping students with learning difficulties (pp. 121-134). Hong Kong: Chinese University Press.

Cho, I.S., Yeo, K.E., Park, H.M. & Lee, H.G. (2005). Education system and current status of Korean special education teacher pre service education. Journal of Education Research, 1 (1), 19-27, Dae-Gu University Education Institute.

Cho, K.S. & Whang, I.K. (2003). The effectiveness of inclusion through on-site in-service for teachers in elementary school inclusive classrooms. Korean Journal of Special Education, 37 (4), 199-217.

Choi, S.S. (2006). Implications and practices of collaborative models for including students with disabilities in inclusive education settings. The Korean Journal of Learning Disabilities, 3 (3), 117-137.

Chung, C.C. (1997). Special education teacher education system. Korean Teacher Education, 14 (2), 103-124.

Clark, C.M. & Peterson, P.L. (1986). Teachers' thought processes. In M.C. Wittrock, (Ed.), Third handbook of research on teaching (pp. 255-296).NY: Macmillan.

Clark, M.D. (1997). Teacher response to learning disability. A test of attributional principles. Journal of Learning Disabilities, 30, 69-79

Clark, M.D. & Artiles, A. J. (2000). A cross-national study of teachers' attributional patterns. The Journal of Special Education, 34, 77-89.

Clarkson, P. & Leder, G.C. (1984). Causal attributions for success and failure in mathematics:Across cultural perspective. Educational Studies in Mathematics, 15, 413-422.

Cobb, P. (1994). Constructivism in mathematics and science education. Educational Researcher, 23 (7), 4.

Cohen, S.A. (1969). Studies in visual perception and reading in disadvantaged children. Journal of Learning Disabilities, 2, 498-507.

Cohen, S.A. (1970). Cause versus treatment in reading achievement. Journal of Learning Disabilities, 3, 163-166.

Cohen, S.A. (1971). Dyspedagogia as a cause of reading retardation: Definition and treatment. In B. Bateman, (Ed.), Learning disorders (Vol.4) (pp. 269-291). Seattle, WA: Special Child.

Cole, D.A., Maxwell, S.E., Martin, J.M., Peeke, L.G., Seroczynski, A.D., Tram, J.M., Hoffman, K.B., Ruiz, M.D., Jacquez, F., & Maschman, T. (2001). The development of multiple domains of child and adolescent self-concept: A cohort sequential longitudinal design. Child Development, 72, 1723-1746.

Coleman, M.C. (1986). Behavior disorders theory and practice. Englewood Cliffs, NJ: Prentice-Hall.

Colvin, R.L. & Helfand, D. (2000). Special education a failure on many fronts. The Los Angeles Times (www.latimes.com/news/state/reports/specialeduc/) (11.05.2007).

Connor, F.P. (1983). Improving school instruction for learning disabled children: The Teachers College Institute. Exceptional Education Quarterly, 4 (1), 23-44.

Conway, A. (1989) Teachers' explanation for children with learning difficulties: An analysis of written reports. Early Child Development and Care, 53, 53-61.

Council for Exceptional Children (2002). No child left behind act of 2001 implication for special education policy and practice (www.cec.sped.org) (07.10.2003).

Covington, M. & Omelich, C. (1984). The trouble with pitfalls: a reply to Weiner's

critique of attribution research, Journal of Educational Psychology, 76, 1199-1213.
Covington, M.V. & Mueller, K.J. (2001). Intrinsic versus extrinsic motivation: an approach avoidance reformulation. Educational Psychology Review, 13 (2), 157-176.
Cox, T. (2000). Introduction. In T. Cox, (Ed.), Combating educational disadvantage: meeting the needs of vulnerable children (pp. 1-14). London: Falmer.
Cruickshank, W.M. (1976). William M. Cruickshank. In J.M. Kauffman & D.P. Hallahan, (Eds.), Teaching children with learning disabilities: Personal perspectives (pp. 94-127). Columbus, OH: Charles E. Merrill.
Cruickshank, W.M. & Hallahan D.P. (1973). Alfred Strauss: Pioneer in learning disabilities. Exceptional Children, 39, 321-327.
Daly, E., Witt, J.C., Martens, B.K. & Dool, E. (1997). A model for conducting functional analysis of academic performance problems. School Psychology Review, 26, 554-574.
DeJong, G. (1979). The movement for independent living: origins, ideology and implications for disability research. University Centre for International Rehabilitation. Michigan State University.
Deno, E. (1970). Special education as developmental capital. Exceptional Children, 37, 229-237.
DeSimone, J. & Parmar, R. (2006). Middle school mathematics teachers' beliefs about inclusion of students with learning disabilities. Learning Disabilities Research & Practice, 21 (2), 98-110.
Dollard, N., Christenssen, L., Colucci, K. & Epanchin, B. (1996). Constructive class room management. Focus on Exceptional Children, 29 (2), 1-12.
Doris, J. (1993). Defining learning disabilities: A history of the search for consensus. In G.R. Lyon, D.B. Gray, J.F. Cavanaugh & N. A. Krasnegor, (Eds.), Better understanding learning disabilities (pp. 97-116). Baltimore: Paul H. Brookes.
Drave, W., Rumpler, F. & Wachtel, P. (2000). Empfehlungen zur sonderpädagogischen Förderung, allgemeine Grundlagen und Förderschwerpunkte (KMK) mit Kommentaren. Würzburg: Edition Bentheim.
Dudley-Marling, C. (2004). The social construction of learning disabilities. Journal of Learning Disabilities, 37 (6), 482-489.
Dudley-Marling, C. & Dippo, D. (1995). What learning disability does: Sustaining the ideology of schooling. Journal of Learning Disabilities, 28, 408-414.
Dudley-Marling, C. & Dippo, D. (1996). What learning disability does: Sustaining the ideology of schooling. In M.S. Poplin & P.T. Cousin, (Eds.), Alternative views of learning disabilities: issues for the 21st century, (pp. 14-57). Austin: Pro.Ed.

Dunbar, L. (1988). The common interest: How our social welfare policies work and what we can do about them. New York: Pantheon.

DuPaul, G.J. & Stonder, G. (2003). ADHD in the schools: assessment and intervention strategies. New York: Guilford Press.

Eber, L., Nelson, C.M., & Miles, P. (1997). School-based wraparound for students with emotional and behavioural challenges. Exceptional Children, 65 (4), 539-555.

Eberwein, H. (1997). Lernbehinderung – Faktum oder Konstrukt? Zeitschrift für Heilpädagogik, 48 (1), 14-22.

Eberwein, H. (1996). Handbuch lernen und lern-behinderungen: Aneignungsprobleme – neues Verständnis von lernen-integrationspädagogische Lösungsansätze. Weinheim: Beltz.

Eccles, J.S. & Wigfield, A. (2002). Motivational Beliefs, values, and goals, Annual Review of Psychology, 53, 109-132.

Eggert,D., Reichenbach,C. & Lückig, C. (2007). Von den Stärken ausgehen: Individuelle Entwicklungspläne (IEP) in der Lernförderungsdiagnostik. Ein Plädoyer für andere Denkgewohnheiten und eine veränderte Praxis. Dortmund: Borgmann.

Ehri, L.C., Nunes, S.R., Stahl, S.R. & Willows, D.M. (2001). Systematic phonics instruction helps students learn to read: Evidence from the National Reading Panel's meta-analysis. Review of Educational Research, 71, 393-447.

Eisenhart, M. A., Shrum, J. L., Harding, J. R., & Cuthbert, A. M. (1988). Teacher beliefs: definitions, findings and directions. Educational Policy, 2(1), 51-70.

Elbaz, F. (1983). Teacher thinking: a study of practical knowledge. NY: Nichols Publishing Company.

Ellsworth, E. (1997). Teaching positions: difference, pedagogy, and the power of address. N.Y: Teachers College Press.

Emmitt, M., Pollock, J., & Komesaroff, L. (2003). Language Variation. Langauge and learning: An Introduction for Teaching (3rd edn.). Melbourne, Victoria, Australia: Oxford University Press

Engelmann, S.E. (1977). Sequencing cognitive and academic tasks.In R.D. Kneedler & S.C. Traver, (Eds.), Changing perspective in special education. Columbus, Ohio: Charles E. Merrill.

Enochs, L.G. & Riggs, I.M. (1990). Further development of an elementary science teaching efficacy belief instrument: A pre-service elementary scale. School Science and Mathematics, 90, 694-706.

Enochs, L.G, Scharmann, L.C. & Riggs, L.M. (1995). The relationship of pupil control to pre-service elementary science teachers self-efficacy and outcome expectation. Science Education, 79, 63-75.

Entwistle, N.J. (1981). Styles of learning and teaching. Chichester: Wiley.

Epps, S., Ysseldyke, J. & McGue, M. (1984). Differentiating LD and non-LD students: "I know one when I see one." Learning Disability Quarterly, 7, 89-101.

European Agency for Development in Special Needs Education. (2003). Inclusive education and classroom practices: Summary report. (http://www.european-agency.org/publications). (15.3.2005).

Ameln, F.v. (2004). Konstruktivismus. Tübingen, Basel: A. Francke Verlag.

Fennema, E., Peterson, P., Carpenter, T. & Lubinski, C. (1990). Teachers' attributions and beliefs about girls, boys, and mathematics. Educational Studies in Mathematics, 21, 55-69.

Fenton, K.S., Yoshida, R.K., Maxwell, J.P. & Kaufman, M.J. (1979). Recognition of team goals: An essential step toward rational decision- making. Exceptional Children, 45, 638-644.

Ferguson, P.M. & Ferguson, D.L. (1995). The interpretivist view of special education and disability: The value of telling stories. In T. Sktic, (Ed.), Disability and democracy: Reconstructing special education for postmodernity (pp. 104-121). NY: Teachers College Press.

Feuerstein, R. (1979). The dynamic assessment of retarded performers: the learning potential assessment device, theory, instruments, and techniques. Baltimore: University Park Press.

Finkelstein, V. (1980). Attitudes and disability: Issues for discussions. New Yorkz: World Rehabilitation Fund.

Finkelstein, V. (1993). Representing disability, In J. Swain, V. Finkelstein, S. French, C. Barnes & C. Thomas, (Eds.), Disabling barriers, enabling environments. London, UK: Sage.

Fishbein, M. & Ajzen, I. (1972). Attitudes and opinions. Annual Review of Psychology, 23, 487-544.

Fletcher, J.M, Coulter, W.A., Reschly, D.J. & Vaughn, S. (2004). Alternative approaches to the definition and identification of learning disabilities: some questions and answers. Annals of Dyslexia, 54 (2), 304-331.

Fletcher J.M., Foorman B.R., Boudousquie A., Barnes M.A., Schatschneider C. & Francis D.J. (2002). Assessment of reading and learning disabilities. A research-based intervention-oriented approach. Journal of School Psychology, 40 (1), 27-63.

Fletcher, J.M., Francis, D.J., Shaywitz, S.E., Lyon, G.R., Foorman, B.R., Stuebing, K.K. & Shaywitz, B.A. (1998). Intelligent testing and the discrepancy model for children with learning disabilities. Learning Disabilities Research & Practice, 13, 186-203.

Flook, L., Repetti, R. & Ullman, J. (2005). Classroom social experiences as predictors of academic performance. Developmental Psychology, 41 (2), 319-327.

Folwer, C. & Wadsworth, J. S. (1991). Individualism and equity: critical values

in North American culture and the impact on disability. Journal of Applied Rehabilitation Counseling, 22 (4), 19-23.
P2 Forness, S. R., & Kavale, K. A. (1996). Treating social skill deficits in children with learning disabilities: A meta-analysis of the research. Learning Disability Quarterly, 19, 2-13.
Fresch, M.J. (2003). A national survey of spelling instruction: Investigating teachers' beliefs and practice. Journal. of Literacy Research, 35 (3), 819-848.
Fuchs, A. (1922). Schwachsinnige Kinder, ihre sittlich-religiöse, itellektuelle und wirtschaftliche Rettung. In S. Ellger-Rüttgart, (Ed.), Lernbehindertenpädagogik. Studientexte zur Geschichte der Behindertenpädagogik (Vol.5) (pp. 72-82). Berlin: Beltz.
Fuchs, D., Fuchs, L., Mathes, P., Lipsey, M. & Roberts, P.H. (2002). Is learning disabilities just a fancy term for low achievement? A meta-analysis of reading differences between low achievers with and without the label. In R. Bradley, L. Danielson & D.P. Hallahan, (Eds.), Identification of Learning Disabilities: Research to Practice (pp. 737-762). Mahwah, N.J: Erlbaum.
Fulk, B.M., Brigham, F.J., & Lohman, D.A. (1998). Motivation and self-regulation: A comparison of students with learning and behavior problems. Remedial and Special Education, 19, 300-309.
Gallhager, D.J. (1998). The scientific knowledge base of special education. Do we know what we think we know? Exceptional Children, 64 (4), 483-502.
Galloway, D., Rogers, C., Armstrong, D. & Leo, E. (1998). Motivating the difficult to teach. London: Longman.
Georgiou, S.N., Christou, C., Stavrinides P. & Panaoura, G. (2002). Teacher attributions of student failure and teacher behavior toward the failing student. Psychology In the Schools, 39, 5, 583-595.
Gerber, M.M. (2000). An appreciation of learning disabilities: The value of blue-green algae.Exceptionality, 8, 29-42.
Gerber, M.M. (2002). A meta-research commentary on MacMillan and Siperstein's "Learning disabilities as operationally defined by schools". In R. Bradley, L. Danielson, D.P. Hallahan, (Eds.), Identification of learning disabilities: research to practice (pp. 341-350). Mahwah, NJ: Lawrence Erlbaum.
Gerken, K. (1988). Best practice in academic assessment. In A. Thomas & K. Grimes, (Eds.), Best practice in school psychology (pp. 157-170). Washington DC: National Association of School Psychologists.
Gibson, S. & Dembo, M. (1984). Teacher efficacy: A construct validation.Journal of Educational Psychology, 76, 569-582.
Gindis, B. (1999). Vygotsky's vision: Reshaping the practice of special education for the 21st century. Remedial And Special Education, 20 (6), 333-340.

Glassberg, L.A. (1994). Students with behavioural disorders: Determinations of placement outcomes. Behavioral Disorders, 19 (3), 181-191.

Gorrell, J. & Hwang, Y.S. (1995). A study of self-efficacy beliefs among pre-service teachers in Korea. Journal of Research and Development in Education, 28, 101-105.

Gottfredson, D.C., Marciniak, E.M., Birdseye, A.T. & Gottfredson, G.D. (1995). Increasing teacher expectations for student achievement. Journal of Educational Research, 88 (3), 155-163.

Graham, S. & Harries, K.R. (2000). Helping children who experience reading difficulties. In L. Baker, M.J. Dreher & J.T. Guthrie, (Eds.), Engaging Young Readers: Promoting Achievement and Motivation (pp. 43-67). New York: Guilford Press.

Gregg, N. (1994). Eligibility for learning disabilities rehabilitation services: Operationalizing the definition. Journal of Vocational Rehabilitation, 4 (2), 86–95.

Gresham, F.M. (2002). Responsiveness to intervention: An alternative approach to the identification of learning disabilities. In R. Bradley, L. Danielson & D. Hallahan, (Eds.), Identification of learning disabilities: Research to practice (pp. 467-519). Mahwah NJ: Erlbaum.

Grigorenko, E.L. (2001). Developmental dyslexia: an update on genes, brains and environments. Journal of Child Psychology and Psychiatry, 42, 91-125.

Gu, B.G., Kim, D.Y., Kim, Y.U., Kim, W.G., Park, H.M., Seok, D.I., Yoon, J.R., Jeong, J.K., Jeong, J.J. & Cho, I.S. (1996). Special education. Seoul: Gyoyuggwajaksa.

Guskey, T. (1982). Differences in teachers' perceptions of personal control of positive versus negative student learning outcomes. Contemporary Educational Psychology, 7, 70-80.

Haeberlin, U., Bless, B., Moser, U., & Klaghofer, R. (1999). Die integration von Lernbehinderten: Versuche, Theorien, Forschungen, Enttäuschungen, Hoffnungen (3rd edn.) Stuttgart: Bern.

Hagborg, W.J. (1996). Self-concept and middle school students wit learning disabilities: a comparison of scholastic competence subgroups. Learning Disability Quarter, 19, 117-126.

Hallahan, D.P. & Cruickshank, W.M. (1973). Psychoeducational foundations of learning disabilities. Englewood Cliffs, NJ: Prentice-Hall.

Hallahan, D.P. & Mercer, C.D. (2002). Learning disabilities: Historical perspectives. In R. Bradley, L. Danielson & D.P. Hallahan, (Eds.), Identification of learning disabilities: Research to practice (pp. 1-67). Mahwah, NJ: Erlbaum.

Hallahan, D.P., Kauffman, J.M. & Lloyd, J.W. (1999). Introduction to learning disabilities (2nd ed.). Boston: Allyn & Bacon.

Hallahan, D.P., Hall, R.J., Ianna, S.O., Kneedler, R.D., Lloyd, J.W., Loper, A.B., et al. (1983). Summary of research findings at the University of Virginia Learning Disabilities Research Institute. Exceptional Education Quarterly, 4 (1), 95-114.

Hamayan, E.V. (1995). Approaches to alternative assessment. Annual Review of Applied Linguistics, 15, 212-226.

Hammill, D.D. (1990). On defining learning disabilities: an emerging consensus. Journal of Learning Disabilities, 23 (2), 74-84.

Hammill, D.D. (1993). A timely definition of learning disabilities. Family and Community Health, 16 (3), 1-8.

Hanson, M.J. & Carta, J.J. (1995). Addressing challenges of families with multiple risks. Exceptional Children, 62 (3), 102-212.

Harries, K.R. & Graham, S. (1996). Constructivism and students with special needs: issues in the classroom. Learning Disabilities Research and Practice, 11 (3), 134-137.

Hasting, N. & Schwieso, J. (1995). Task and tables: the effects of seating arrangements in primary classrooms. Educational Research, 37 (3), 279-291.

Haynes, C., Hook, 1., Macaruso, P., Muta, E., Hayashi, Y., Kato, J., et al. (2000). Teachers' skill ratings of children with learning disabilities: A comparison of the United States and Japan. Annals of Dyslexia, 50, 215-238.

Heider, F. (1958). The psychology of interpersonal relations. New York: John Wiley & Sons Inc.

Helmke, A. & Weinert, F.E. (1997). Bedingungsfaktoren schulischer Leistungen. In F.E. Weinert, (Ed.), Psychologie des Unterrichts und der Schule. Enzyklopädie der Psychologie: Pädagogische Psychologie (3rd edn.) (pp. 71-176). Göttingen: Hogrefe.

Henderson, R.W. (2002). Queensland Year 2 Diagnostic Net and teachers' explanations of literacy failure. Australian Journal of Education, 46 (1), 50-64.

Henning, M. (2006). Individuen und ihre sozialen Beziehungen. Wiesbaden: VS Verlag für Sozialwissenschaften.

Heshusius, L. (1984). Why would they and I want to do it? A phenomenological-theoretical view of special education. Learning Disability Quarterly, 7, 363-368.

Heshusius, L. (1995). Holism and special education: There is no substitute for real life purposes and processes. In T.M. Skrtic, (Ed.), Disability and democracy: Reconstructing (special) education for postmodernity (pp. 166-189). NY: Columbia University, Teachers College.

Hinshaw, S.P. (1992). Externalizing behavior problems and academic underachievement in childhood and adolescence: Causal relationships and underlying mechanisms. Psychological Bulletin, 111, 127-155.

Ho, I. (2004). A comparison of Australian and Chinese teachers' attributions for student problem behaviour. Educational Psychology, 24 (3), 375-391.

Hobbs, N. (1966). Helping disturbed children: psychological and ecological strategies. American Psychologist, 21, 1105-1115.
Hofsäss, Th. (1993). Die Überweisung von Schülern auf die Hilfsschule und die Schule für Lernbehinderte. Eine historisch-vergleichende Untersuchung. Berlin: Edition Marhold.
Hofsäss, Th. (1999). Aktuelle Fragestellungen der Lernbehindertenpädagogik. In L. Pflüger, (Ed.), Sonderpädagogik auf dem Weg ins 21. Jahrhundert: Förderung von Kindern und Jugendlichen mit Lernbeeinträchtigungen. Festschrift für Winfried Kerkhoff zum 65. Geburtstag (pp. 155-175). Berlin: VWB-Verlag.
Hofsäss, Th. (2003). Didaktische Konzepte der Oberstufe an der Schule für Lernbehinderte: Schulentwicklung zwischen Tradition und Innovation. Zeitschrift für Heilpädagogik, 54 (5), 180-182.
Holbrook, M. (1999). Vygotsky's methodological contribution to sociocultural theory. Remedial & Special Education, 20 (6), 341-360.
Holbrook, M.C. (2003). Teachers' perceptions of using the mountbatten brailler with young children. Journal of Visual Impairment & Blindness, 97 (10), 1-15.
Hooper, S., Montgomery, J., Swartz, C., Reed, M., Sandler, A.D., Levine, M.D., Waston, T.E. & Wasileski, T. (1994). Measurement of written language expression. In Lyon, G.R., (Ed.), Frames of reference for the assessment of learning disabilities. New views on measurement issues (pp. 375-417). Baltimore, London, Sydney: Brookes.
Hoskyn, M. & Swanson, H.L. (2000). Cognitive processing of low achievers and children with reading disabilities: a selective meta-analytic review of the published literature. School Psychology Review, 29, 102-119.
Hoy, C. & Gregg, N. (1994). Assessment: The special educator's role. Pacific Grove, CA: Brooks/Cole.
Hurrelman, K. (2002). Einführung in die Sozialisationstheorie, (8th ed.). Weinheim, Basel: Beltz Verlag.
Hurrelman, K. & Ulich, D. (2002). Handbuch der Sozialisationsforschung. Studienausgabe, (6th ed.). Weinheim, Basel: Beltz Verlag.
Hursh, N.C. (1995). Essential competencies in industrial rehabilitation and disability management practices: A skill-based training model. In D.E. Shrey & M. Lacerte, (Eds.), Principles and practices of disability management in industry (pp. 303-352). Winter Park, FL: GR Press.
Hwang, J.W. (1995). Investigation of learning disabilities: definitions of learning disabilities. The 5th Emotional Learning Disability Symposium. Korean Emotional Learning Disability Research, 143-172.
Ireson, J., Evans, P., Redmond, P. & Wedell, K. (1992). Developing the Curriculum for Pupils Experiencing Difficulties in Learning in Ordinary Schools: A

Systematic, Comparative Analysis. British Educational Research Journal, 18, (2), 155-173.

Jammill, D.D., Leigh, J.E., McNutt, G. & Larsen, S.G. (1981). A new definition of learning disabilities. Learning Disability Quarterly, 4, 336-342.

Jenkins, J.R. & O'Connor, R. (2002). Early identification and intervention for young children with reading, learning disabilities (pp. 99-148). In R. Bradley, L. Danielson & D.P. Hallahan, (Eds.), Identification of learning disabilities: Research to practice. Mahwah, NJ: Erlbaum.

Jenkins, J.R., Antil, L.R., Wayne, S.K. & Vadasy, P.F. (2003). How cooperative learning works for special education and remedial students. Exceptional Children, 69, 3, 279-292.

Jeong, K.S. & Kim, A.H. (2006).Teachers' perceptions regarding instructional adaptation for student with learning disabilities. The Korean Journal of Learning Disabilities, 3 (1), 29-52.

Jones, E.E., Kanouse, D.E., Kelley, H.H., Nisbett, R.E., Valins, S. & Weiner, B. (1972). Attribution: Perceiving the causes of behavior. Morristown, NJ: General Learning Press.

Jordan, A., Kirkaali-Iftar, G. & Diamond, C.T.P. (1993). Who has a problem, the student or the teacher? Differences in teachers' beliefs about their work with at-risk and integrated exceptional students. International Journal of Disability, Development and Education, 40, 45-62.

Jordan, A., Lindsay, L. & Stanovich, P. (1997) Classroom teachers' instructional interactions with students who are exceptional, at risk and typically achieving. Remedial and Special Education, 18, 82-93.

Jung, D.Y. (1991). A research on theoretical model for learning disability concept. Korean Journal of Special Education, 12, 89-105.

Jung, D.Y. (2005). Review on the concept and classification of learning disabilities. The Korean Journal of Learning Disabilities, 2 (2), 1-29.

Jung, D.Y. (2007). South Korean perspective on learning disabilities. Learning Disabilities Research & Practice, 22 (3), 183-188.

Jung, D.Y. & Kim, J.Y. (1999). Operating the committee on special education. Research Report (vol. 4). Ansan: KISE.

Kang J.G., Kim J.H. & Foley, D. (2004). Rethinking of the concept of learning disabilities appropriate to social context of South Korea. The Journal of Special Education: Theory and Practice, 5 (3), 285-300.

Kang, K.S., Kweon, T.H., Kim, S.Y. & Kim, E.J. (2000). Managing inclusive education: Three school cases studies. Ansan: KISE.

Kang, W.Y. (1992). Educational approach on learning disabilities, Deahak-Special Eduation Association, Special education reform and task, 51-65.

Kaplan, E., Fein, D., Kramer, J., Delis, D. & Morris, R. (1999). The WISC-III as a process instrument. San Antonio, TX: The Psychological Corporation.
Kataoka, M., Kraayenoord, C.E. & Elkins, J. (2004). Principals and teachers' perceptions of learning disabilities: a study form Nara prefecture, Japan. Learning Disability Quarterly, 27, 161-175.
Kavale, K.A. (2002). Discrepancy models in the identification of learning disability. In R. Bradley, L. Danielson & D.P. Hallahan, (Eds.), Identification of learning disabilities: Research to practice (pp. 369-426). Mahwah, NJ: Lawrence Erlbaum.
Kavale, K.A. (2003). The Feasibility of a Responsiveness to Intervention Approach For The Identification of Specific Learning Disability: A Psychometric Alternative. Responsiveness-to-Intervention Symposium. Kansas City, Missouri. (http://www.nrcld.org/symposium2003/kavale/kavale.pdf). (1.2.2008)
Kavale, K.A. & Forness S.R. (1985). Learning disability and the history of science: Paradigm or paradox? Remedial and Special Education, 6 (4), 12-23.
Kavale, K.A. & Forness, S.R. (2000a). What definitions of learning disability say and don't say: A critical analysis. Journal of Learning Disabilities, 33, 239-256.
Kavale, K A. & Forness, S.R. (2000b). History, rhetoric, and reality: Analysis of the inclusion debate. Remedial and Special Education, 21, 279-296
Kavale, K.A. & Reese, J.H. (1991). Teacher beliefs ad perceptions about learning disabilities: a survey of Iowa practitioners. Learning Disability Quarterly, 14 (2), 141-160.
Kavale, K.A. & Reese, J.H. (1992). The character of learning disabilities: An Iowa profile. Learning Disability Quarterly, 15, 74-94.
Kavale, K.A., Forness, S.R. & Lorsbach, T.C. (1991). Definition for definitions of learning disabilities. Learning Disability Quarterly, 14, 257-266.
Kavale, K.A., Fuchs, D. & Scruggs, T. (1994). Setting the record straight on learning disability and low achievement: Implications for policy making. Learning Disabilities Research & Practice, 9, 70-77.
Kavale, K.A., Holdnack, J.A. & Mostert, M.P. (2005). Responsiveness to intervention and the identification of specific learning disability: A critique and alternative proposal. Learning Disability Quarterly. 28 (1), 2-16.
Keller, J. A. & Novak, F. (2000). Kleines pädagogisches Wörterbuch (7th edn.). Freiburg im Breisgau: Herder.
Kelley, H.H. (1967). Attribution theory in social psychology. In D. Levine, (Ed.), Nebraska Symposium on Motivation, (vol. 15) (pp. 192-238). Lincoln, NE: University of Nebraska Press.
Keogh, B.K. (1983). A lesson from Gestalt Psychology. Exceptional Education Quarterly, 4 (1), 115-127.

Keogh, B.K. (1986). Classification, compliance, and confusion. Journal of Learning Disabilities, 16, 25.
Kerschner, R. (2000). Teaching children whose progress in learning is causing concern. In D. Whitebread, (Ed.), The Psychology of Teaching and Learning in the Primary School (pp. 277-299). London: Routledge-Falmer.
Kim, A.H. (2006). Development of early screening test for students with mathematics difficulties: Curriculum-based measurement of number sense. Korean Journal of Special Education, 40 (4), 103-133.
Kim, A.H. & Lee, D. M. (2005). A synthesis on classification of learning disabilities. Korean Journal of Special Education, 40 (3), 191-230.
Kim, D.I. & Lee, I.H. (2003). Teachers' perception on the explicit and implicit elements of learning disabilities. The Journal of Yeoulin Education, 11 (1), 63-79.
Kim, D.I. & Lee, T.S. (2003). Analysis of the special education program for the teaching licensure in Korean universities. Special education, 2 (2), 5-33, Ewha Woman's University Special Education Institute.
Kim, D.I., Lee, D.S. & Shin, J.H. (2003). Understanding and education of children with learning disabilities. Seoul: Hakjisa.
Kim, E.J. (2007). Understanding of "individuals with disabilities special education act", (1-6). Author: MOE&HRD, Special Education Policy Division. (http://www.moe.go.kr/common/download.jsp?savePath=/data/upFile/ekms/2007/06/29/726&fileName=070528%20현장특수교육_장애인%20등에%20대한%20특수교육법」의%20이해(김은주).hwp&upfileName=070528%20현장특수교육_장애인%20등에%20대한%20특수교육법」의%20이해(김은주).hwp). (06.01.2008)
Kim, J.K. (2001) A Study on the Identification Methods and Procedures of Learning Disabilities. Korean Journal of Special Education, 36 (1), 101-126.
Kim, J.K. (2005). Review on the concept and classification of learning disabilities: Discussion. 2005 Spring Symposium, 35-39. The Korea Learning Disabilities Association. Seoul: Hanhakmunhwa.
Kim, J.Y., Lee, M.S., Lee, Y.H. & Choi, S.M. (2001). Strategies for improving the management of the special classes in secondary schools, Research Report (vol. 4). Ansan: KISE.
Kim, M.S. & Park, E.M. (2007). A study on educational support in special and regular class for students with mild learning disabilities. The Korean Journal of Learning Disabilities, 4 (1), 25-44.
Kim, S.A. & Sung, J.G. (2005). Education for students with learning disabilities in Germany. The Korean Journal of Learning Disabilities, 2 (2), 55-81.
Kim, S., Kim, K.O., Kim, S.D., Lee, S.D., Lim, H.S. & Han, S.M. (2001). Understanding and education of learning difficulties. Seoul: Hakjisa.

Kim, Y.O. (1992). Definition issues in learning disabilities regarding IQ and attention deficit hyperactivity. Educational Research, 30 (4), 233-241.
Kim, Y.O. & Bong, W.Y. (2004). Discrepancy between scholarly definition of learning disabilities and elementary special educators' diagnostic practices on LD. Korean Journal of Special Education, 39 (2), 85-103.
Kim, Y.W., Kim, D.Y. & Kim, S.S. (2002). A study on Standardized model of Training for special education teachers. Korean Journal of Special Education, 37 (1), 101-130.
Kirk, S.A. (1963). Behavioral diagnosis and remediation of learning disabilities. In Anonymous, Proceedings of the conference on exploration into problems of the perceptually handicapped child. Chicago: Perceptually Handicapped Children.
KISE. Law Database. Special Education Promotion Act (http://www.kise.go.kr/html/). (02.06.2007)
Klatt, H.J. (1991). Learning disabilities: A questionable construct. Educational Theory, 41, 47-60.
Klein, G. (2001). Sozialer Hintergrund und Schullaufbahn von lernbehinderten Förderschülern 1969 und 1997. Zeitschrift für Heilpädagogik, 52, 51-61.
Klotz, J. (2004). Socio-cultural study of intellectual disability: moving beyond labeling and social constructionist perspectives. British Journal of Learning Disabilities, 32, 93-104.
KMK. (1994). Empfehlungen zur sonderpädagogischen Förderung in den Schulen in der Bundesrepublik Deutschland. Beschluss der Kultusministerkonferenz vom 6.5.1994 (http://www.kmk.org/doc/beschl/sopae94.pdf). (08.07.2006).
KMK. (1999). Empfehlungen zum Förderschwerpunkt Lernen (Beschluss der Kultusministerkonferenz vom 1.10.1999) (http://www.kmk.org/doc/beschl/sopale.pdf). (08.07.2006).
KMK (Die Ständige Konferenz der Kultusminister der Länder in der Bundesrepublik Deutschland). The Education System in the Federal Republic of Germany 2005: A description of the responsibilities, structures and developments in education policy for the exchange of information in Europe (http://www.kmk.org/dossier/special.pdf.). (07.092007)
Knitzer, J. (1993). Children's mental health policy: challenging the future. Journal of Emotional and Behavioral Disorders, 1, 8-16.
KOIS (Korean Overseas Information Service Government Information Agency). (2007a)(http://www.kois.go.kr/korea/kor_loca.asp?code=A0101). (20.01.2008)
KOIS. (2007b). Facts about Korea. Seoul: KOIS.
Korea inclusive education association. (2006). Introduction to special education for teachers: Inclusive education. Seoul:Hakjisa.

Korgel, B. (2002). Nurturing Faculty-Student Dialogue, Deep Learning and Creativity through Journal Writing Exercises, Journal of Engineering Education, 91(1), 143-146.
KISE. (2001). Prevalence of children with special educational needs. Gyunggido Ansan: KISE.
KISE. (2002). 2002 Special education indicators of Korea, Gyunggido Ansan: KISE.
Kossar, K., Mitchem, K. & Ludlow, B. (2005). No Child Left Behind: a national study of its impact on special education in rural schools. Rural Special Education Quarterly, 24 (1), 66-69.
Kwak, S.C., Paik, E.H., Jeon, B.U., Lee, B.I., & Lee, Y.H. (2002). The current status and future direction of in-service training program for special education teachers. Korean Journal of Special Education, 37 (1), 25-60.
Lago-Dello, E. (1998). Classroom dynamics and the development of serious emotional disturbance. Exceptional Children, 64 (4), 479-492.
Lauth, G. (2000). Lernbehinderungen, In J. Borchert, (Ed.), Handbuch der sonderpädagogischen Psychologie, Göttingen: Hogrefe.
Lee, D.S. (2001). Diagnosing and screening learning disabilities. Korean Journal of Emotional Disturbance. Learning disability Research, 17 (2), 19-41.
Lee, M.R. & Kwon, Y.H. (2006). An analysis of special education teachers' assessment factors in referral of students in need of special education. Korean Journal of Special Education, 41 (3), 229-249.
Lee, S.H. (1999). Discussion on definition and assessment of learning disabilities. Emotional Learning Disability Research, 15 (2), 101-120.
Lerner, J. (2000). Learning disabilities: theories, diagnosis and teaching strategies (8th ed.). Boston: Houghton Mifflin Company.
Lesar, S., Trivette, C.M. & Dunst, C.J. (1995). Families of children and adolescents with special needs across the life span. Exceptional Children, 62 (3), 197-199.
Lin, H. & Gorrell, J. (2001). Explatory analysis of pre-service teacher efficacy in Taiwan. Teaching and Teacher Education, 17, 623-635.
Lin, H., Gorrell, J. & Taylor, J. (2002). Influence of culture and education on U.S. and Taiwan pre-service teachers' efficacy beliefs. The Journal of Educational Research, 96, 37-46.
Lindemann, H. & Vossler, N. (1999). Die Behinderung liegt im Auge des Betrachters. Konstruktivistisches Denken für die pädagogische Praxis. Darmstadt, Neuwied: Luchterhand.
Löhrmann, S. (2009). http://www.sylvia-loehrmann.de/aktuelles/re_ldkhagen.html (01.03.2009)
Lopez-Reyna, N.A., Bay, M. & Patrikakou, E.N. (1996). Use of assessment procedures: learning disabilities teachers' perspectives. Diagnostique, 21 (2), 35-50.

Love, P.D. (2003). Supporting children's social, and emotional growth, School Age Connections, 12 (3), 1-4.

Lovitt, T.C. (1975). Applied behavior analysis and learning disabilities – specific research recommendation, and suggestions for practitioners. Journal of Learning Disabilities, 8 (8), 504-518.

Luhmann, N. (1977). Interpenetration. Zum Verhältnis personaler und sozialer Systeme. Zeitschrift für Soziologie, 6(1), 62-76

Luhmann, N. (1993). Soziale Systeme. Grundriß einer allgemeinen Theorie (4th edn.). Frankfurt am Main: Suhrkamp.

Lyle, S. (1996). An analysis of collaborative group work in the primary school and factors relevant to its success. Language and Education, 10 (1), 13-31.

Lyon, G R. (1996). Learning disabilities. In E.J. Marsh & R.A. Barkely, (Eds.), Child psychopathology (pp. 390-435). NY: The Guilford Press.

Lyon, G.R. (1996). Learning disabilities. The future of children: special Education for Students with Disabilities, 6 (1), 54-75.

Lyon, G.R., Fletcher, J.M., & Barnes, M.C. (2003). Learning disabilities. In E.J. Mash & R.A. Barkely, (Eds.), Child psychopathology (2nd ed.) (pp. 520-586). N.Y: Guildford Press.

Lyon, G.R., Fletcher, J.M., Shaywitz, S.E., Shaywitz, B.A., Torgesen, J.K., Wood, F.B., Schulte, A. & Olson, R. (2001). Rethinking Learning Disabilities. In C.E. Finn, A.J. Rotherham, C.R. Hokanson, (Eds.), Rethinking Special Education for a New Century (pp. 259-287). Fordham Foundation, Washington, DC.; Progressive Policy Inst., Washington, DC.

Maier, S.F. & Seligman, M.E. (1976). Learned Helplessness: Theory and evidence. Journal of Experimental Psychology, 105 (1), 3-46.

MacMillan, D. L. & Siperstein, G. N. (2002). Learning disabilities as operationally defined by schools. In R. Bradley, L. Danielson & D.P. Hallahan, (Eds.), Identification of learning disabilities: Research to practice (pp. 287-333). Mahwah, NJ: Erlbaum.

Madon, S., Jussim, L. & Eccles, J. (1997). In search of the powerful self-fulfilling prophecy. Journal of Personality & Social Psychology, 72 (4), 791-809.

Marschark, D. (2003). No Child Left Behind: a foolish race into the past. Phi Delta Kappan, 85 (3), 229-231.

Makin, L. & McNaught, M. (2001). Multiple perspectives on early literacy: Staff and parents speak out. Australian Journal of Language and Literacy, 24(2), 133.

Martin, K.F., Lloyd, J.W., Kauffman, J.M., & Coyne, M. (1995). Teachers' perceptions of educational placement decisions for pupils with emotional or behavioral disorders. Behavioral Disorders, 20, 106-117.

Masten, A.S. (1994). Resilience in individual development: successful adaptation despite risk and adversity. In M.C. Wang & E.W. Gordon, (Eds.) Educational resilience in inner-city America: challenges and prospects (pp. 3-26). N.J: Erlbaum.

Mavropoulou, S. & Padeliadu, S. (2002). Teachers' causal attributions for behavior problems in relation to perceptions of control. Educational Psychology, 22 (2), 191-202.

McDermott, P.A., Goldberg, M.M., Watkins, M.W., Stanley, J.L. & Glutting, J.J. (2006). A nationwide epidemiologic modeling study of learning disabilities: Risk, protection, and unintended impact. Journal of Learning Disabilities, 39, 230-251.

McDermott, R. & Varenne, H. (1995). Culture as disability. Anthropology &Education Quarterly, 26, 324-348.

McDermott, R. & Varenne, H. (1999). Adam, Adam, Adam, and Adam: The cultural construction of a learning disability. In H. Varenne & R. McDermott, (Eds.), Successful failure: The school America builds (pp. 25-44). Boulder, CO: Westview Press.

McDermott, R.P. (1993). The acquisition of a child by a learning disability. In S. Chaiklin & J. Lave, (Eds.), Understanding practice (pp. 269-305). New York: Cambridge University Press.

McKnight, R.T. (1982). The learning disability myth in American education. Journal of Education, 164, 351-359.

McLaren, P. (1998). Life in schools: an introduction to critical pedagogy in the foundations of education (3rd ed.). NY: Longman.

McLaughlin, M.J. (1999). Access to the general education curriculum: Paperwork and procedure or redefining special education. Journal of Special Education Leadership, 12 (1), 9-14.

Mcloughlin, C.S. (1985). Evaluating the ecology of the young child: internal and external environments. In C.S. Mcloughlin & D.F.Gullo, (Eds.), Young children in context Impact of self, family and society on development (pp. 277-309). Springfield, IL: C.C. Thomas.

McLoyd, V. (1998). Socioeconomic disadvantage and child development. American Psychologist, 53,185-204.

Medway, F. (1979). Causal attributions for school related problems: Teacher perceptions and teacher feedback. Journal of Educational Psychology, 71, 809-818

Mellard, D.F. (1990). The eligibility process: Identifying students with learning disabilities in California's community colleges. Learning Disabilities Focus, 5, 75-90.

Mercer, C.D. (1997). Students with learning disabilities (5th ed.). Upper Saddle River, NJ: Prentice-Hall.

Mercer, C.D., Jordan, L. & Miller, S.P. (1996). Constructive math instruction for diverse learners. Learning Disabilities Research and Practice, 11 (3), 147-156.

Mercer, C.D., Jordan, L., Allsopp, D.H. & Mercer, A.R. (1996). Learning disabilities definitions and criteria used by state education departments. Learning Disability Quarterly, 19, 217-232.

Miles, S. (2005). Inclusive Education Key issues and debates: Mainstreaming Disability in Development. The example of Inclusive Education. (http://www.disabilitykar.net/docs/inclusive_ed_paper.doc) (04.07.2010).

Moats, L.C. (2002). Learning disabilities and low-achievement are not meaningfully different categories for classification or treatment of reading disabilities. In R. Bradley, L. Danielson & D.P. Hallahan, (Eds.), Identification of Learning Disabilities: Research to Practice (pp. 777-782). Mahwah, NJ: Erlbaum.

MOE & HRD (2004). 2004 Annual report on special education. Seoul: MOE & HRD.

MOE & HRD (2005a).Education in Korea 2005-2006. (http://www.studyinkorea.go.kr/english/sub-2/link_url.jsp?ma_url=sub_6) (2007.10.01).

MOE& HRD (2005b).2005 Annual report on special education.

MOE & HRD (2005c). Special Education Promotion Act. Seoul: MOE & HRD.

MOE & HRD (2006a).2006 Annual report on special education.

MOE & HRD (2006b).2005 Annual academic performance evaluation: assessment on student academic performance.

MOE & HRD (2007a).Annual report on special education.Seoul: MOE & HRD.

MOE & HRD (2007b).Education in Korea 2007-2008.Seoul: MOE & HRD.

MOE & HRD (2007c). Revision of Special Education Promotional Act ("Individuals with Disabilities Special Education Act") (http://www.moe.go.kr/main.jsp?idx=0306010101). (02.07.2008).

MOE & HRD & Korean Educational Development Institute, KEDI. (2005).Brief statistics on Korean education, statistical materials 2005-4. Seoul: MOE & HRD & KEDI.

Montgomery, M.S. (1994). Self-concept and children with learning disabilities: observer-child concordance across six context-dependent domains. Journal of Learning Disabilities, 27(4), 254-262.

Morison, P., White, S.H. & Fever, M.J. (1996). The use of IQ tests in special education decision making and planning. Washington, DC: National Academy Press.

Morris, D. (2003). Reading instruction in first grade. In D. Morris & R.E. Slavin, (Eds.), Every Child Reading (pp. 33-57). Boston: Allyn & Bacon.

Moser, V. & Sasse, A. (2008). Theorien der Behindertenpädagogik. München, Basel: Reinhardt.

Nagi, S. (1991). Disability concepts revisited: Implications for prevention. In A. Pope & A. Tarlov (Eds.), Disability in America: Toward a National Agenda for Prevention. Washington, D.C: National Academy Press.

Naglieri, J.A. (2003). Current advances in assessment and intervention for children with learning disabilities. In T.E. Scruggs & M.A. Mastropieri, (Eds.), Advances in learning and behavioral disabilities: Identification and assessment (Vol. 16, pp. 163-190). Oxford, England: Elsevier Science.

National Center for Learning Disabilities (NCLD). (2002). Early help for struggling learners: A national survey of parents and educators.Author. (http://www.ld.org/press/PR2003/survey_findings.pdf). (01.02.2008)

National Dissemination Center for Children with Disabilities (NICHCY).(1997). Assessing children for the presence of a disability, 1-51. (http://www.nichcy.org/pubs/newsdig/nd23txt.htm). (19.08.2004)

Nespor, J. (1987). The role of beliefs in the practice of teaching. Journal of Curriculum Studies, 19 (4), 317-328.

Noddings, N. (1991). Stories in dialogue: Caring and interpersonal reasoning. In C. Witherell & N. Noddings, (Eds.), Stories lives tell: Narrative and dialogue in education (pp. 157-170). NY: Teachers College Press.

Norwich, B. (1994). Predicting girls' learning behaviors in secondary school mathematics lessons from motivational and learning environment factors, Educational Psychology, 14, 291-306.

Norwich, B. & Rovoli, I. (1993). Affective factors and learning behavior in secondary school mathematics and English lessons for average and low attainers, British Journal of Educational Psychology, 63, 308-321.

O'shaughnessy, T.E. & Swanson, H.L. (1998). Do immediate memory deficits in students with learning disabilities in reading reflect a developmental lag or deficit? A selective meta analysis of the literature. Learning Disability Quarterly, 21, 123-148.

Office of Special Education Programs, U.S. Department of Education, (http://idea.ed.gov/explore/view/p/\%2Croot\%2Cdynamic\%2CTopicalBricf\%2C23\%2C) (10.04.2006)

Oliver, M. (1986). Disability and social policy: some theoretical issues. Disability, Handicap and Society, 1 (1), 5-18.

Oliver, M. (1989). Disability and dependency: a creation of industrial societies? In L. Barton, (Ed.), Disability and Dependency (pp. 6-22), Bristrol, PA: Taylor & Francis/ Falmer Press.

Oliver, M. (1992). Changing the social relations of research production? Disability, Handicap & Society, 7 (2), 101-114.

Oliver, M. (1993). If I had a hammer; the social model in action, In J. Swain,

V. Finkelstein, S. French, C. Barnes & C. Thomas, (Eds.), Disabling barriers, enabling environments. London, UK: Sage.

Oliver, M. (1996). A sociology of disability or a disablist sociology? In L. Barton, (Ed.), Disability & Society: Emerging Issues and Insights (pp. 18-42), Edinburgh Gate, Harlow, Essex: Addison Westley Longman Limited.

Oliver, M. & Zarb, G. (1989).The politics of disability: a new approach. Disability, Handicap & Society, 4, 221-239.

Opp, G. (1992). A German perspective on learning disabilities. Journal of Learning Disabilities, 25, 351-360.

Opp, G. (1994). Historical roots of the field of learning disabilities: some nineteenth-century German contributions. Journal of Learning Disabilities, 27 (1), 10-19.

Ormrod, J.E. (2003). Educational Psychology:developing learners (4th edn.). Upper Saddle River, NJ: Merrill-Prentice Hall.

Ortner, R. (1979). Enflüße der schulischen Umwelt auf das Erziehungsgeschehen. Pädagogische Welt, 31, 483-488.

Painter, C. (1999). Preparing for School: developing a semantic style for educational knowledge, In F.Christie (Ed.), Pedagogy and the Shaping of Consciousness (pp. 66-87). London: Continuum.

Palmowski, W. (1996). Anders handeln. Lehrerverhalten in Konfliktsituationen. Dortmund: Borgmann.

Park, J.Y. (2002). Special education in South Korea. Teaching Exceptional Children, 34 (5), 28-33.

Park, H.S. (1992). Comparative study on identification of children with learning disabilities. Gyughaknonjib (Korean Journal of Education), 61 (3), 205-229.

Park, H.S. (1999). Analysis of studies on program effect on full inclusion of students with mild disabilities in primary schools. Korean Journal of Special Education, 34 (1), 1-29.

Park, H.S. & Cho, Y.G. (2004). A Qualitative Analysis on Support System for Students with Learning Disabilities Based on the Interviews with Their Teachers. Korean Journal of Special Education, 39 (1), 121-142.

Pavri, S. & Luftig, R. (2000). The social face of inclusive education: are students with learning disabilities really included in the classroom? Preventing School Failure, 45, 8-14.

Peters, S.J, Klein, A., & Shadwick, C. (1998). From our voices: special education and the alter-eagle problem. In B. Franklin (Ed.), When children don't learn (pp. 99-115), NY: Teachers College Press.

Pierangelo, R. & Giuliani, G.A. (2008). Teaching Students With Learning Disabilities: A Step-by-Step Guide for Educators, CA: Corwin Press.

Pintrich, P.R., Anderman, E/M. & Klobucar, C. (1994). Intra-individual differences

in motivation and cognition in students with and without learning disabilities. Journal of Learning Disabilities, 27 (6), 360-370.
Podell, D.M. & Soodak, L.C. (1993). Teacher efficacy and bias in special education referrals. Journal of Educational Research, 86, 247-253.
Poplin, M.S. (1984a). Summary rationalizations, apologies and farewell: what we don't know about the learning disabled. Learning disability Quarterly, 7(2), 130-135.
Poplin, M.S. (1984b). Toward a holistic view of persons with learning disabilities. Learning Disability Quarterly, 7(4), 290-294.
Poplin, M.S. (1988a). The reductionist fallacy in learning disabilities: replicating the past by reducing the present. Journal of Learning Disabilities, 21, 389-400.
Poplin, M.S. (1988b). Holistic/constructivist principles of the teaching/learning process: implication for the field of learning disabilities. Journal of Learning Disabilities, 21, 401-416.
Poplin, M.S. (1995). Looking through other lenses and listening to other voices: stretching the boundaries of learning disabilities. Journal of Learning Disabilities, 28, 392-398.
Poulou, M. & Norwich, B. (2002). Cognitive, emotional, and behavioural responses to students with emotional and behavioural difficulties: a model of decision-making, British Educational Research Journal, 28 (1), 111-138.
Proctor, B. & Prevatt, F. (2003). Agreement among four models used for diagnosing learning disabilities, Journal of Learning Disabilities, 36 (5), 459-466.
Prosser, M. and Trigwell, K. (1999) Understanding Learning and Teaching: The experience in higher education. Buckingham: Open University Press
Prücher, F. & Langfeldt, H-P. (2002). How German teachers in special education perceive and describe children with a learning disability. International Journal of Disability, Development and Education, 49 (4), 399-411.
Ramsden, P. (1992). Learning to Teach in Higher Education. London: Routledge.
Reid, D.K. & Valle, J.W. (2004). The discursive practice of learning disabilities. Journal of Learning Disabilities, 37 (6), 466-481.
Reschly, D.J. & Hosp, J.L.(2004). State SLD identification policies and practices. Learning Disability Quarterly, 27 (4), 197-213.
Rhodes, W.C. (1972). Interventions. In W.C. Rhodes & M.L. Tracy, (Eds.), A study of child variance (Vol.2). Ann, Arbor: University of Michigan Press.
Richardson, M. (1997). Addressing barriers: disabled rights and the implications for nursing of the social construct of disability. Journal of Advanced Nursing, 25, 1269-1275.
Roeltgen, D. & Heilman, K.M. (1984). Lexical agraphia. Brain, 107, 811-827.
Rogers, C. (1974). Lernen in Freiheit. Zur Bildungsreform in Schule und Universität. München: Kösel

Rogers, C. (1969). Freedom to learn: A view of what education might become. OH: Charles E. Merrill.
Rogers, H. & Saklofske, D.H. (1985). Self-concepts, locus of control and performance expectations of learning disabled children. Journal of Learning Disabilities, 18, 273-279.
Roit, M.L. & McKenzie, R.G. (1985). Disorders of written communication: An instructional priority for LD students. Journal of Learning Disabilities, 19, 258-260.
Sächsisches Staatsministerium für Kultus (2005). Handbuch zur Förderdiagnostik. (http://www.sachsen-macht-schule.de/smk/610.htm?id=82). (08.02.2006)
Saldern, M.v. (1987). Sozialklima von Schulklassen. Überlegungen und meherbenanalztische Untersuchungen zur subjektiven Wahrnehmung von Lernumwelten. Reihe11: Pädagogik Band 302. Frakfurt/M., Bern, New York: Peter Lang.
Sander, A. (1999). Ökosystemische Ebenen integrativer Schulentwicklung – ein organisatorisches Innovationsmodell. In U. Heimlich (Ed.), Sonderpädagogische Fördersysteme. Auf dem Weg zur Integration (pp. 33-44). Stuttgart: Kohlhammer.
Sander, A. (2003). Über die Integration zur Inklusion. St. Ingbert: Röhrig.
Santrock, J.W. (2001). Educational Psychology. NY: McGraw-Hill.
Sarason, I.G., Glaser, E.M. & Fargo, G.A. (1972). Reinforcing productive classroom behavior. NY: Behavioral Publications.
Schechtman, Z., Reiter, S. & Schanin, M. (1993). Intrinsic motivation of teachers and the challenge of mainstreaming: an empirical investigation. Special Services in the Schools, 7(1), 107-121.
Schlichting, H. & Schulz, P. (2000). Empfehlungen zu den Förderschwerpunkten im Bereich des Lernund Leistungsverhaltens, insbesondere des schulischen Lernens und des Umgehen – Könnens mit Beeinträchtigungen beim Lernen. In W. Drave, F. Rumpler & P. Wachtel, (Eds.), Empfehlungen zur sonderpädagogischen Förderung. Allgemeine Grundlagen und Förderschwerpunkte (KMK) mit Kommentaren (pp. 317-322). Würzburg: edition Bentheim.
Schründer-Lenzen, A. (2007). Schriftspracherwerb und Unterricht. Bausteine professionellen Handlungswissens (2nd edn.). Wiesbaden: Verlag für Sozialwissenschaften.
Schumm, J.S., Vaughn, S., Haager, D., McDowell, J., Rothlein, L. & Saumell, L. (1995). General education teacher planning: What can students with learning disabilities expect? Exceptional Children, 61 (4), 335-352.
Scott, M. (1980). Ecological theory and methods of research in special education. Journal of Special Education, 4, 279-294.
Sessa, V.I & London, M. (2006). Continuous Learning in Organizations: Individ-

ual, Group, And Organizational Perspectives. Mahwah, NJ: Lawrence Erlbaum Associates.

Segal, N. (2005). Mapping the field of inclusive education: A review of the Indian literature. International Journal of Inclusive Education, 9, 331-350.

Shakespeare, T. (2006). The social model of disability. In L.J. Davis, (Ed.), The disability studies reader (2nd Ed.) (pp. 197-204). NY: Taylor & Francis Group.

Shavelson, R.J. & Stern, P. (1981). Research on teachers' pedagogical thoughts, judgments, decisions, and behavior. Review of Educational Research, 51, 4, 455-498.

Shaywitz, B.A., Fletcher, J.M., Holahan, J.M. & Shaywitz, S.E. (1992). Discrepancy compared to low-achievement definitions of reading disability: Results from the Connecticut longitudinal study. Journal of Learning Disabilities, 25, 10, 639-648.

Sideridis, G.D., & Scanlon, D. (2006). Motivational Issues in Learning Disabilities, editors' introduction to special issue. Learning Disability Quarterly, 29, 131-135.

Shields, N. (1995). The link between student identity, attributions, and self-esteem among adult, returning students. Sociological Perspectives, 38 (2), 261-272.

Shin, H.K. & Jung, J.Y. (2002). The perception of regular teachers about evaluation adaptation for students with developmental delayed in elementary inclusive classroom. Korean Journal of Emotional and Learning Disabilities, 18 (1), 247-268.

Shin, J.H. (1999). Reading difference between students (groups) with learning disabilities and low-achievement, a serial analysis: discussion on conceptualization of leaning disability. Korean Journal of Special Education Research, 34 (2), 277-295.

Shin, J.H. (2005). Review on the concept and classification of learning disabilities: Discussion. 2005 Spring Symposium, 32-34. The Korea Learning Disabilities Association. Seoul: Hanhakmunhwa.

Sicbcrs, T. (2001). Disability in Theory: from social constructionism to the new realism of the body. American Literary History, 13 (4), 737-754.

Siegel, L.S. (1988). Evidence that I.Q. scores are irrelevant to the definition and analysis of reading disability. Canadian Journal of Psychology, 42, 201-215.

Siegel, L.S. (1989). IQ is irrelevant to the definition of learning disabilities. Journal of Learning Disabilities, 22, 469-478, 486.

Siegel, L.S. (1990). IQ and learning disabilities: R.I.P. In H.L. Swanson & B. Keogh, (Eds.), Learning disabilities: Theoretical and research issues (pp. 111-128). Hillsdale, NJ: Erlbaum.

Siegel, L.S. (1999). Issues in the definition and diagnosis of learning disabilities:

A perspective on Guckenberger v. Boston University. Journal of Learning Disabilities, 32, 304-319.

Siegel, L.S. (2003). IQ-discrepancy definitions and the diagnosis of LD: Introduction to the special issue. Journal of Learning Disabilities, 36, 2-3.

Silver, A.A. & Hagin, R.A. (2000).Disorders of learning in childhood (2nd edn.). New York: Wiley.

Silver, L.B. (1990). Attention deficit-hyperactivity disorder: is it a learning disability or related disorder? Journal of Learning Disabilities, 23 (7), 394-397.

Simmons, D.C., Kameenui, E.J. & Chard, D.J. (1998). General education teachers' assumptions about learning and students with learning disabilities: Design-of-instruction analysis. Learning Disability Quarterly, 21, 6-21.

Simpson, D. (2005). Phrenology and the neurosciences: contributions of F.J. Gall and J.G. Spurzheim. ANZ J. Surg. 75, 475-482

Skinner, E.A. (1995). Perceived control, motivation, and coping. London: Sage Publications.

Skrtic, T.M. (1991). Behind special education: a critical analysis of professional culture and school organization. Denver: Love.

Skrtic, T.M. (1999). Learning disabilities as organizational pathologies. In R.J. Sternberg & L. Spear-Swerling, (Eds.), Perspectives on learning disabilities: biological, cognitive, contextual (pp. 193-226). Colorado, Oxford: Westview Press.

Slavin, R. & Karweit, N. (1992). Preventing early school failures: What works? Educational Leadership, 50, 10-18.

Slavin, R.E. (1994). Preventing early school failure. In R.E. Slavin, N.L. Karweit & B.A. Wasik, (Eds.), Preventing early school failure (pp. 1-12). Boston: Allyn & Bacon.

Slavin, R.E. (2006). Student diversity. Educational psychology theory and practice eighth edition (pp. 96-131). Boston: Pearson Education, Inc.

Sleeter, C.E. (1986). Learning disabilities: the social construction of a special education category. Exceptional Children, 53 (1), 46-54.

Sleeter, C.E. (1995). Radical structuralist perspectives on the creation and use of learning disabilities. In T.M. Skrtic, (Ed.), Disability and democracy: Reconstructing special education for postmodernity (pp. 153-165). NY: Teachers College Press.

Smart, J. (2002). Disability, society, and the individual. Austin, TX: Pro-ED.

Smart, J.F. (2006). Challenging the Biomedical Model of Disability. Advances in Medical Psychotherapy and Psychodiagnosis, American Board of Medical Psychotherapists, 12, 41-44.

Smart, J.F. & Smart, D.W. (2006). Models of disability: Implications for the counseling profession. Journal of Counseling and Development, 84, 29-40.

Soderlund, J., Bursuck, B., Polloway, E.A. & Foley, R.A. (1995). A comparison of homework problems of secondary school students with behavior disorders and non-disabled peers. Journal of Emotional and Behavioral Disorders, 3 (3), 150-155.

Soodak, L.C. (2000). Performance assessment and students with learning problems: promising practice or reform rhetoric? Reading & Writing Quarterly, 16, 257-280.

Soodak, L.C. & Podell, D.M. (1994). Teachers' thinking about difficult-to-teach students'. Journal of Educational Research, 88 (1), 44-51.

Speck, O. (1996). System Heilpädagogik. Eine ökologisch reflexive Grundlegung. München: Reinhardt.

Speck, O. (2003). System Heilpädagogik. Eine ökologisch reflexive Grundlegung (5th ed.). München: Reinhardt.

Stanovich, K.E. (1991). Discrepancy definitions of reading disability: Has intelligence led us astray? Reading Research Quarterly, 26, 7-29.

Stanovich, K.E. (1999). The sociopsychometrics of learning disabilities. Journal of Learning Disabilities, 32, 350-361.

Stone, D. A. (1985). The disabled state. London: Macmillan.

Stone C.A., Silliman, E.R., Ehren, B.J., Apel, K (2006) Handbook of Language and Literacy: Development and Disorders (1st edn.). UK: Guilford Press.

Storch, S.A., & Whitehurst, G.J. (2001). The role of family and home in the developmental course of literacy in children from low-income backgrounds. New Directions in Child Development (pp. 51-73). New York: Wiley.

Stötzner, H.E. (1864). Schulen für schwachbefähigte Kinder. In S. Ellger-Rüttgart, (Ed.), Lernbehindertenpädagogik.Studientexte zur Geschichte der Behindertenpädagogik (Vol.5). Berlin:Beltz Verlag.

Swain, J. (1993). International perspectives on disability, In J. Swain, V. Finkelstein, S. French, C. Barnes & C. Thomas, (Eds.), Disabling barriers, enabling environments. London, UK: Sage.

Swanson, H.L. (1991). Operational definitions and learning disabilities: an overview.Learning Disability Quarterly, 14 (4), 242-254.

Swanson, H.L. (1994a). Short term memory and working memory: do both contribute to our understanding of academic achievement in children and adults with learning disabilities? Journal of Learning Disabilities, 27 (1), 34-50.

Swanson, H.L. (1994b). The role of working memory and dynamic assessment in the classification of children with learning disabilities. Learning Disabilities Research and Practice, 9 (4), 190-202.

Swanson, H.L. (2000a). What instruction works for students with learning disabilities? In R. Gersten, E. Schiller & S. Vaughn, (Eds.), Contemporary special education research (pp. 1-30). Mahwah, NJ: Erlbaum.

Swanson, H.L. (2000b). Issues facing the field of learning disabilities. Learning Disabilities Quarterly, 23, 37-50.

Swanson, H.L. & Saez, L. (2003). Memory difficulties in children and adults with learning disabilities. In H.L. Swanson, K.R., Harris & S. Graham, (Eds.), Handbook of learning disabilities (pp. 182-198). N.Y: Guilford Press.

Sylwester, R. (1997). The neurobiology of self-esteem and aggression. Educational Leadership, 54(4), 75-79.

Tabachnick, B.G. & Fidell, L.S. (2007).Using multivariate statistics (5th edn.). Boston:Allyn & Bacon.

Taylor S.J &. Bogdan R. (1989). On accepting relationships between people with mental retardation and non-disabled people: towards an understanding of acceptance. Disability, Handicap & Society, 4 (1), 21-36.

Thomas, D. & Woods, H. (2003). Working with people with learning disabilities: theory and practices. London: Jessica Kingsley Publishers.

Thomas, E.D. & Marshall, M.J. (1977). Clinical evaluation and coordination of services. An ecological model. Exceptional Children, 44, 16-22.

Thomas, G. & Loxley, A. (2007). Deconstructing special education and constructing inclusion (2nd edn.). Maidenhead: Open University Press.

Thurman, S.K. (1977). Congruence of behavioral ecologies: A model for special education programming. Journal of Special Education, 11, 329-333.

Tollefson, N. & Chen, J. (1988). Consequences of teacher attribution for student failure. Teaching and Teacher Education, 4, 259-265.

Tomilnson, C.A. (1999). The Differentiated Classroom: Responding to the Needs of All Learners. Alexandria, VA: ASCD.

Tomilson, C. (2004). The Möbius effect: Addressing learner variance in schools. Journal of Learning Disabilities, 37 (6), 516-524.

Torgesen, J.K. (1986). Learning disabilities theory: its current state and future prospects. Journal of Learning Disabilities, 79 (7), 399-407.

Tschannen-Moran, M. & Woolfolk-Hoy, A. (2001). Teacher efficacy: Capturing an elusive construct. Teaching and Teacher Education, 77, 783-805.

Tschannen-Moran, M., Woolfolk-Hoy, A. & Hoy, W.K. (1998). Teacher Efficacy: Its Meaning and Measure. Review of Educational Research, 68, 202-248.

U.S Department of Education (http://idea.ed.gov/explore/view/p/\%2Croot\ %2Cstatute\%2CI\%2CB\%2C614\%2Cb\%2C). (11.02.2007).

VanOudenhoven, J.P. (1985). Evaluative feedback as a determinant of the Pygmalion effect. Psychological Reports, 57 (3, part 1), 755-761.

Varenne, H. & McDermott, R. (1999). Introduction. In H. Varenne & R. McDermott, (Eds.), Successful failure: The school America builds (pp. 1-21). Boulder, CO: Westview Press.

Vaughn, S. & Schumm, J.S. (1995). Responsible inclusion for students with learning disabilities. Journal of Learning Disabilities, 28 (5),264-70.
Verhulst, F.C., Koot, H.H. & Van der Ende, J. (1994). Differential predictive value of parents' and teachers' reports of children's problem behaviors: a longitundial study. Journal of abnormal child psychology 22 (5) 531-546.
Vernon-Feagans, L., Hammer, C.S., Miccio, A.W., & Manlove, E. (2001). Early literacy in low income and bilingual children. In S. Neuman, & D. Dickinson (Eds.), Handbook on research in early literacy (pp. 192-210). NY: Guilford Publications.
Waldron, N.L. & McLeskey, J. (2000). Preventing academic failure. In K.M. Minke & G.C. Bear, (Eds.), Preventing school problems: promoting school success (pp. 171-209). Bethesda, MD: National Association of School Psychologists.
Walter, H. (1981). Region und Sozialisation. Ein neuer Schwerpunkt zur Erforschung der Voraussetzung menschlicher Entwicklung. In H. Water, (Ed.), Region und Sozialisation. Beiträge zur sozialökologischen Präzisierung menschlicher Entwicklungsvoraussetzungen Band? (pp. 1-55). Stuttgart, Frommann-Holzboog.
Weiner, B. (1974). Achievement motivation and attribution theory. Morristown, N.J.: General Learning Press.
Weiner, B. (1979). A theory of motivation for some classroom experiences. Journal of Educational Psychology, 71, 3-25.
Weiner, B. (1980a). A cognitive (attribution)-emotion-action model of motivated behavior: An analysis of judgments of help giving, Journal of Personality and Social Psychology, 39, 186-200.
Weiner, B. (1985). An attributional theory of achievement motivation and emotion.Psychological Review, 92, 548-573.
Weiner, B. (1993). On sin versus sickness: a theory of perceived responsibility and social motivation. American Psychologist, 48, 957-965.
Weiner, B. & Graham, S. (1989). Understanding the motivational role of affect: life-span research from an attributional perspective, Cognition and Emotion, 3 (4), 401-419.
Weiner, B., Graham, S. & Chandler, C. (1982). Pity, Anger, and Guilt. Personality and Social Psychology Bulletin, 8 (2), 226-232.
Weiner, B. & Kukla, A. (1970). An attributional analysis of achievement motivation. Journal of Personality and Social Psychology, 15, 1-20.
Weiner, B., Nierenberg, R. & Goldstein, M. (1976). Social learning (locus of control) versus attributional (causal stability) interpretations of expectancy of success, Journal of Personality, 44, 52-68.
Wenz-Gross, M. & Siperstein, G.N. (1998). Students with learning problems at

risk in middle school: Stress, social support, and adjustment. Exceptional Children, 65 (1), 91-100.
Werning, R. (1989). Das sozial auffällige Kind.Lebensweltprobleme von Kindern und Jugendlichen als interdisplinäre Herausforderung. Münster, New York: Verlag.
Werning, R. (1996): Das sozial auffällige Kind. Lebensweltprobleme von Kindern und Jugendlichen als interdisziplinäre Herausforderung (2nd ed.). Münster, New York: Waxmann.
Werning, R. (2002). Lernen und Behinderung des Lernens. In R. Werning, R. Balgo, W. Palmowski & M. Sassenroth, (Eds.), Sonderpädagogik. Lernen, Verhalten, Sprache, Bewegung und Wahrnehmung (pp. 129-189). München Wien: R. Oldenbourg.
Werning, R., Löser, J.M., & Urban, M. (2008). Cultural and Social Diversity: An Analysis of Minority Groups in German Schools. The Journal of Special Education, 42, 47-54.
Werning, R. & Lütje-Klose, B. (2003). Enführng in die Lernbehindertenpädagogik. München: Ernst Reinhardt.
Werning, R. & Lütje-Klose, B. (2006). Enführng in die Pädagogik bei Lernbeeinträchtigungen. München: Ernst Reinhardt.
Werning, R. & Wischer, B. (2002). Kindliche Lebenswelten und Planungskompetenz. Lernchancen, 25, 40-45.
Westwood, P. (1995). Teachers' beliefs and expectations concerning students with earning difficulties. Australian Journal of Remedial Education, 27 (2), 19-21.
Westwood, P. (2004). Learning and learning difficulties: a handbook for teachers.London: David Fulton Publishers.
Westwood, P. & Graham, L. (2000). How many children with special needs in regular classes: Official predictions vs. teachers' perceptions in South Australia and New South Wales. Australian Journal of Learning Disabilities, 5 (3), 24-35.
Westwood, P.S. (1993). Striving for positive outcomes for students with learning difficulties. Special Education Perspectives, 2 (2), 87-94.
Westwood, P.S. (1996). Current issues in effective teaching and learning. In New South Wales Board of studies: nature of the learner forum (pp. 28-43). Sydney: Board of Studies New South Wales.
Wiener, J & Schneider, B. (2002). A multisource exploration of friendship patterns of children with learning disabilities. Journal of Abnormal Child Psychology, 30(2), 127-141.
Wiener, J. & Tardif, C. (2004). Social and emotional functioning of children with learning disabilities: Does special education placement make a difference? Learning Disabilities Research and Practice, 19, 20-32.

Wilson, D.R. & William, J.D. (1994). Academic intrinsic motivation and attitudes towards school and learning of learning disabled students. Learning Disabilities Research and Practice, 9 (3), 148-156.

Witherell, C. & Noddings, N. (1991). Prologue: an invitation to our readers. In C.Witherell & N. Noddings, (Eds.), Stories lives tell: narrative and dialogue in education (pp. 1-12). NY: Teachers College Press.

Wocken, H. (2000). Leistung, Intelligenz und Soziallage von Schülern mit Lernbehinderungen. Vergleichende Untersuchungen an Förderschulen in Hamburg, Zeitschrift für Heilpädagogik, 51, 492-503

Woolfolk, A.E. & Hoy, W.K. (1990). Prospective teachers' sense of efficacy and beliefs about control. Journal of Educational Psychology, 82, 81-91.

World Health Organization (WHO). (http://www.who.int/classifications/apps/icd/icd10online/) (2.10.2005).

Wunderlich, G.S., Rice, D.P., & Amado, N.L (Eds.). (2002). The dynamics of disability: Measuring and monitoring disability for social security programs. Washington, D.C.: National Academy Press. Retrieved from http://www.nap.edu/openbook.php?record_id=10411 (01.03.2010)

Yang, M.H. & Landrum, T. (2005). Identification and instruction of learning disabilities under IDEA reauthorization 2004. The Korean Journal of Learning Disabilities, 2 (2), 103-121.

Yeung, K. & Watkins, D. (2000). Hong Kong student teachers' personal construction of teaching efficacy. Educational Psychology, 20, 213-236.

Yoshida, R.K., Fenton, K.S., Maxwell, J.P. & Kaufman, M.J. (1978). Group decision – making in the planning team process: Myth or reality? Journal of School Psychology, 16, 237-244.

Ysseldyke, J. & Algozzine, R.B. (2006). The legal foundations of special education: a practical Guide for every teacher. London: Sage Publication Ltd.

Ysseldyke, J., Algozzine, B. & Thurlow, M. (2000). Critical Issues in Special Education (3rd edn). Boston: Houghton Mifflin.

Ysseldyke, J., Algozzine, B., Shinn, M. & McGue, M. (1982). Similarities and differences between low achievers and students classified as learning disabled. The Journal of Special Education, 16, 73–85.

Ysseldyke, J. E., Thurlow, M., Graden, J., Wesson, C., Algozzine, B. & Deno, S. L. (1983). Generalizations from five years of research on assessment and decision making: The University of Minnesota Institute. *Exceptional* Education Quarterly, 4 (1), 75-93.

Zander, M. (2008). Armes Kind-starkes Kind? Die Chance der Resilienz. Wiesbaden: VS Verlag für Sozialwissenschaften.

Zimring, F. (1994). Carl Rogers. UNESCO Prospects: The quarterly review of comparative education, vol. XXIV, no. 3/4, 411-422.

Appendix A

Appendix A

Ⅰ. Teacher information sheet

* Please Click "⊙" your answer according to the following questions

1. School location

1) Provincial Office of Education

o Seoul	o Busan	o Daegu	o Incheon
o Gwangju	o Daejeon	o Ulsan	o Gyeonggi
o Gangwon	o Chungbuk	o Chungnam	o Jeonbuk
o Jeonnam	o Gyeongbuk	o Gyeongnam	o Jeju

2) Regional location

o Seoul	o Kwang-yeoug-si	o Si	o Gun - Ub

2. Grade levels taught

o the lower grades	o the higher grades

3. Qualifications

o Special education teacher certification
o General education teacher + special education teacher certification
o General education teacher + over 60 hours in-service education
o General education teacher + under 60 hours in-service education

4. Years of teaching experience

o under 1 year	o over 1 – under 2 years	o over 2 – under 3 years
o over 3 – under 5 years	o over 5 – under 10 years	o over 10 years

5. Number of students with learning disabilities taught

o above 1 student	o 2 – 4 students	o over 5 students

6. Pre-service education in the area of learning disabilities

o **Yes**	o **No**

7. In-service education in the area of learning disabilities

o **Yes**	o **No**

To what extent do you **agree** to be including the **components** stated below in the **definition of 'learning disability (LD)'**?

	Strongly Disagree (absolutely not including)	Disagree	Undecided	agree	Strongly Agree (absolutely Including)
① Academic learning problem	O	O	O	O	O
② Discrepancy between intellectual ability and academic achievement	O	O	O	O	O
③ Normal or above average intelligence	O	O	O	O	O
④ Disorder in basic psychological processes	O	O	O	O	O
⑤ Central nervous system dysfunction	O	O	O	O	O
⑥ It is not the direct result of other handicapping conditions	O	O	O	O	O
⑦ It is not the direct result of environmental, cultural, social or economic disadvantages	O	O	O	O	O

Appendix A

To what extent do you agree that the **individual variables** stated below **contribute to LD?**

	Strongly disagree	Disagree	Undecided	Agree	Strongly agree
① Attention problem	O	O	O	O	O
② Memory problem	O	O	O	O	O
③ Perceptual disorder (ex: visual · auditory)	O	O	O	O	O
④ Phonological · language disorder	O	O	O	O	O
⑤ Neurological impairment	O	O	O	O	O
⑥ Emotional· behavioral problems	O	O	O	O	O
⑦ Lack of pre-knowledge	O	O	O	O	O
⑧ Poor motivation	O	O	O	O	O
⑨ Poor self-confidence	O	O	O	O	O
⑩ Poor learning style	O	O	O	O	O

To what extend do you agree that the **environmental variables** stated below **contribute to LD?**

	Strongly disagree	Disagree	Undecided	Agree	Strongly agree
① Unsuitable curriculum	O	O	O	O	O
② Inappropriate teaching method	O	O	O	O	O
③ Lack of textbook · materials	O	O	O	O	O
④ Inappropriate assessment method	O	O	O	O	O
⑤ Poor student-teacher relationship	O	O	O	O	O
⑥ Inadequate physical classroom environment	O	O	O	O	O
⑦ Inappropriate social classroom environment	O	O	O	O	O
⑧ Lack of regular-special teacher cooperation	O	O	O	O	O
⑨ Lack of special teacher-parents cooperation	O	O	O	O	O
⑩ Special teachers' lack of professional knowledge of LD	O	O	O	O	O
⑪ Regular teachers' lack of understanding of LD	O	O	O	O	O
⑫ Poor economic home background	O	O	O	O	O
⑬ Unsupportive parent (ex: Family breakdown, Indifferent)	O	O	O	O	O

APPENDIX A

How **frequently** are you using the **assessment methods** below during the **LD assessment** in your school?

	Not at all	Not often	normal	Often	Very often
① Standardized Test	○	○	○	○	○
② Observation in regular classroom	○	○	○	○	○
③ Interview with regular teacher	○	○	○	○	○
④ Interview with parent of LD	○	○	○	○	○
⑤ Interview with the student (LD)	○	○	○	○	○
⑥ Look pattern of errors in student's work	○	○	○	○	○
⑦ Regular-special teacher team approach	○	○	○	○	○
⑧ Curriculum based assessment	○	○	○	○	○
⑨ Learning style assessment	○	○	○	○	○
⑩ Dynamic assessment (test-train/intervention – retest)	○	○	○	○	○

Do you consider **yourself competent** in using the following assessment methods?

	Not at all	Little competent	Undecided	Competent	Very Competent
① Standardized test	○	○	○	○	○
② Observation skill	○	○	○	○	○
③ Interview skill	○	○	○	○	○
④ Error analysis	○	○	○	○	○
⑤ Collaboration with regular teacher for team approach	○	○	○	○	○
⑥ Curriculum based assessment	○	○	○	○	○
⑦ Learning style assessment	○	○	○	○	○
⑧ Dynamic assessment	○	○	○	○	○

Appendix A

Please click the answer which is most in conformity with **your school situation** when interpreting assessment results

	Not at all	Not often	normal	Often	Very often
① Check assessment results which appear to be contradictory (ex. error measurement)	○	○	○	○	○
② Discuss with parent about results related to family situation that may contribute to student's academic problem	○	○	○	○	○
③ Discuss with regular teacher about results regarding the classroom environment (ex. modifying classroom rules or conditions)	○	○	○	○	○
④ Discuss with regular teacher about results regarding the teaching method (ex: using different instructional grouping or alternative textbooks or materials)	○	○	○	○	○
⑤ Discuss with regular teacher about results regarding the general curriculum modification (ex: developing instructional objectives specific for the student)	○	○	○	○	○
⑥ Discuss with regular teacher about results regarding the assessment method (ex: using various test form or situation specific for the student)	○	○	○	○	○
⑦ Discuss with the principal about results to work on the student's academic problem	○	○	○	○	○
⑧ Discuss with other special education personnel about results to work on the student's problem (in- or extern school i.e. school psychologist, doctor, therapist etc.)	○	○	○	○	○
⑨ Have meetings as a team which are prepared in written report or oral presentation	○	○	○	○	○

Appendix B

Factor analysis: special education teachers' perceptions of the causes of LD
Table B 4.1 Factor analysis: PCA with forced extraction of 4 components (23 items)

Rotated Component Matrix[a]

	Component			
	1	2	3	4
3.4 inappropriate assessment method	.835			
3.5 poor student teacher relationship	.824			
3.11 regular teachers' lack of understanding of LD	.812			
3.8 lack of regular-special teacher cooperation	.808			
3.2 inappropriate teaching method	.769			
3.7 inadequate social classroom environment	.748			
3.10 special teachers' lack of proffesional knowledge of LD	.717			
3.9 lack of special teacher-parents cooperation	.553		-.465	.413
2.9 poor self confidence		.888		
2.7 lack of preknowledge		.846		
2.8 poor motivation		.787		
2.10 poor learning style		.667		
2.6 emotional behavioral problems		.525		
2.3 perceptual disorder			.683	
2.5 neurological impairement			.679	
2.2 memory problem			.632	
3.1 unsuitable curriculum			-.560	
2.1 attention problem			.443	
3.13 unsupportive parent				.768
3.12 poor economic home background		.440		.667
2.4 phonological language disorder		.428		-.659
3.3 lack of text book materials			-.424	.546
3.6 inadequate physical classroom environment				.442

Extraction Method: Principal Component Analysis.
Rotation Method: Varimax with Kaiser Normalization.
a. Rotation converged in 5 iterations.

Factor analysis: special education teachers' perceptions of the causes of LD
Table B 4.2   Factor analysis: PCA with forced extraction of 4 components (21 items) Exclusion of items: 2.4, 3.1.

Rotated Component Matrix[a]

	Component			
	1	2	3	4
3.4 inappropriate assessment method	.842			
3.11 regular teachers' lack of understanding of LD	.809			
3.5 poor student teacher relationship	.800			
3.8 lack of regular-special teacher cooperation	.784			
3.2 inappropriate teaching method	.780			
3.7 inadequate social classroom environment	.749			
3.10 special teachers' lack of proffesional knowledge of LD	.688			
3.9 lack of special teacher-parents cooperation	.613		-.426	
2.9 poor self confidence		.886		
2.7 lack of preknowledge		.854		
2.8 poor motivation		.796		
2.10 poor learning style		.642		
2.6 emotional behavioral problems		.551		
2.2 memory problem			.712	
2.5 neurological impairement			.693	
2.3 perceptual disorder			.684	
2.1 attention problem			.504	
3.13 unsupportive parent				.807
3.12 poor economic home background		.402		.698
3.3 lack of text book materials				.499
3.6 inadequate physical classroom environment				.471

Extraction Method: Principal Component Analysis.
Rotation Method: Varimax with Kaiser Normalization.
  a. Rotation converged in 6 iterations.

Appendix B

Factor analysis: special education teachers' perceptions of the causes of LD
Table B 4.3 Factor analysis: PCA with forced extraction of 4 components (19 items). Exclusion of items: 2.4, 3.1, 3.3, 3.6. Suppressed absolute values less than 0.40

Rotated Component Matrix[a]

	Component			
	1	2	3	4
3.4 inappropriate assessment method	.839			
3.5 poor student teacher relationship	.808			
3.11 regular teachers' lack of understanding of LD	.801			
3.8 lack of regular-special teacher cooperation	.797			
3.2 inappropriate teaching method	.776			
3.7 inadequate social classroom environment	.737			
3.10 special teachers' lack of proffesional knowledge of LD	.702			
3.9 lack of special teacher-parents cooperation	.618		-.439	
2.9 poor self confidence		.886		
2.7 lack of preknowledge		.838		
2.8 poor motivation		.809		
2.10 poor learning style		.625		
2.6 emotional behavioral problems		.578		
2.2 memory problem			.739	
2.5 neurological impairement			.700	
2.3 perceptual disorder			.689	
2.1 attention problem			.530	
3.13 unsupportive parent				.877
3.12 poor economic home background				.750

Extraction Method: Principal Component Analysis.
Rotation Method: Varimax with Kaiser Normalization.
  a. Rotation converged in 6 iterations.

Regression: Binary Logistic (Enter) Regression
Special education teachers' perception of LD and their definition of LD

Table B 5.1 Logistic regression analysis: component 'Average or above average Intelligence'

Predictor	B	S.E.	Wald	df	p	Exp(B) odds ratio
Teacher factor	-0.9414	0.3473	7.3473	1	0.0067	0.3901
Personality factor	-0.4837	0.2765	3.0602	1	0.0802	0.6165
Constant	18.8075	23113.0380	0.0000	1	0.9994	147232017.2173

Test

Omnibus Tests of Model Coefficients

	Chi-square	df	p
Model	23.8869	11	0.0132

Model Summary

-2 Log likelihood	174.2432
Cox & Snell R Square	0.0730
Nagelkerke R Square	0.1564

Goodness-of-fit test

Hosmer and Lemeshow Test

Chi-square	df	p
3.6321	8	0.8887

Table B 5.2 Logistic regression analysis: component: 'Disorder in basic psychological processes'

Predictor	B	S.E.	Wald	df	p	Exp(B) odds ratio
Personality factor	-0.4918	0.1878	6.8577	1	0.0088	0.6115
Family factor	0.7537	0.1594	22.3495	1	0.0000	2.1250
Grade levels taught	-0.8651	0.3656	5.5990	1	0.0180	0.4210
Teaching years	0.8599	0.4188	4.2160	1	0.0400	2.3630
Constant	19.9372	22698.5822	0.0000	1	0.9993	455642748.5811

Test

Omnibus Tests of Model Coefficients

	Chi-square	df	p
Model	65.7858	11	0.0000

Model Summary

-2 Log likelihood	265.4051
Cox & Snell R Square	0.188478
Nagelkerke R Square	0.28972

Goodness-of-fit test

Hosmer and Lemeshow Test

Chi-square	df	p
18.3085	8	0.0190

APPENDIX B

Regression: Binary Logistic (Enter) Regression
Special education teachers' perception of LD and their definition of LD
Table B 5.3 Logistic regression analysis: component: exclusion clause ('It is not the direct result of environmental ·cultural ·economic influences).

Predictor	B	S.E.	Wald	df	p	Exp(B) odds ratio
Teacher factor	0.4221	0.1512	7.7958	1	0.0052	1.5251
Personality factor	-1.1508	0.1904	36.5276	1	0.0000	0.3164
Family factor	-0.4810	0.1612	8.9007	1	0.0029	0.6182
Constant	-19.1065	23197.8354	0.0000	1	0.9993	0.0000

Test
Omnibus Tests of Model Coefficients

	Chi-square	df	p
Model	79.8841	11	0.0000

Model Summary

-2 Log likelihood	307.4684
Cox & Snell R Square	0.2240
Nagelkerke R Square	0.3166

Goodness-of-fit test
Hosmer and Lemeshow Test

Chi-square	df	Sig.
2.5846	8	0.9577

Table B 5.4 Logistic regression analysis: component 'Central Nervous System (CNS) dysfunction'

Predictor	B	S.E.	Wald	df	p	Exp(B) odds ratio
Teacher factor	-0.9710	0.3524	7.5925	1	0.0059	0.3787
Cognitive factor	1.2161	0.2767	19.3148	1	0.0000	3.3741
Family factor	0.5231	0.2029	6.6492	1	0.0099	1.6873
Constant	16.2444	22828.4474	0.0000	1	0.9994	11346751.4496

Test
Omnibus Tests of Model Coefficients

	Chi-square	df	p
Model	74.8410	11	0.0000

Model Summary

-2 Log likelihood	210.6163
Cox & Snell R Square	0.211474
Nagelkerke R Square	0.354853

Goodness-of-fit test
Hosmer and Lemeshow Test

Chi-square	df	p
3.1543	8	0.9243

Regression (Enter) Linear Regression
Special education teachers' perception of LD and LD assessment
Table B 5.5 Linear regression analysis: Standardized test

Model Summary(b)

Model	R	R Square	Adjusted R Square	Std. Error of the Estimate	Durbin-Watson
1	0.565	0.319	0.308	0.742	1.756

a Predictors: (Constant), family, personality, cognitive, teacher-school
b Dependent Variable: standardized test

ANOVA(b)

Model		Sum of Squares	df	Mean Square	F	p
1	Regression	60.681	4.000	15.170	27.571	0.000
	Residual	129.303	235.000	0.550		
	Total	189.983	239.000			

a Predictors: (Constant), family, personality, cognitive, teacher-school
b Dependent Variable: standardized test

Coefficients(a)

Model		Unstandardized Coefficients		Standardized Coefficients	t	p	95% Confidence Interval for B	
		B	Std. Error	Beta			Lower Bound	Upper Bound
1	(Constant)	3.810	0.050		75.917	0.000	3.711	3.909
	teacher-school	0.122	0.070	0.105	1.741	0.083	-0.016	0.259
	personality	-0.283	0.052	-0.310	-5.426	0.000	-0.385	-0.180
	cognitive	0.242	0.071	0.198	3.406	0.001	0.102	0.383
	family	0.328	0.053	0.372	6.191	0.000	0.223	0.432

a Dependent Variable: standardized test

Regression Linear (Enter) Regression
Special education teachers' perception of LD and LD assessment
Table B 5.6 Linear regression analysis: Observation in regular classroom

Model Summary(b)

Model	R	R Square	Adjusted R Square	Std. Error of the Estimate	Durbin-Watson
1	0.380	0.145	0.130	1.121	1.255

a Predictors: (Constant), family, personality, cognitive, teacher-school
b Dependent Variable: observation in regular classroom

ANOVA(b)

Model		Sum of Squares	df	Mean Square	F	p
1	Regression	49.907	4.000	12.477	9.931	0.000
	Residual	295.255	235.000	1.256		
	Total	345.163	239.000			

a Predictors: (Constant), family, personality, cognitive, teacher-school
b Dependent Variable: observation in regular classroom

Coefficients(a)

Model		Unstandardized Coefficients		Standardized Coefficients	t	p	95% Confidence Interval for B	
		B	Std. Error	Beta			Lower Bound	Upper Bound
1	(Constant)	3.102	0.076		40.899	0.000	2.952	3.251
	teacher-school	-0.559	0.106	-0.357	-5.295	0.000	-0.767	-0.351
	personality	0.182	0.079	0.148	2.309	0.022	0.027	0.337
	cognitive	-0.291	0.108	-0.176	-2.702	0.007	-0.502	-0.079
	family	-0.034	0.080	-0.029	-0.425	0.672	-0.191	0.124

a Dependent Variable: observation in regular classroom

Regression Linear (Enter) Regression
Special education teachers' perception of LD and LD assessment

Table B 5.7 Linear regression analysis: Interview with regular teacher, interview with parent, interview with the student (LD)

Model Summary(b)

Model	R	R Square	Adjusted R Square	Std. Error of the Estimate	Durbin-Watson
1	0.363	0.132	0.117	0.389	1.556

a Predictors: (Constant), family, personality, cognitive, teacher-school
b Dependent Variable: interview

ANOVA(b)

Model		Sum of Squares	df	Mean Square	F	p
1	Regression	5.303	4	1.326	8.783	0.000
	Residual	34.869	231	0.151		
	Total	40.171	235			

a Predictors: (Constant), family, personality, cognitive, teacher-school
b Dependent Variable: interview

Coefficients(a)

Model		Unstandardized Coefficients		Standardized Coefficients	t	p	95% Confidence Interval for B	
		B	Std. Error	Beta			Lower Bound	Upper Bound
1	(Constant)	3.583	0.027		135.022	0.000	3.531	3.636
	Teacher-school	0.043	0.037	0.080	1.173	0.242	-0.029	0.115
	personality	0.085	0.027	0.201	3.093	0.002	0.031	0.139
	cognitive	0.062	0.038	0.110	1.654	0.099	-0.012	0.136
	family	0.084	0.028	0.206	3.004	0.003	0.029	0.139

a Dependent Variable: interview

Regression Linear (Enter) Regression
Special education teachers' perception of LD and LD assessment
Table B 5.8 Linear regression analysis: Look pattern of errors in student's work

Model Summary(b)

Model	R	R Square	Adjusted R Square	Std. Error of the Estimate	Durbin-Watson
1	0.515	0.265	0.253	0.752	1.372

a Predictors: (Constant), family, personality, cognitive, teacher-school
b Dependent Variable: look pattern of errors in student's work

ANOVA(b)

Model		Sum of Squares	df	Mean Square	F	Sig.
1	Regression	47.920	4.000	11.980	21.187	0.000
	Residual	132.876	235.000	0.565		
	Total	180.796	239.000			

a Predictors: (Constant), family, personality, cognitive, teacher-school
b Dependent Variable: look pattern of errors in student's work

Coefficients(a)

Model		Unstandardized Coefficients		Standardized Coefficients	t	Sig.	95% Confidence Interval for B	
		B	Std. Error	Beta			Lower Bound	Upper Bound
1	(Constant)	3.181	0.051		62.515	0.000	3.080	3.281
	Teacher-school	0.076	0.071	0.067	1.078	0.282	-0.063	0.216
	personality	0.186	0.053	0.209	3.528	0.001	0.082	0.290
	cognitive	0.450	0.072	0.377	6.239	0.000	0.308	0.592
	family	0.125	0.054	0.146	2.334	0.020	0.019	0.231

a Dependent Variable: look pattern of errors in student's work

Regression Linear (Enter) Regression
Special education teachers' perception of LD and LD assessment

Table B 5.9 Linear regression analysis: Alternative methods; Curriculum based assessment, Learning style assessment, Dynamic assessment

Model Summary(b)

Model	R	R Square	Adjusted R Square	Std. Error of the Estimate	Durbin-Watson
1	0.545	0.297	0.285	0.476	1.287

a Predictors: (Constant), family, personality, cognitive, teacher-school
b Dependent Variable: alternative method

ANOVA(b)

Model		Sum of Squares	df	Mean Square	F	p
1	Regression	22.478	4.000	5.620	24.819	0.000
	Residual	53.209	235.000	0.226		
	Total	75.687	239.000			

a Predictors: (Constant), family, personality, cognitive, teacher-school
b Dependent Variable: alternative method

Coefficients(a)

Model		Unstandardized Coefficients		Standardized Coefficients	t	Sig.	95% Confidence Interval for B	
		B	Std. Error	Beta			Lower Bound	Upper Bound
1	(Constant)	1.973	0.032		61.294	0.000	1.910	2.037
	Teacher-school	0.032	0.045	0.043	0.707	0.480	-0.057	0.120
	personality	-0.251	0.033	-0.437	-7.522	0.000	-0.317	-0.186
	cognitive	0.318	0.046	0.411	6.969	0.000	0.228	0.408
	family	-0.130	0.034	-0.234	-3.831	0.000	-0.197	-0.063

a Dependent Variable: alternative method

Spearman correlation Special education teachers' self-competence to utilize the assessment methods
Table B 5.13 Spearman correlation: self-competence and use of assessment methods (frequency of use)

Correlations

			confid summarized method competence
Spearman's rho	q3_4_1 4.1 standardized test	Correlation Coefficient	-.034
		Sig. (2-tailed)	.596
		N	240
	q3_4_2 4.2 observation in regular classroom	Correlation Coefficient	-.109
		Sig. (2-tailed)	.093
		N	240
	dvmeth1 dv interview	Correlation Coefficient	.075
		Sig. (2-tailed)	.249
		N	236
	q3_4_6 4.6 look pattern of errors in student's work	Correlation Coefficient	.301**
		Sig. (2-tailed)	.000
		N	240
	q3_4_7 4.7 regular-special teacher team approach	Correlation Coefficient	.278**
		Sig. (2-tailed)	.000
		N	240
	dvmeth2 dv alternative method	Correlation Coefficient	.129*
		Sig. (2-tailed)	.045
		N	240

**. Correlation is significant at the 0.01 level (2-tailed).
*. Correlation is significant at the 0.05 level (2-tailed).

Correlations

			confid summarized method competence
Spearman's rho	q3_4_1 4.1 standardized test	Correlation Coefficient	-.034
		Sig. (2-tailed)	.596
		N	240
	q3_4_2 4.2 observation in regular classroom	Correlation Coefficient	-.109
		Sig. (2-tailed)	.093
		N	240
	q3_4_3 4.3 interview with regular teacher	Correlation Coefficient	.213**
		Sig. (2-tailed)	.001
		N	236
	q3_4_4 4.4 interview with parent of LD	Correlation Coefficient	.017
		Sig. (2-tailed)	.789
		N	240
	q3_4_5 4.5 interview with the student(LD)	Correlation Coefficient	.000
		Sig. (2-tailed)	.999
		N	240
	q3_4_6 4.6 look pattern of errors in student's work	Correlation Coefficient	.301**
		Sig. (2-tailed)	.000
		N	240
	q3_4_7 4.7 regular-special teacher team approach	Correlation Coefficient	.278**
		Sig. (2-tailed)	.000
		N	240
	q3_4_8 4.8 curriculum based assessment	Correlation Coefficient	.224**
		Sig. (2-tailed)	.000
		N	240
	q3_4_9 4.9 learning style assessment	Correlation Coefficient	-.107
		Sig. (2-tailed)	.099
		N	240
	q3_4_10 4.10 dynamic assessment	Correlation Coefficient	.366**
		Sig. (2-tailed)	.000
		N	240

**. Correlation is significant at the 0.01 level (2-tailed).

Descriptive statistics: Special education teachers' definition of LD
Table B 5.11 Descriptive statistics :definition of LD reported by special education teachers to be utilized in practice

		academic learning problem	discrepancy between intellectual and academic achievement	normal or over average intelligence	disorder in basic psychological processes	central nervous system dysfunction	it is not the direct result of other handicapping conditions	it is not the direct result of environmental cultural economic influences
	missing	317	317	317	317	317	317	317
		0	0	0	0	0	0	0
Mean		5.00	5.00	4.81	4.56	4.66	5.00	4.39
Median		5.00	5.00	4.81	4.56	4.66	5.00	4.39
SD		0.00	0.00	0.59	0.83	0.75	0.00	0.92
Minimum		5	5	3	3	3	5	3
Maximum		5	5	5	5	5	5	5
Undecided		0	0	30 (9.5%)	70 (22.1%)	54 (17%)	0	97 (30.6%)
Strongly agree		317	317	287 (90.5%)	247 (77.9%)	263 (83%)	317	220 (60.4%)

Descriptive Statistics Collaboration in assessment process
Table 5.14 Descriptive statistic: Special education teacher reported collaboration situation in interpreting assessment results

	N	Min	Max	Mean	SD
Check assessment results which appears to be contradictory (error)	240	1	5	3.94	0.68
Discuss with parent about assessment results related to family situation that may contribute to student's academic problem	240	3	5	4.35	0.50
Discuss with regular teacher about assessment results regarding the classroom environment	240	3	5	3.63	0.73
Discuss with regular teacher about results regarding the teaching method	240	1	4	2.32	0.75
Discuss with regular teacher about results regarding the general curriculum modification	240	1	4	1.78	1.00
Discuss with regular teacher about results regarding the assessment method	240	1	3	1.73	0.45
Discuss with principal about the results to work on student's academic problem	240	1	3	1.80	0.55
Discuss with other special educational personnel about the results to work on student's problem	240	1	3	1.83	0.41
Have meetings together which are prepared in written report or oral presentation	240	1	2	1.71	0.46

Descriptive statistics: Special education teachers' definition of LD
Table B 5.12 Descriptive statistics: Tests on normal distribution–special teachers' self-competence to use the method

One-Sample Kolmogorov-Smirnov Test

		standardized test	observation skill	interview skill	error analysis	collaboration with regular teacher for team approach	curriculum based assessment	learning style assessment	dynamic assessment
N		240	240	240	240	240	240	240	240
Normal Parameters(a,b)	Mean	3.53	3.08	3.25	3.05	2.64	2.91	2.29	2.06
	SD	0.71	0.70	0.53	0.90	0.70	0.97	0.63	0.42
Most Extreme Differences	Absolute	0.40	0.26	0.39	0.25	0.30	0.34	0.48	0.47
	Positive	0.25	0.26	0.39	0.24	0.30	0.34	0.48	0.47
	Negative	-0.40	-0.25	-0.27	-0.25	-0.22	-0.29	-0.32	-0.40
Kolmogorov-Smirnov Z		6.25	3.99	5.98	3.92	4.71	5.24	7.37	7.31
p (2-tailed)		0	0	0	0	0	0	0	0